A WORLD ATLAS OF MILITARY HISTORY: 1945–1984

A WORLD ATLAS

By TOM HARTMAN
Maps by JOHN MITCHELL
Introduction by
MAJOR-GENERAL J. D. LUNT

OF MILITARY HISTORY

1945–1984

A DA CAPO PAPERBACK

Library of Congress Cataloging in Publication Data

Hartman, Tom, 1935-
  A world atlas of military history, 1945-1984.

  Reprint. Originally published: London: L. Cooper,
1985.
  Includes index.
  1. Geography, Historical—Maps. 2. Military history,
Modern—20th century—Maps. I. Mitchell, John.
II. Title.
G1030.H37 1988   911   87-37108
ISBN 0-306-80316-X (pbk.)

Published by Da Capo Press, Inc.
A Subsidiary of Plenum Publishing Corporation
233 Spring Street, New York, N.Y. 10013

CONTENTS

INTRODUCTION

by

MAJOR-GENERAL JAMES LUNT, CBE, OBE, FRGS

It is a sobering thought that there has hardly been a day since the guns stopped firing at the end of the Second World War when a war of some kind or other has not been taking place. At the moment of writing there is war in Afghanistan, Chad, Lebanon, Mauritania, Namibia, Central America and between Iraq and Iran. Men are being killed in battle, women and children are being made homeless, towns and villages are being devastated and vast sums are being spent on arms and ammunition. Much time and thought has been devoted to the outlawry of war between nations, so far with little effect. A League of Nations was established after the First World War with the intention of resolving disputes by peaceful means but it proved to be singularly unsuccessful in deterring Japan from attacking China or Italy from invading Abyssinia; nor did the League prevent Hitler from rearming Germany or the Civil War in Spain.

Nevertheless, despite this experience, a second attempt was made after the Second World War and a United Nations Organization was set up in the hope that mankind would find a better way of settling differences than had hitherto been the case. However, the succession of wars since the UN's inception provide mute testimony to the fact that when states consider their national interests to be at risk, or when people conclude that their life is so intolerable that only force will lead to an improvement, they will resort to armed action in exactly the same fashion as their forebears. "Jaw, jaw may be better than war, war," but there comes a moment when the talking ceases and men reach for their weapons. The UN may succeed in extending the talking process, but, as was evident in the dispute between Britain and Argentina over the Falkland Islands, there are limits beyond which neither side is prepared to go. War then becomes inevitable, although it is virtually certain that it will create as many problems in its aftermath as those it was intended to resolve. "Getting off the hook" is frequently more difficult than the original involvement. Since 1945 the world has been divided between the two Superpowers, the United States and the Soviet Union, each as fearful and suspicious as the other. However, despite many causes for conflict, neither has fought the other, other than by proxy. It is interesting to consider why this should have been the case. It is equally noteworthy that in Western Europe, for centuries the cockpit of the Nations, there has been no war since 1945, apart from the struggles for liberty in Hungary and Czechoslovakia, so brutally suppressed by the Russians – and it is in Western Europe that the two Superpowers stand face to face. How is it, then, that, despite such provocations as the blockade of West Berlin, the missile crisis in Cuba, Soviet support for the Hanoi régime in Vietnam, and now Soviet meddling in Central America, the two Superpowers have never yet come to blows?

The answer lies in the Balance of Power or, as some may prefer to describe it, the Balance of Terror. Nations as powerful as the United States and Soviet Union do not go to war in the expectation that they may lose, but when the end result may well be the nuclear exchange, victory by either side will provide little cause for jubilation. The danger lies in war by miscalculation, as could happen if the Arab states, with overt Russian support, force Israel into the sea, or if Russia, holding the keys to West Berlin, were to lock and bar the doors, hoping to hold to ransom the three Western occupying Powers – America, France and Britain. Since neither of these situations seems likely to occur, the principal threat posed by nuclear weapons is not so much the ability of America and Russia to destroy each other as the proliferation of nuclear weapons among the other nations.

It is the possession of nuclear weapons by such nations, who might in desperation be driven to use them, which poses a far greater threat to peace than their possession by Russia and America, always provided that the balance between Russia and America remains equal. It is too often forgotten that in November, 1950, the United States preferred to risk the overrunning of the Eighth US Army in Korea by the Chinese rather than have recourse to the nuclear bomb, and who chose national humiliation rather than employ it against the North Vietnamese. Seldom if ever before in history has a nation abjured the use of a battle-winning weapon; some may feel, with the wisdom of hindsight, that the world would have been a better place had similar forbearance been shown before Hiroshima and Nagasaki were incinerated.

Whereas in Russia public opinion has little choice but to follow the party line, in the West liberal consciences tend to be selective. Those who parade the streets to denounce the iniquities of South African involvement in southern Angola seldom raise their voices to denounce the activities of the 5th Brigade in Zimbabwe, nor is the indignation aroused by US involvement in Central America accompanied by protest against Soviet involvement in the same area; the fact that the Russians are fuelling the flames by their supply of weapons seems to be taken for granted.

It is this woolliness of thought that leads some good people to assume that the unilateral abandonment of nuclear weapons by the West will automatically result in peace on earth, regardless of Russia's oft-repeated intention to turn us all into communists eventually. When no less an authority than the former American Secretary of State, Dean Rusk, asserts categorically that in 1961 the West was on the brink of war with Russia over the approaches to West Berlin, one may legitimately ask how or why these good people think war was avoided? Not on account of any preponderance of conventional arms on the part of the West, that is certain. And do the unilateralists ever ask themselves why a predominantly land power like the Soviet Union considers it necessary to build up the second largest navy in the world, including a great number of submarines?

Mankind's natural yearning for peace has yet to produce results in practical terms. The world's religions preach peace – in two of them the daily greeting *is* "Peace" – and yet war is all too familiar to far too many. Nearly forty years have passed since Lord Mountbatten accepted in Singapore the unconditional surrender of the Japanese land, sea and air forces in South-East Asia. Throughout this time the British people have known peace, as well as a remarkable improvement in their living standards. Nevertheless, the British armed forces have fought no less than ten campaigns since 1945 – in Malaya and the Dutch East Indies, Cyprus, Kenya, Oman, Korea, Aden and South Arabia, Borneo, the Falkland Islands and Northern Ireland (which still continues). However these campaigns may be described in official parlance – emergencies, confrontations or peacekeeping operations – men have been killed or wounded, women have become widows and children made fatherless or orphaned. But because these acts of war have made little impact on the daily life of the mass of the nation, we consider we have been living at peace. There was a time when the killing of a single soldier in Northern Ireland was headline news, but today it requires a massacre such as Warren Point to evoke much indignation. There have been many to criticize the sinking of the *General Belgrano* off the Falklands because the warship was not precisely within the war zone, but that was war. Apart from the I.R.A. few people in Britain consider the situation in Northern Ireland to be a state of war and yet far more British servicemen have been killed and wounded in Northern Ireland than was the case in the Falklands. The casualties in Northern Ireland between 1969 and 1980 amounted to 400 killed and 3,000 wounded, and there were of course many more civilian casualties.

However, these figures pale into insignificance when compared with other and more terrible wars fought since 1945.

The Chinese Civil War from 1945–49 resulted in millions of casualties and the devastation of entire provinces. The US lost 34,000 killed and had 105,000 wounded in Korea; Chinese losses in that war were estimated at 900,000. The French lost 21,000 killed in Indo-China and 17,500 in Algeria. In Vietnam from start to finish the Americans lost 47,000 killed, the North more than a million, and the South about 400,000. There were, of course, tens of thousands of civilian casualties, as there have been more recently in war-torn Lebanon.

Vietnam introduced a new and powerful element into warfare – the television camera. Day after day, night after night, the American people watched the progress of the war on their TV screens. They saw, close up, the carnage of battle, the total exhaustion of the soldiers after hours of shelling and bombing, the desperate women and children running for cover, and the remorseless questioning by television reporters of officers and soldiers at the extreme limit of their endurance. Since bad news is sometimes as welcome to editors as good news, this on-the-spot reporting often had an adverse effect on morale, particularly on the home front. It accounted in large measure for the American public's steady disillusionment in the war, which in turn inevitably affected the morale of the combat troops. Whereas in previous wars the main aim of the propaganda effort had been to sustain morale, in Vietnam the reverse seemed to be the case.

The British Army, learning from this American experience, took special steps to instruct the troops in Northern Ireland in the handling of television interviews, but not before suffering some uncomfortable shocks. There were even more uncomfortable moments during the Falklands campaign when there was almost endless speculation about the courses open to the respective field commanders. Since surprise is one of the cardinal principles of war it remains to be seen to what extent this can be achieved when the public's demand for television news appears to be insatiable. Certainly the navy's attempt to ensure secrecy during the campaign did little to enhance that service's image in the eyes of the accompanying reporters.

The same can be said of the effect on viewers of action which may be taken for sound political or military reasons but which is repugnant on humanitarian grounds. An example of this was the bombardment of Beirut by Israel in July, 1982, resulting in a great many civilian casualties which caused complete revulsion when seen on the screen. The bombardment may have achieved Israel's aim of driving the P.L.O. from Beirut but in so doing it lost Israel's cause thousands of sympathizers throughout the world. Only a totalitarian government can afford to take such risks, and then only at its peril. Russia, for example, has few inhibitions in the handling of operations in Afghanistan, but by its actions Russia is storing up a legacy of hatred that will long outlast its occupation of the country. In this connection the British experience in Afghanistan should serve as a dreadful warning to every aspiring Soviet general and proconsul.

When we talk of war in peace we need to remind ourselves

that India has been involved four times in war since independence in 1947 – three times against Pakistan and once against China. As a consequence of the latter, India, with a volunteer army nearly one million strong, spends far more money than she can afford in order to maintain substantial garrisons in the Himalayas, in some cases at altitudes of 20,000 ft. The logistic problems involved in the supply and reinforcement of these garrisons are a constant headache for Staffs who know only too well the debilitating effects on morale of "mountain sickness". Even mules have to be acclimatized gradually on their way from the plains to the heights if they are to function efficiently.

It was Glubb Pasha who observed that there were three different kinds of war – general or global war, civil war and United Nations war. He described the latter as "a political war, where small armies are directed against some comparatively unimportant position, in order to exploit a political objective". The truth of this observation has been borne out in the series of wars fought between the Arab states and Israel. In every instance the Security Council has intervened to impose a truce, the intention being to bring the contestants to the council table in order to negotiate a lasting peace. In fact, however, Israel has invariably been left with the territory seized in battle. There have been five Arab–Israeli wars since 1948, both sides deploying increasingly sophisticated weapons which have been supplied for the most part by the Soviet Union and the United States. After the Six-Day War in 1967 Jordan lost the West Bank and Arab Jerusalem, Syria part of the Golan Heights. After the Yom Kippur War in 1973 Israel consolidated these gains, after what were probably the greatest tank battles in history. Later, as a result of the Camp David agreements negotiated between Israel and Egypt, Israel gave up Sinai in return for a peace treaty with Egypt, but no one believed that would be the end of the story. Since then Israel has invaded Lebanon and seized yet more territory, at the same time expelling the P.L.O. from Beirut, but the commitment to defend her ever-extending borders is placing a considerable economic strain on a population as small as Israel's. Nor are the Arab states ever likely to agree to negotiate peace so long as the whole of Jerusalem and Jordan's West Bank remains in Israeli hands.

A marked feature of the Arab–Israel wars has been the rapid replenishment of the combatants' armouries as soon as the fighting has ceased. For example, in 1973 the Soviet Union supplied Egypt and Syria with the most sophisticated weapons available, including surface-to-air and surface-to-surface missiles, without which the battle could hardly have begun. When war broke out a massive Soviet sea and air lift helped to maintain the momentum of the Arabs' attack. After some initial hesitation the United States came to the aid of Israel; in less than one month the U.S.A.F. flew in 22,000 tons of arms and ammunition which included tanks, artillery, helicopters and many other items of equipment. Nor did it end there. Within a few months of the fighting dying down, Russia had resupplied Syria with all the tanks lost in the war, some 1,200, and has since provided more. It is this apparent willingness on the part of the Superpowers to stock the armouries of their client states that has added yet another dimension to war in the second half of the

twentieth century, rendering ever more distant the prospect of a negotiated peace. A self-denying ordinance in the sphere of arms sales by the principal manufacturing nations would do more to deter the waging of war than any unilateral abandonment of the nuclear weapon by countries like Britain and France.

This ability to provide so many tanks "off the shelf" should arouse much more concern in the West than it has done. The international arms trade is now in the hands of governments, each competing to sell to Third World countries and to the wide variety of "Liberation Movements" the tools of war. Whereas formerly the arms trade was operated by a relatively few entrepreneurs, such as the mysterious naturalized Frenchman, Basil Zaharoff, nowadays entire government departments exist only to sell arms. This serves two purposes. Firstly, by selling arms abroad the arms-producing countries finance their own armaments, at the same time acquiring influence with the purchasers. Secondly, the latest type of military equipment can be tested under battle conditions at the least cost to the suppliers. It is yet another instance of war by proxy.

There have been many examples of this since 1945. In 1977, during the Ogaden War between Somaliland and Ethiopia, Russia supplied the Ethiopians with long-range medium artillery, T62 and T54 tanks and MiG-21 fighter planes. Even more importantly, they provided the field commander, General Vasily Petrov, and as many as 11,000 troops from their client state, Cuba. A large airlift from bases in Eastern Europe and the Soviet Union was organized, utilizing the former British base at Khormaksar (Aden) as a staging post. Cuban involvement in Angola was equally effective, although the Cubans would never have got there or fought there without Russian transportation and the provision of modern weapons.

A new departure has been the peace-keeping missions of international contingents operating under the aegis of the United Nations. These have proved effective in reducing tension in many areas, particularly in Cyprus, the Congo and the Middle East. It was the surprising willingness of the Secretary-General, U Thant, to withdraw the UN peace-keeping force from Sinai at Nasser's request that sparked off the Six-Day War in 1967 which resulted in Egypt's and Jordan's defeat. Peace-keeping has resulted in the development of special techniques; it has also created its own myths. Whereas the UN lacks the military staffs necessary for the efficient organization and control of such forces, it is obvious that without the cooperation of the governments involved, so often Israel and the Arab states, peace-keeping forces are at best deterrents, to be swept aside contemptuously should the need arise. This happened to UNIFIL when Israel invaded the Lebanon in 1982. Nevertheless, UN peace-keeping forces have had as many triumphs as failures, and where they have been properly organized and effectively commanded they have been instrumental in reducing tension.

The break-up of the former colonial empires of Britain, France, Holland, Belgium, Spain and Portugal has inevitably contributed to the world's instability since 1945. Frontiers drawn by the former colonial powers to suit themselves, as in the 'Scramble for Africa,' have come to be regarded as sacrosanct by the successor states. In many instances the consequences have been tragic, as in the Nigerian Civil War from 1967–70 and in the Horn of Africa in 1977. The long-drawn-out war in Eritrea still continues and it required seventeen years of bitter fighting before the northern and southern Sudan became reconciled. All too frequently the arms acquired by "Freedom Fighters" were used instead for banditry or acts of terrorism. It has become the norm rather than the exception for governments to be overthrown by military coups; what was once regarded as a purely Latin-American disease has spread across the world, fomented by the conflicting ideologies of the Superpowers.

It has become the fashion for Liberation Movements, such as the I.R.A., to attract publicity by acts of terrorism ostensibly directed against the Security Forces but in fact causing most damage among the civilian population. For every soldier killed in Northern Ireland there have been four or five times as many innocent civilian victims; for every Israeli killed by the P.L.O. dozens of Arab civilians have suffered. The streets and airports of the world's capital cities have become the terrorists' battlefields in pursuit of causes degraded by the callous indifference of those who claim to fight for them.

Violence begets violence. In a period of human history when the living standards of the mass of mankind have improved beyond any previous expectation, there are probably more refugees than at any time since Genghis Khan ravaged Central Asia. Millions of Palestinians live out a diaspora made no more acceptable by the knowledge that the Jews before them were forced to do the same. The "Boat People" of Vietnam, the Bengalis who fled from East Pakistan to the slums of Calcutta, the Poles who will never see Poland again, and with them the Czechs and Hungarians who have fled from Russian tyranny, and now today the wretched people of Chad, are living witnesses of man's inhumanity to man. So too are the people of Central America whose turn it is to see their homes wrecked, their streets turned into battlefields and their futures reduced to the hunger and stupefying boredom of refugee camps. And while they squat in squalor the Superpowers fight it out by proxy in the mountains, fields and forests.

Paradoxically, in an age when religion appears to be losing ground to materialism, wars continue to be fought for religious reasons. The tragic confrontation in Northern Ireland owes a great deal to religion, as did the war between India and Pakistan which resulted in the emergence of the state of Bangladesh. In recent years there appears to have been a swing back to religion, even in Russia, as a protest against the purely materialistic society. Nowhere is this more evident than in the Muslim countries where the Islamic Revival continues to gather strength. In Iran the austere dictates of the Mullahs rule the people with medieval severity, sending boys to fight the Iraqis in a war which seemingly has no end.

Modern warfare has been transformed by technological advances. As was evident during the Falklands campaign, naval tactics will have to be drastically revised to deal with the missile. During the Yom Kippur War the use of missiles by both sides has inevitably affected tactics in the air and on the ground. Surely the time is not far distant when the tank will be driven from the battlefield as surely as the horse by the well-concealed infantry soldier operating an anti-tank weapon which can kill at extreme ranges with 100% accuracy?

War grows increasingly deadly and more and more costly. Far too much money is spent on weaponry which would be far better spent on medicine, education and the improvement of living standards. However, it seems unlikely that wars will cease, despite man's terrifying ability to destroy mankind. Not surprisingly, the majority would like to see the nuclear weapon banished for ever from the earth, but the fact remains that it has been invented, tested and tried, and nothing now will make it go away. Somehow or other we have to learn to live with it. It is a sombre thought.

James Lunt

AUTHOR'S NOTE

Sadly, it is inevitable that such a book as this will be out of date before it is published, since fighting is still going on in at least seven of the conflicts in the following pages. It is to be hoped that, if and when a second edition is called for, peace will have returned to those troubled areas; but, as General Lunt points out in his Introduction, the odds are that there will be other "savage wars of peace" to consider. Happily, however, the major part of the book is concerned with conflicts which have now passed from the field of current events into the pages of history.

It is hoped that this book will be of use not only as an independent work of reference but also as an additional aid to those studying other and fuller accounts of the campaigns covered but which may not have such detailed maps. With this in mind, we have tried in the main to stick to the spelling of place names generally used in comtemporary accounts. There is not much point, for instance talking about Beijing when discussing the Chinese Civil War, at which time the city was still known as Peking. In such instances, where the names of important towns or cities have been changed, the earlier or later form is shown in brackets, depending on which name was being used at the time.

Tom Hartman

PART I

Europe

THE COD WAR

NORTHERN
IRELAND

THE PARTITION
OF GERMANY

THE INVASION OF
CZECHOSLOVAKIA

THE HUNGARIAN
NATIONAL RISING

TRIESTE

THE GREEK
CIVIL WAR

CYPRUS

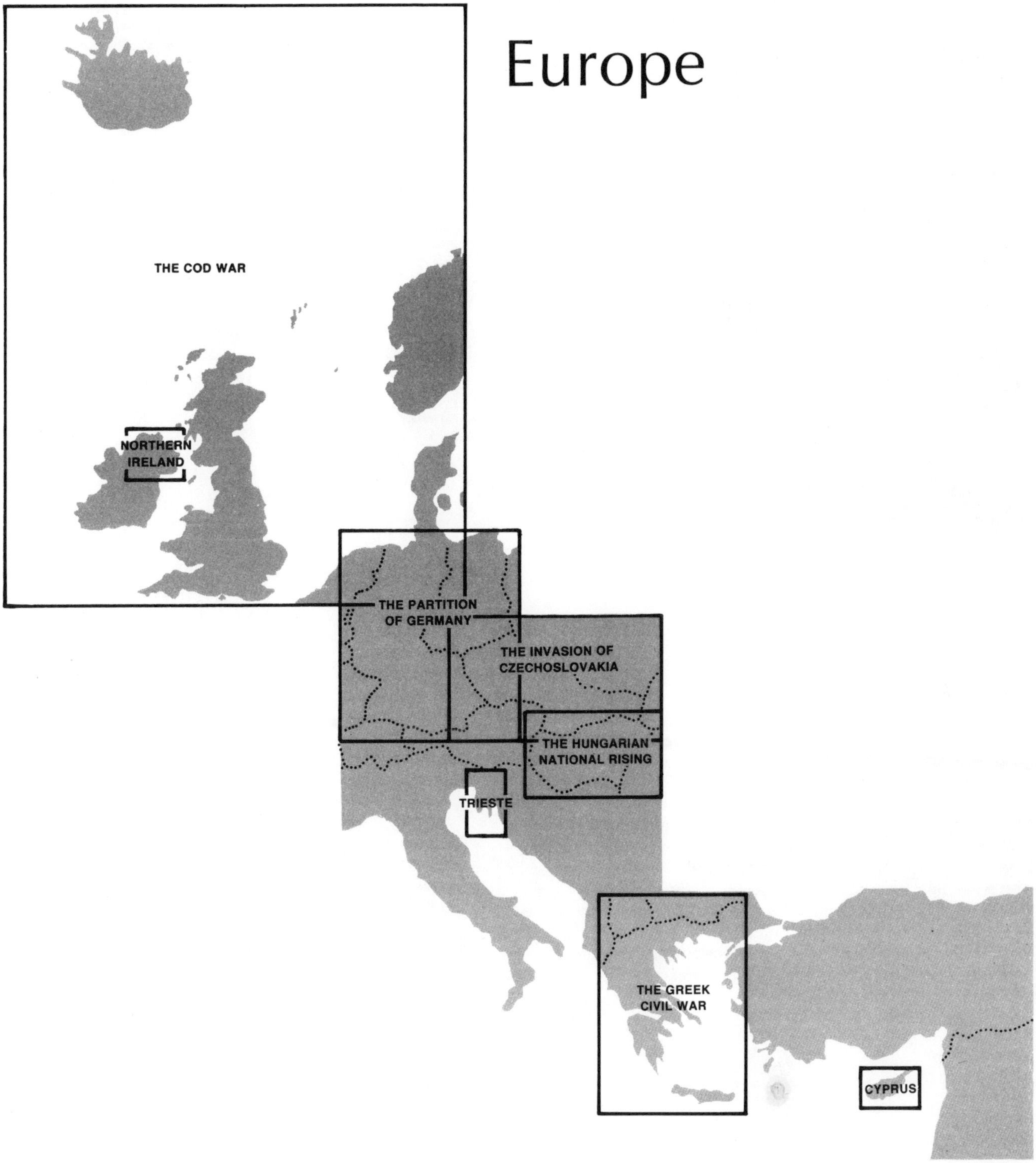

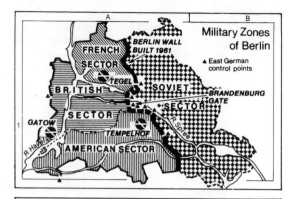

Military Zones of Berlin

▲ East German control points

The Partition of Germany 1945

In 1945, following the unconditional surrender of Germany, the country was divided into four zones, responsibility for the government of which was assumed by the four occupying powers: the United States, France, the Soviet Union and Great Britain. Berlin, though in the Soviet Zone, was occupied by all four powers, pending the then envisaged reunification of Germany.

In June 1948, the Soviet Union, in an attempt to prevent a West German state from coming into being, blocked all road, rail, and canal traffic into West Berlin. Thereupon the Allies launched the Berlin Airlift and the city was supplied by air with all essential supplies until May 1949 when the Russians lifted the blockade, but future disputes made it necessary for the airlift to be continued until September.

Between 1945 and 1961 about 3,000,000 people left East Germany for the West, many of whom were highly trained technicians. The main route of departure was through Berlin so, in August 1961, the East German Government sealed off West Berlin by erecting a barbed wire barrier, later replaced by a concrete wall – the notorious 'Berlin Wall'.

Between 1949 and 1971 harassment of traffic on the land approaches to Berlin was a regular occurrence. In 1971 a new agreement was reached with East Germany, since when such harassment has ceased.

Saarland was politically reunited with Germany in 1957.

The first West German Federal Election was held in August 1949.

The German Democratic Republic was set up by the Russians in October 1949.

Trieste 1947–54

Trieste, the prosperous main port of the Austro-Hungarian Empire, was occupied by Italian troops in 1918, taken by the Germans in 1943 and occupied by Marshal Tito's Yugoslav troops in 1945. The Paris Peace Treaties of 1947 established Trieste as a free port, temporarily divided into two zones: Zone A under Anglo/US military administration; Zone B under Yugoslav administration. But the free territory status was unworkable; tension ran high and rioting occurred sporadically until 1954 when an agreement was reached between Italy, Yugoslavia, Britain and the U.S.A. by which, with a minor border adjustment, Zone A was handed over to Italy and Zone B to Yugoslavia. Italy agreed to maintain Trieste as a free port and the Italian and Yugoslav governments agreed to a special statute regulating the rights of national minorities on both sides of the demarcation line.

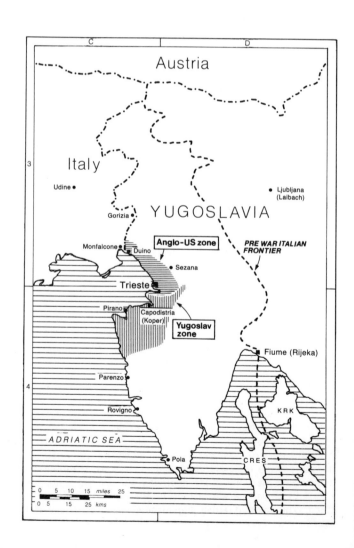

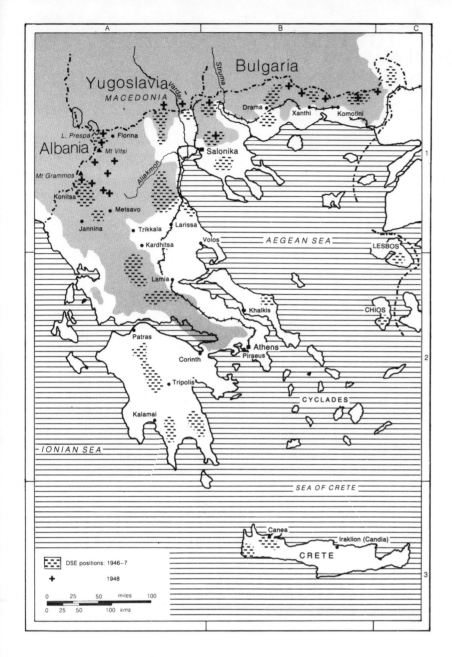

Map labels:

Yugoslavia
MACEDONIA
Bulgaria
Struma
Vardar
Drama
Xanthi
Komotini
L. Prespa
Florina
Albania
Mt Vitsi
Salonika
Mt Grammos
Aliakmon
Konitsa
Metsavo
Jannina
Trikkala
Larissa
Kardhitsa
Volos
AEGEAN SEA
LESBOS
Lamia
Khalkis
CHIOS
Patras
Athens
Corinth
Piraeus
Tripolis
CYCLADES
Kalamai
IONIAN SEA
SEA OF CRETE
Canea
Iraklion (Candia)
CRETE

DSE positions: 1946–7
+ 1948

0 25 50 *miles* 100
0 25 50 100 *kms*

The Greek Civil War 1943–49

The Greek Civil War started in 1943 but did not finish until 1949, so can fairly be considered to fall within the scope of this book. When the Second World War started in 1939 Greece remained neutral, but, on 28 October, 1940, Mussolini, the Italian dictator, launched a treacherous attack, without declaration of war, across the Albanian frontier into Greece, having invaded and occupied the former country in April, 1939. Mussolini expected only token resistance but the 'Greeks fought back stubbornly, drove back the Italians and had conquered nearly one third of Albania before the Italian forces recovered and the war was reduced to a deadlock until April, 1941, when German troops crossed the Bulgarian frontier into Macedonia, not because Hitler was anxious to come to the aid of Mussolini, but to secure his own southern flank in readiness for his projected invasion of Russia. Within a few weeks the whole of Greece was in German hands. After 15 months of Axis occupation 10% of Athens' population of 1m had died of starvation. Guerrilla warfare was waged continuously by the *Antartes* (irregular bands), despite savage reprisals, but, as time went by, differences of political opinion undermined the unity of the guerrillas who started fighting each other, despite efforts by British liaison officers to get them to cooperate in fighting the Germans. The main guerrilla organization was the National Popular Liberation Army (ELAS), controlled by the National Liberation Movement (EAM), the resistance organization of the Greek Communist Party (KKE). When the Germans began to withdraw ELAS prepared to take over the country but was defeated, after fierce fighting in Athens and Piraeus, by British troops. ELAS was destroyed as a fighting force but a few hard-core elements took to the hills. The regular Greek Army was re-established. In September, 1945, the Monarchy was restored by plebiscite and King George II returned to Greece. In the second stage of the Civil War, which started in 1946, the contestants being the KKE and Greek government forces, the main difference was that the KKE's support came from the newly communist states of Albania, Bulgaria and Yugoslavia. The Democratic Army of Greece (DSE), successor to ELAS, was led by General Markos Vaphiadis who seized control of major northern border regions, while fighting broke out all over Greece, but was fiercest in the Vardos Valley.

1946

10 December UN Security Council begins investigations into Greek charges that Yugoslavia, Albania and Bulgaria were supporting guerrillas in N. Greece. In March, 1947, the Security Council agreed that those countries had violated the UN Charter.

1947

12 March British aid having ceased, owing to her own economic problems, President Truman promised aid to both Greece and Turkey to fight communist insurgents.

1948

1 January Government troops relieve Konitsa after long seige, driving guerrillas into Albania.

19 June Greek Army takes the offensive; heavy fighting starts in Mount Grammos area.

28 June Yugoslavia is expelled from Cominterm and ceases to support the DSE.

27 November UN again condemns Albania, Bulgaria and Yugoslavia (wrongly) for helping Greek guerrillas.

31 January 1949: Nikos Zakhariadis replaces Markos as head of DSE

28 August Greek troops take Mount Grammos.

16 October End of the Greek Civil War.

"In January, 1951, the Greek General Staff weekly newspaper *Stratiokita* published a summary of losses during the war. It gave Greek Army deaths at 12,777, with 37,732 wounded and 4,527 missing. It said a further 4,124 civilians and 165 priests had been executed by the communists.... Estimates of the number of communists killed vary greatly, but 38,000 is considered a reliable figure. 40,000 were captured or surrendered" (*War in Peace* ed: Sir Robert Thompson).

The Hungarian National Rising
23 October–14 November 1956

The Turks, who had conquered most of southern and eastern Hungary in 1526, were gradually expelled by the Hapsburgs at the end of the 17th century and the country was then incorporated into the Austrian Empire. In 1867, as a sop to Hungarian nationalist aspirations, the dual monarchy of Austria-Hungary was created and Hungary became internally autonomous. It proclaimed its independence after the First World War and, after a short-lived communist republic under Béla Kun (1919), a constitutional monarchy was set up under the regency of Admiral Miklós Horthy. During the Second World War the country reluctantly sided with Germany and was occupied by Soviet troops in 1945. In 1949 the Hungarian Communist People's Republic was proclaimed. The head of the Workers' Party, in whom all power resided, was Mátyás Rákosi, who remained, under Moscow, all-powerful until the death of Stalin in March, 1953, when a period of fluctuation set in. In July, 1953, Rákosi was replaced by Imre Nagy who instituted a more liberal régime which did much to fan the embers of Hungarian nationalist and anti-communist sentiments; but Moscow hesitated to support him and in April, 1955, he was dismissed from his post and expelled from the Party. The hated Rákosi was reinstated and at once reinstituted his old hard-line policies. Then, in July, 1956, he was dismissed in disgrace by the new Soviet leader, Nikita Khruschev; Hungarian hopes rose again, but it transpired that he had merely been sacked as a gesture to President Tito of Yugoslavia, whom he had offended and who Khruschev wished to indulge. The new boss was Ernö Gerö, a man almost as detested as Rákosi himself. On 23 October students and workers demonstrated in Budapest, pulling down a massive statue of Stalin as a symbol of their protest. They

sought the reappointment of Nagy as Prime Minister, an end to Soviet domination and the removal of Soviet troops from Hungarian territory. Gerö, in a truculent speech, rejected their demands and his police fired into the crowd, thus turning a demonstration into a revolution. Gerö asked the Soviet troops for aid; fighting broke out in Budapest and in a few days had spread throughout the country. On 24 October Nagy was named Prime Minister and Soviet troops started leaving the country, which, by 30 October, was almost completely liberated. Fighting, intense between 25 and 30 October and costing about 10,000 lives, died down between 30 October and 4 November. On 31 October Cardinal Jószef Mindszenty, liberated from prison, made a triumphal entry in Budapest. On 1 November Nagy announced Hungary's withdrawal from the Warsaw Pact and asked the UN to recognize Hungary as a neutral state. This was too much for the Russians and by the night of 3–4 November their tanks were in position around the main towns and cities of Hungary. At 4am on the 4th they entered Budapest and seized control of all main roads and railways. Severe fighting occurred in a number of towns, particularly in Tata, Dorog and Györ, costing thousands more lives, but by 14 November all major resistance had been crushed and a new government installed under János Kádár. Over 150,000 Hungarians seized the opportunity to seek refuge in the West – thereby depriving the country of a substantial proportion of her educated classes – but there was never any likelihood of Western intervention since the rising coincided exactly with the Suez Crisis (see p. 11). Imre Nagy, who had taken sanctuary in the Yugoslav Embassy, was tricked into leaving it by the Russians, taken to Romania and shot. Russia's grip on Hungary has not noticeably slackened since 1956.

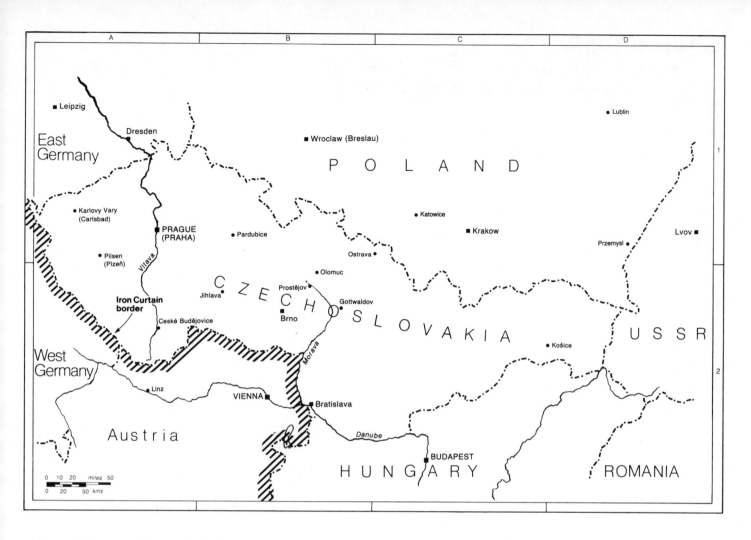

The Russian Invasion of Czechoslovakia 1968

The Republic of Czechoslovakia was created in 1918 from the former Western Slavonic provinces of Austria-Hungary. One-fifth of the population was of German descent and opposed to their inclusion in the new state, thereby providing the flimsy excuse which led to Hitler's annexation of the Sudetenland in 1938 and the rest of Czechoslovakia in March, 1939. Nevertheless, throughout the Second World War the mass of the people remained bitterly hostile to the Germans, and Czechs living abroad rendered valuable service to the Allies. By May, 1945, US troops were only 50 miles from Prague, but there, in accordance with the Yalta Agreement (by which Stalin, Roosevelt and Churchill had determined the spheres of influence in liberated Europe), they stopped, thereby allowing the Russians to enter the city on 9 May and ensure that Czechoslovakia would remain behind the Iron Curtain. In February, 1948, President Eduard Beneš was forced by the Prime Minister, Klement Gottwald, to appoint a virtually all-communist ministry, the exception being Jan Masaryk, son of the first President, Tómas Masaryk, who became Foreign Minister. However, he was murdered on 10 March, though the communists said he had committed suicide. Beneš resigned on 7 June and died on 2 August. Gottwald became President and communist control unqualified, the official Stalinist line being scrupulously observed. When Gottwald died in March, 1953, he was succeeded as virtual dictator by Antonin Novotný who remained in power until early 1968, being replaced by Alexander Dubček as First Secretary in January and by General Svoboda as President in March. For some time before that, however, the Czech leadership had permitted a considerable degree of liberalization to take place, a tendency which received further impetus under Dubček whose liberalizing reforms of April, 1968, ushered in the period known as the "Prague Spring". Despite warnings from Moscow and his other Warsaw Pact allies, Dubček stood firm. "We do not wish to yield anything at all on our principles," he declared. This was too much for Moscow and on the night of 20/21 August about 250,000 Soviet troops, accompanied by token contingents from Poland, Hungary, Bulgaria and E. Germany, crossed the frontier and took over the country with amazing efficiency. The Czechs were spared the bloodbath which followed the Hungarian National Rising of 1956, but Russia had nonetheless made it clear that no degree of liberalization would be tolerated. Dubček was removed in April, 1969, and replaced by Gustav Husák who remains in office (1983).

Cyprus 1955–77

Cyprus was under Turkish rule from 1570 until 1878, when the administration of the island was taken over by Britain, but it was not formally annexed to the British Crown until 1914, when, on the outbreak of the First World War, Turkey joined the Central Powers. This annexation was recognized at the Treaty of Lausanne in 1923 and in 1925 the island became a Crown Colony. Though it has never been part of modern Greece, the majority of Greek Cypriots supported the idea of the union of Cyprus with Greece (*enosis*). The movement had existed since before 1878 but it was not until 1931, when *enosis* demonstrators burnt down Government House in Nicosia, that its militant face began to show. Quiescent during the Second World War, *enosis* gained a powerful leader when Makarios became Archbishop of Cyprus in 1950. In April, 1955, an organization called EOKA (*Ethniki Organosis Kyprion Agoniston* – National Organization of Cypriot Fighters) began its campaign of sabotage and murder, the aim of which was to force Britain to relinquish Cyprus and grant *enosis*. EOKA's leader was a fanatical right-wing ex-Greek army officer of Cypriot birth, Colonel George Grivas.

MAIN EVENTS

1955

1 April	EOKA carry out bombing raids in Nicosia, Limassol and Larnaca.
3 October	Field-Marshal Harding becomes Governor and Commander-in-Chief.
November	First murders of British off-duty servicemen by EOKA.
27 November	Britain proclaims State of Emergency.

1956

9 March	Makarios is sent into 'restricted residence' on Seychelles Islands.
November	Grivas uses British involvement in Suez War to intensify EOKA activity. 416 incidents this month. 20,000 British servicemen now in Cyprus.

1957

March	Makarios is flown back to Athens.
November	Sir Hugh Foot replaces Harding as Governor.

1958

April	Week of rioting follows general strike ordered by Grivas.
June	Mr Macmillan puts forward plan for separate Greek and Turkish assemblies: serious intercommunal rioting follows.
August	Turkey announces support for British plan.
September	Makarios abandons *enosis* in favour of independent Republic of Cyprus. Violence follows.

1959

February	The London/Zurich Agreements between Britain, Greece and Turkey set up an independent Republic with British Sovereign Base Areas at Dhekelia and Episkopi.
March	Makarios returns to Cyprus. Grivas sent back to Greece.
December	State of Emergency ended.

1960

16 August	Cyprus attains full independence. Makarios becomes first President.

The granting of independence did not, however, see an end to violence in Cyprus; tension between the Greek and Turkish communities mounted steadily and by 1963 the island was on the verge of civil war. The population then was about 590,000 of whom 78% were Greek, 18% Turkish, 4% others.

1963

December	British troops called in to contain serious rioting in Nicosia.

1964

April	UN Peacekeeping force (UNFICYP) sent to Cyprus.
June	Grivas returns to Cyprus to encourage fight for *enosis*; is appointed Commander of Greek Cypriot National Guard.
August	Violent fighting in Kokkina. Greeks start 4-year blockade of this Turkish village. Turkish planes bomb Greek villges in retaliation.

Serious intercommunal clashes occurred in the following places (dates in brackets): Famagusta (11/65); Mora, Melousha (7/66); Lefka (12/66); Mari (4/67); Ayios Theodoros, Kophinou (11/67); Limassol (5/70); Trikomo (8/70).

1967

November	Grivas recalled to Greece.

1969

Rise of the National Front, pro-*enosis* faction formed by EOKA extremists.

1974

27 January	Death of Grivas.
15 July	National Guard ousts Makarios who escapes to Paphos, thence to London. Nikos Sampson, ex-EOKA leader, named President.
20 July	Turkish troops land near Kyrenia, paratroops near Geunyeli.
22 July	Glavkos Klerides takes over from Sampson. Greeks order ceasefire which Turks ignore.
16 August	Turkey orders ceasefire, by which time one-third of the island is in Turkish hands.
7 December	Makarios returns to Nicosia.

1975

13 February	Turks declare Turkish Federated State of Cyprus.

1977

3 August	Archbishop Makarios dies and is succeeded by Spyros Kyprianou.

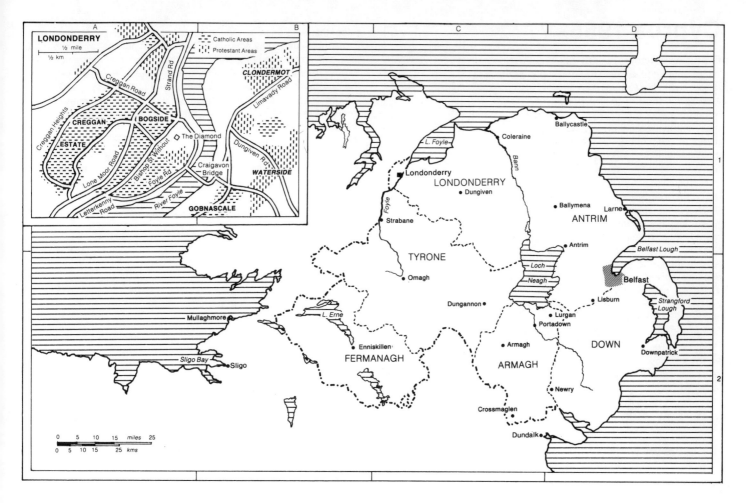

Northern Ireland

The trouble in Northern Ireland has its roots deeper in the past than any other conflict mentioned in this book. In 1172 the kings of Ireland were forced to acknowledge King Henry II of England as their overlord and seldom has there not been friction between Ireland and England thereafter. The fight for 'Home Rule' during the latter part of the 19th century culminated in 1914 in the Home Rule for Ireland Bill, but its operation was suspended owing to the outbreak of the First World War. After the war and the general election of December, 1918, members of the victorious Sinn Féin party set up a National Parliament (*Dáil Éireann*) in Dublin, the independent status of Ireland was unilaterally affirmed and there followed a period of guerrilla warfare between the forces of the Crown in Ireland and the forces of the new republican government. In 1921 the British Government offered dominion status to Southern Ireland while the six predominantly Protestant counties of Ulster were to remain British. A Northern Ireland Parliament, in which the Protestant Unionist party, in favour of continued union with Britain, had a large majority, was duly elected on 24 May, 1921, and on 6 December a treaty was signed between Great Britain and representatives of *Dáil Éireann*, whereby dominion status was accepted for the Irish Free State, known after 1937 as Eire. In 1948 the name was changed to the Republic of Ireland and association with the British Commonwealth was severed. Conversely, in the previous year the 'Attlee Declaration', which guaranteed that 'in no event will Northern Ireland or any part therefore cease to be part of the United Kingdom without the consent of the parliament of Northern Ireland', had bound Ulster even more firmly to Great Britain. Apart from the legacy of the frequently ruthless assertion of English rule in Ireland, the more proximate cause of the present trouble in the North lay in the relegation of Ulster's Catholic minority to the status of second-class citizens, which in turn led to the division of the province into mutually hostile religious communities. By blatant gerrymandering the Protestants had denied the Catholics any say in the running of the province and had seen to it that they came last in the queue for housing and jobs. Furthermore, the steady but inexorable rise in the Catholic population made it clear to the Protestants that within a foreseeable time it would be the Catholics who would predominate. Out of this situation, further exacerbated in 1966 by the emergence of the Rev Ian Paisley as the leader of extreme Protestant-Unionist opinion, grew the Northern Ireland Civil Rights Association (CRA), formed in January, 1967. On 5 October, 1968, the CRA staged a march in Londonderry, in defiance of an order forbidding it, which led to a riot in which 88 people were injured. This marks the true beginning of the Ulster crisis. The Irish Republican Army (IRA), a child of the Easter Rising of 1916, and bitterly opposed to partition, saw the CRA as a useful front, but soon the IRA split and a new ultra-militant and pro-violence wing, styling itself the Provisional IRA, commonly called the Provos, began in the winter of 1968–9 to take up arms, the funds being supplied by the misguided Irish-American community. Civil unrest intensified and on 12 August, 1969, the barricades went up for the first time in the Catholic Bogside area of Londonderry. British troops moved into Londonderry on 14 August and into Belfast on the following day. At first the troops were welcomed by the Catholic community but in July, 1970, the Army carried out the first house-to-house search in the Falls area of Belfast, found a considerable quantity of arms and the honeymoon was over. On 6 February, 1971, the first British soldier was killed on duty by the IRA; on 11 March the first three British soldiers off duty were killed. Since then it has been war, though, as so often in these situations, the British Army has to pay scrupulous heed to a book of

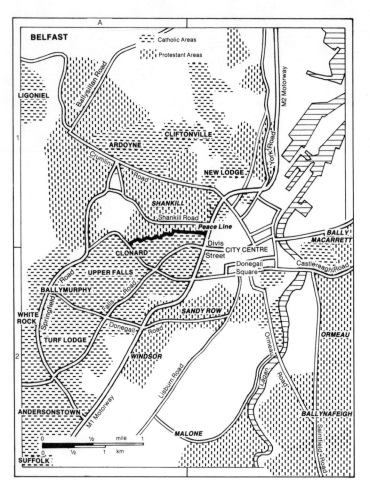

rules the existence of which is acknowledged, by Catholic and Protestant alike, only when it suits them. All political endeavours to end the fighting have come to nothing and the luckless British soldier remains in the buffer zone between the Provisional IRA on the one hand and on the other Protestant, or 'Loyalist', paramilitary groups such as the Ulster Volunteer Force and the conventional forces of law and order such as the Royal Ulster Constabulary and the Ulster Defence Regiment. Paul Johnson in *Ireland, Land of Troubles* says of the British Army in Ulster: "Seldom, perhaps never before, in history has a military force been subjected to such close scrutiny of its conduct, over so long a period, and by such a variety of umpires, and emerged with such credit." It is a fair judgment.

Deaths in Ulster 1969–1982				
	RUC	Army & UDR	Civilian	Total
1969	1	0	12	13
1970	2	0	23	25
1971	11	48	115	174
1972	17	129	322	468
1973	13	66	171	250
1974	15	25	166	206
1975	11	20	216	247
1976	23	29	245	297
1977	14	29	69	112
1978	10	21	50	81
1979	14	48	51	113
1980	9	16	50	75
1981	21	23	54	98
1982	28		57	85

The Cod War 1972–73

The dispute between Iceland on the one hand and the United Kingdom and West Germany on the other, which came to be known as the 'Cod War', arose from Iceland's unilateral decision on 1 September 1972, to extend her territorial waters from 12 to 50 miles (19–80km). A growing number of clashes between British and West German trawlers continuing to fish within the 50-mile (80km) limit and Icelandic gunboats trying to prevent this by cutting the trawlers' fishing nets and other gear led, after much pressure from the fishing ports, to the dispatch on 23 January 1973, of a fast ocean-going tug, the *Statesman*, to protect British trawlers, and on 18 March the first live warning shots to be used in the 'Cod War' were fired across the bows of the *Statesman* by the Icelandic gunboat *Odinn*.

The first serious incident occurred on 26 May when the Icelandic gunboat *Aegir* fired six or eight live shots which holed the British trawler *Everton* in the forecastle and below the waterline.

The first incident between a British frigate and an Icelandic gunboat occurred on 7 June when HMS *Scylla* collided with the *Aegir* off the north-west coast of Iceland: the damage was slight and there were no casualties. But the use of frigates to protect the trawlers changed the nature of the dispute and in mid-October the two Prime Ministers, Mr Olafur Johannesson and Mr Edward Heath, reached agreement on general terms and brought the 14-month Cod War to an end.

PART II
The Middle East

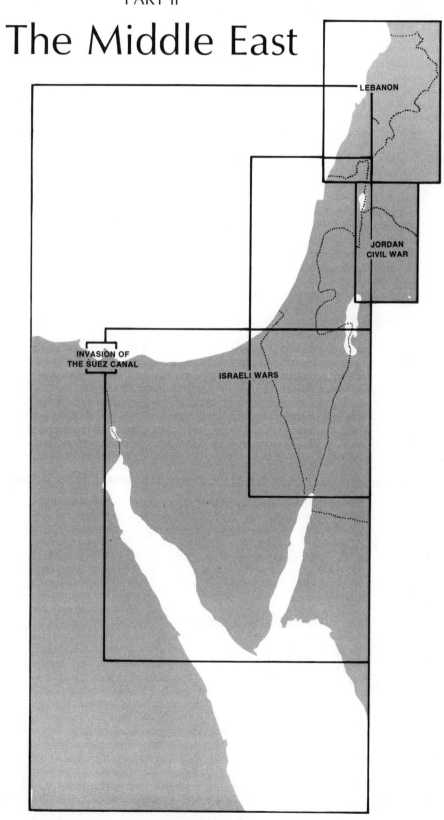

LEBANON

JORDAN
CIVIL WAR

INVASION OF
THE SUEZ CANAL

ISRAELI WARS

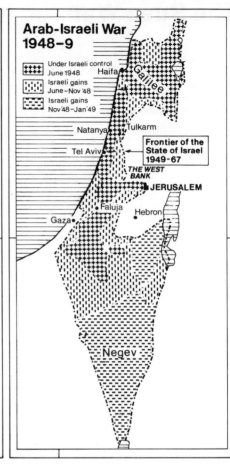

Mandated Palestine 1920–48

In October 1917 British troops entered Palestine, until then under Turkish rule, Britain and Turkey being on opposing sides in the First World War. In November the Balfour Declaration promised British support for a Jewish national home in Palestine, provided that 'nothing shall be done which may prejudice the civil and religious rights of existing non-Jewish communities in Palestine.' In 1920 Palestine became a British mandated territory.

Between the two World Wars Britain tried with decreasing success to prevent violence between Jews and Arabs. Terrorism, suspended during the Second World War, broke out again in 1946 as Jewish determination to establish a national home hardened; but British security forces now became their targets. The Jews believed that Britain's post-War Labour Government was stalling.

Violence was organized by three groups: Hagana (Defence), Irgun Zvei Leumi (National Military Organization) and the Stern Gang.

22 July 1946: Irgun blow up King David Hotel, Jerusalem. 91 killed.

The United Nations Partition Proposal 29 November 1947

On 29 November 1947 the United Nations approved a plan to partition Palestine between the Jews and the Arabs. The plan was unacceptable to the Arabs who were almost in a majority even in the land allotted to the Jews, and who in any case still rejected the notion of a Jewish national home. However, on 14 March 1948 the State of Israel was proclaimed and on 15 May Britain announced the end of the mandate.

31 March 1947: Irgun blow up oil refinery at Haifa.
May 1947: Irgun release 100 Jews and 171 Arabs from the supposedly impregnable Acre prison.
30 July 1947: Irgun hang two British sergeants near Natanya as an act of reprisal.
1944–48: Over 300 British killed by Jewish terrorists.

The Arab-Israeli War 14 May 1948– 5 January 1949

The day the mandate ended Israel was invaded by troops from Egypt, Jordan, Syria, Lebanon and Iraq. All, save the British-trained Arab Legion of Jordan, were soon repulsed. By December Israel controlled all the territory allotted to her by the UN as well as most of Western Galilee and the modern part of Jerusalem. Jordan had taken most of the eastern part of Palestine allotted by the UN to the Arabs. The separate armistice agreements signed by Egypt, Lebanon, Jordan and Syria in 1949 left Israel in possession of all the land it had conquered. The 'West Bank' and the Old City of Jerusalem voted to accede to Jordan. Palestine ceased to exist. Arab refugees flooded into Jordan, Syria, Lebanon and Egypt, where they were kept in refugee camps near the Israeli frontier, a source of continuing friction and bitterness.

The Suez War

After the deposition of King Farouk in 1952 and the assumption of power by President Nasser in 1954 Egypt became the main force behind Arab nationalist ambitions, and frequent Egyptian-inspired raids were mounted against Israel from the Gaza Strip. In September 1955 Egypt closed the Straits of Tiran to Israeli shipping. In June 1956 the last British troops, whose presence had hitherto restrained Egypt from attacking Israel, left the Canal Zone and Egypt started to prepare for war. In July Nasser nationalized the Suez Canal and in September Israel, France and Britain began planning a joint attack on Egypt.

CHRONOLOGY

29 Oct 1659	Israeli Para Bn lands at E. end of Mitla Pass. Rest of 202 Para Bde crosses frontier at Kuntilla.
30 Oct am	7th Armd Bde attacks Um Qataf.
1800	Britain and France issue ultimatum to both sides to withdraw 10 m either side of the Canal.
2230	202 Para Bde reaches Mitla Pass
31 Oct	9 Inf Bde begins advance to Sharm el Sheikh. 7 Armd Bde outflanks Abu Abweigila. 1 Inf and 27 Armd Bdes attack Rafah.
1 Nov	Nasser orders Egyptian troops to withdraw. Israelis take Rafah, advance to El Arish.
2 Nov	Egyptians abandon Abu Abweigila. Israelis take El Arish. 12 Inf Bde moves into Gaza to find Egyptians gone.
5 Nov	British and French paratroops land at Suez. Israelis take Sharm el Sheikh.
7 Nov	Ceasefire announced.
Dec	Israel withdraws from all Sinai except the Gaza Strip and Sharm el Sheikh.
March '57	Israel withdraws to prewar frontiers.

CASUALTIES

	Dead	Wounded	Prisoners
Israel	181	620	
Egypt	c.2500	undisclosed	c.6000

Egypt also abandoned some $50 m worth of military equipment in Sinai.

The Invasion of the Suez Canal

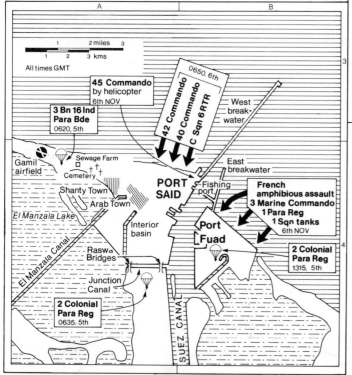

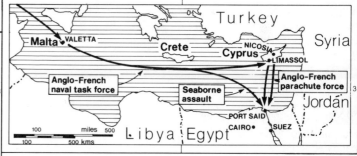

Angered by Nasser's nationalization of the Suez Canal on 26 July 1956 and concerned about Egypt's growing armoury of Soviet-supplied weapons, Britain and France decided to reoccupy the Canal Zone, the operation being thinly disguised as an attempt to halt the Israeli invasion of Sinai on the grounds that it threatened the canal. In fact the operation had been planned jointly by the three invaders, but the deception demanded that the seaborne part of the operation, which had to be staged from Malta, six day's steaming from the canal, could not start until the invasion of Sinai was under way. Thus Israel's attack was launched on 29 October and the Anglo-French forces went in on 5 November. The seaborne part of the attack was codenamed Operation Musketeer. Though militarily successful, the incident aroused such worldwide condemnation that Britain and France were compelled to agree to a ceasefire on 7 November, having advanced only 23 miles down the canal. It is estimated that 90,000 French and British servicemen took part in the operation, of whom 32 were killed and 130 wounded. Egyptian dead in Sinai and on the Canal were between 2,500 and 3,000.

The Six Day War 1967

After the Suez War of 1956 the presence of a UN force in Sinai kept the peace on Israel's southern border, but by 1966 Nasser, smarting from successive rebuffs to his ambition to lead a union of all the Arab states, decided that Egypt was again strong enough to provoke and win a decisive clash with Israel. In the meantime incidents between Israel and her other neighbours, particularly Syria, had intensified.

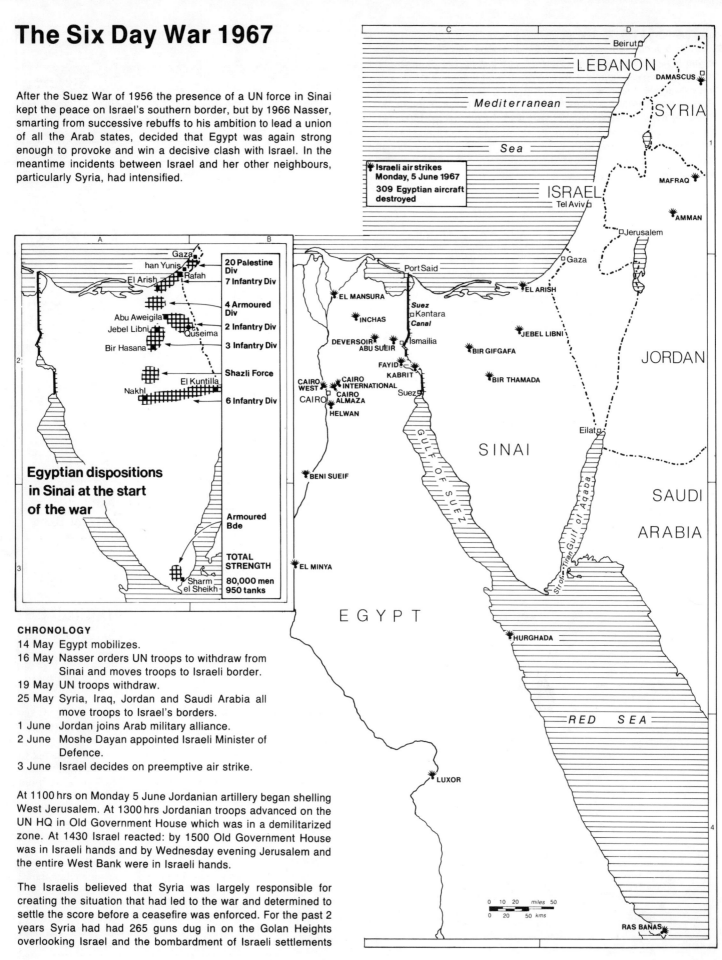

Israeli air strikes
Monday, 5 June 1967
309 Egyptian aircraft destroyed

Egyptian dispositions in Sinai at the start of the war

20 Palestine Div	
7 Infantry Div	
4 Armoured Div	
2 Infantry Div	
3 Infantry Div	
Shazli Force	
6 Infantry Div	
Armoured Bde	
TOTAL STRENGTH	**80,000 men 950 tanks**

CHRONOLOGY

14 May Egypt mobilizes.
16 May Nasser orders UN troops to withdraw from Sinai and moves troops to Israeli border.
19 May UN troops withdraw.
25 May Syria, Iraq, Jordan and Saudi Arabia all move troops to Israel's borders.
1 June Jordan joins Arab military alliance.
2 June Moshe Dayan appointed Israeli Minister of Defence.
3 June Israel decides on preemptive air strike.

At 1100 hrs on Monday 5 June Jordanian artillery began shelling West Jerusalem. At 1300 hrs Jordanian troops advanced on the UN HQ in Old Government House which was in a demilitarized zone. At 1430 Israel reacted: by 1500 Old Government House was in Israeli hands and by Wednesday evening Jerusalem and the entire West Bank were in Israeli hands.

The Israelis believed that Syria was largely responsible for creating the situation that had led to the war and determined to settle the score before a ceasefire was enforced. For the past 2 years Syria had had 265 guns dug in on the Golan Heights overlooking Israel and the bombardment of Israeli settlements near the border had intensified during the first four months of 1967. By 5 June there were 40,000 Syrian troops with 260 tanks on the Golan Heights and during 6, 7 and 8 June the Syrians bombarded all settlements within range of their guns; but Israel made no move until it was clear that the war in Sinai was won. The first Israeli troops crossed the border at 1130 hrs on 9 June. When the war officially ended at 1930 hrs on 10 June about 1000 Syrians had been killed and 500 taken prisoner. Israeli losses were 115 killed and 306 wounded.

Total casualties in the Six Day War

	Died	Wounded	Prisoners
Israeli	275	800	21
Egyptian	10–15,000	50,000 +	11,500

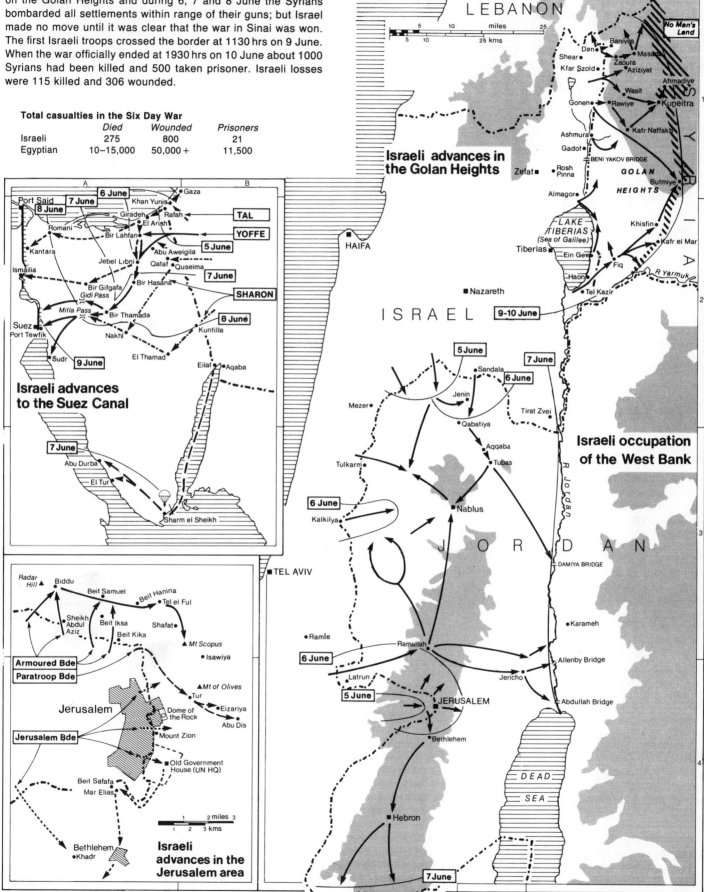

Israeli advances to the Suez Canal

Israeli advances in the Golan Heights

Israeli occupation of the West Bank

Israeli advances in the Jerusalem area

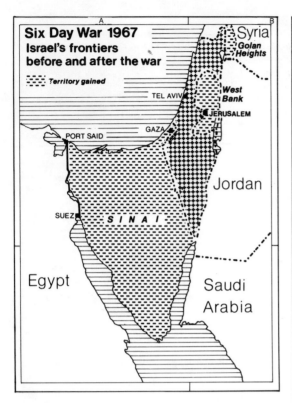

Six Day War 1967
Israel's frontiers before and after the war

Territory gained

Syria
Golan Heights
TEL AVIV
West Bank
JERUSALEM
PORT SAID
GAZA
Jordan
SUEZ
SINAI
Egypt
Saudi Arabia

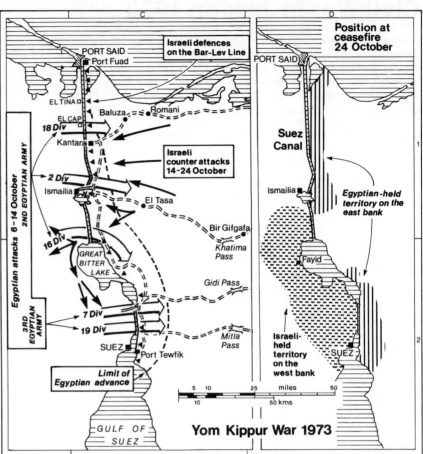

Yom Kippur War 1973

Israeli defences on the Bar-Lev Line

PORT SAID
Port Fuad
EL TINA
Baluza   Romani
EL CAP
18 Div
Kantara

Israeli counter attacks 14–24 October

Egyptian attacks 6–14 October
2ND EGYPTIAN ARMY
2 Div
Ismailia   El Tasa
Bir Gifgafa
Khatima Pass
16 Div
GREAT BITTER LAKE
Gidi Pass
3RD EGYPTIAN ARMY
7 Div
19 Div
Mitla Pass
SUEZ   Port Tewfik
Limit of Egyptian advance
GULF OF SUEZ

Position at ceasefire 24 October

PORT SAID
Suez Canal
Ismailia
Egyptian-held territory on the east bank
Fayid
Israeli-held territory on the west bank
SUEZ

miles
5 10 25 50
10 50 kms

The Yom Kippur War 1973

The Six Day War solved no problems in the Middle East. Israel would not return to the pre-1967 borders. The Arabs refused to recognize the new boundaries and insisted on a solution which acknowledged the rights of the Palestinians, both refugees and those still in Israel. During the ensuing political deadlock Israel constructed a chain of defended posts along the east bank of the Suez Canal, known as the Bar-Lev Line, and established defensive positions on the Golan Heights. Egypt reacted with commando raids, artillery bombardments and the installation of a Russian-equipped air defence system. This period between October 1968 and August 1970 was known as the War of Attrition. In September 1970 President Nasser died and was succeeded by Anwar Sadat, who, in October 1972, decided on war with Israel. After meticulous planning, in which Russia, Syria and Jordan were involved, it was decided to attack on the Day of Atonement (Yom Kipppur), the holiest day in the Jewish calendar – 6 October, 1973. The advances on both the Egyptian and Syrian fronts were initially successful, but when a ceasefire was enforced on 24 October the Israelis had repulsed the Egyptians and Syrians and gained further territory.

Total Israeli losses in the Yom Kippur war were 2,378. Arab losses were never announced but it is estimated that Egypt and Syria each lost about 8000 men.

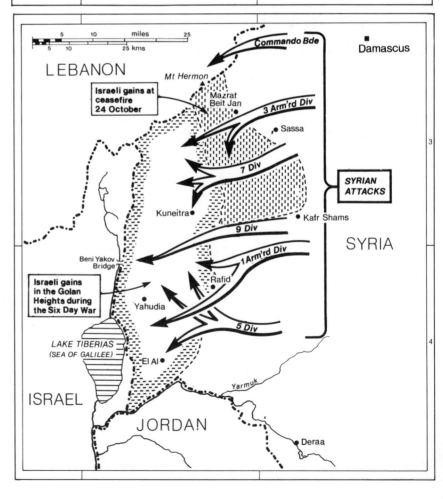

Yom Kippur War 1973

miles
5 10 25
5 10 25 kms

Commando Bde   Damascus
LEBANON   Mt Hermon

Israeli gains at ceasefire 24 October
Mazrat Beit Jan
3 Arm'rd Div
Sassa
7 Div
SYRIAN ATTACKS
Kuneitra   Kafr Shams
9 Div
SYRIA
Beni Yakov Bridge
1 Arm'rd Div
Israeli gains in the Golan Heights during the Six Day War
Rafid
Yahudia
5 Div
LAKE TIBERIAS (SEA OF GALILEE)
El Al
Yarmuk
ISRAEL
JORDAN
Deraa

Civil War in Jordan 1970

Relations between the Jordan Government and the Palestinian Arab guerrillas degenerated during 1970 into full-scale civil war. In February the ten Palestinian guerrilla organizations in Jordan, of which *Al Fatah*, led by Yassir Arafat, was the largest and most important, banded together to form the Palestine Armed Struggle Command (PASC) after the Government had banned, among other things, the carrying of weapons in public and the publication of unlicensed newspapers. Clashes occurred at once and the Government was forced to suspend the order three days later. Further clashes occurred between 7 and 11 June, sparked off when commandos of the Popular Front for the Liberation of Palestine (PFLP) tried to storm a prison in which guerrillas were held. The fighting brought normal life in Amman to a standstill and King Hussein was obliged to give in to many of the guerrillas' demands, including the dismissal of his uncle, Major-General Sherif bin Jamal, from command of the Army, in order to obtain a ceasefire. More serious trouble started when, between 6 and 9 September, the PFLP hijacked four large passenger aircraft – a Pan Am jumbo jet which was blown up at Cairo airport and three planes belonging to British Airways, Swissair and TWA which were flown to an airstrip 25 miles from Amman – and used them to bargain for the release of *fedayeen* prisoners held in Britain, Israel, Switzerland and W. Germany. The passengers and crews were eventually released but the planes were blown up. Fighting began again and on 15 September Hussein formed a military government. By 17 September the fighting was general but was heaviest around Amman, near which the Army continually shelled the refugee camps of Jebel Wahdat and Jebel Hussain, where the guerrillas had their strongholds. In the north, reinforced by Syrian armoured units, they held the towns of Irbid and Ramtha. Spurred on by fear of intervention by the US 6th Fleet and/or the Israeli Army, an inter-Arab mission succeeded in obtaining a ceasefire on 25 September. Estimates of casualties vary. In a message to President Nasser on 23 September Yassir Arafat put the death toll at 10,000. *The Times* on 24 September said, 'Casualties will not be less than 15,000 – a high proportion of them deaths'. On 4 October the Information Minister in the new cabinet, Mr Abou Odeh, said that the casualties had been vastly exaggerated and did not exceed 700 killed and 1300 wounded. Guerrilla spokesmen, however, insisted that up to 25,000 people had been killed and injured throughout Jordan during the Civil War.

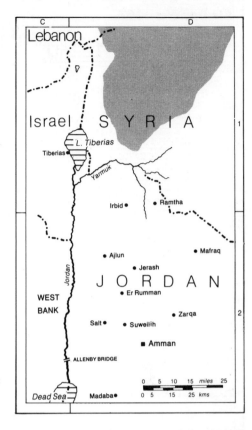

The Israeli Withdrawal from Sinai, 1974–82

When the ceasefire which marked the end of the Yom Kippur War came into effect on 24 October, 1973, Egyptian forces held a thin strip of Sinai along the East Bank of the Suez Canal, while, behind them, Israeli troops held areas of Egyptian territory on the West Bank. Under the disengagement agreements of 18 January, 1974, and 1 September, 1975, Israel withdrew from North-West Sinai, and the rest of the peninsula was restored to Egypt in seven stages, as laid down at the Israeli–Egyptian peace treaty of 26 March, 1979, which itself arose out of the Camp David agreement between Mr Begin and President Sadat of 17 September, 1978.

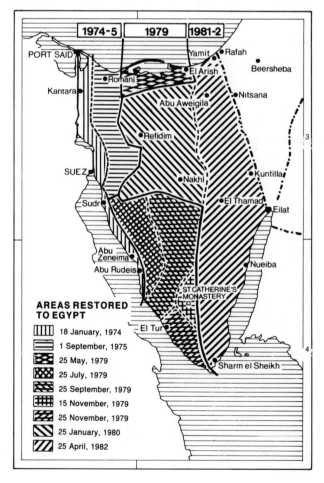

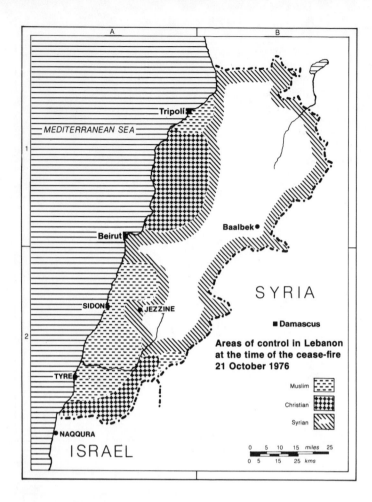

Areas of control in Lebanon
at the time of the cease-fire
21 October 1976

Muslim
Christian
Syrian

0 5 10 15 miles 25
0 5 15 25 kms

Lebanon 1958–81

Until 1864 Lebanon was part of the Syrian province of the Ottoman Empire, but in that year 'Mount Lebanon' was separated from the rest of Syria and became an autonomous sanjaq. After the First World War it came under French mandate and in 1920 France created the present Lebanon by adding to the predominantly Christian sanjaq the predominantly Muslim territories to the north, east and south. In 1940 it was held by the Vichy French, but was taken by British troops in 1941. They and the French troops were withdrawn in 1946 and Lebanon became completely independent for the first time in its history. The country had come into being on the basis of a compromise between Muslims and Christians, who formed almost equal proportions of the population. Early in 1958 opposition by both Christians and Muslims to the Maronite Christian President Camille Chamoun hardened, both on account of his pro-Western attitude during the Suez Crisis and because it was thought that he planned to amend the constitution in order to remain in office. In May the Muslims of Tripoli rose in armed revolt and the trouble soon spread to the Muslim quarters of Beirut, also to Sidon and the Shi'ite region of Baalbek. UAR units from Syria took over peripheral parts of the country in aid of the insurgents. President Chamoun appealed to the U.S. for military assistance and U.S. troops landed at Beirut on 14 July. However, the insurrection continued on a reduced scale until September when General Chehab took over from Chamoun and the country soon returned to nearly normal conditions. American troops were withdrawn gradually, the last leaving on 25 October, 1958.

Civil War broke out again in April, 1975, between the right-wing Christian Phalangist party and left-wing Muslim groups, a feud which owed its origins to the distribution of power in Lebanon but was not aided by the fact that over 200,000 Palestinian refugees were allowed to live there virtually as a state within a state. Heavy Israeli raids on S. Lebanon in retaliation for Palestinian guerrilla attacks caused scores of casualties and the evacuation of numerous border villages. Sectarian fighting began in Tripoli in mid-March and spread to Beirut in April. On 15 May the government of Rashid Solh resigned and President Franjieh appointed a military government led by Brigadier Nowreddin Rifai on 23 May; it lasted 3 days. On 30 June a new cabinet was formed, led by Rashid Karami, but it was powerless to stop the fighting which intensified in October. Elements of the PLO, which, until then had played a peace-keeping role, entered the battle for control of Beirut, in which scores of buildings were totally destroyed. During the first half of January, 1976, there was fighting throughout the country as Phalangist right-wing Christian forces blockaded the Palestinian refugee camps and the Palestinians responded by attacking Christian villages on the coast. A Syrian-sponsored cease-fire lasted from 22 January to 13 March when fighting began again. In April a constitutional amendment facilitated the early retirement of President Franjieh who was succeeded by Elias Sarkis. On 1 June Syrian troops made their first large-scale intervention, advancing to occupy the Bekaa Valley in the face of tough resistance from Palestinian forces. At Riyadh on 17 October the leaders of Saudi Arabia, Syria, Egypt, Lebanon and the PLO agreed terms for a cease-fire which came into effect on 21 October, enforced by the Arab Deterrent Forces (ADF), composed mainly of Syrian troops. This ended, temporarily 19 months of civil war which had cost some 45,000 lives, left 100,000 wounded and caused another 500,000 to emigrate.

1977
Fierce fighting between Christian rightists and Palestinians broke out in February round Marjayoun and continued throughout the summer. Israel supported the Christians with artillery and tanks. The murder of the leftist Druze leader, Kamal Jumblatt, on 16 March was followed by Druze attacks on Christian villages and counter-reprisals which continued throughout the year.

1978

February	Serious fighting between Syrian forces of the ADF and right-wing Lebanese militia.
14 March	Israel launches full-scale attack into S. Lebanon to destroy PLO bases.
19 March	Israelis now hold all of S. Lebanon south of the Litani except for a small enclave round Tyre. Troops of UN Interim Force in Lebanon (UNIFIL) begin to arrive and Israelis withdraw by mid-June. An estimated 1000 people were killed in this invasion; 200,000 Lebanese and 65,000 Palestinians fled north.
Early July	Syrian forces bombard E. Beirut in revenge for the murder, allegedly by Phalangists, of Tony Franjieh, son of the ex-President, a close friend of President Assad of Syria.
5 August	Further intense bombardment of Beirut.
9 August	Cease-fire.
6 October	Syrian troops surround E. Beirut.
17 October	Syrian troops withdraw a few hundred yards to allow Lebanese Christian civilians to leave Beirut.

1979

17 April	Former Lebanese Army Major Sa'ad Haddad, leader of the Israeli-equipped right-wing Maronite Christian militia in S. Lebanon, declares the 350-square mile (900 sq.km) border area under his control to be the independent state of 'Free Lebanon'. 500 Lebanese Army troops move into S. Lebanon and Haddad's artillery shells UNIFIL HQ at Naqqura.
5 June	Israeli jets bomb Nabatiyeh.
19 June	Israeli forces attack S. Lebanon. Fighting with Palestinian commandos lasts for 5 days before a cease-fire is arranged through U.S. mediation.

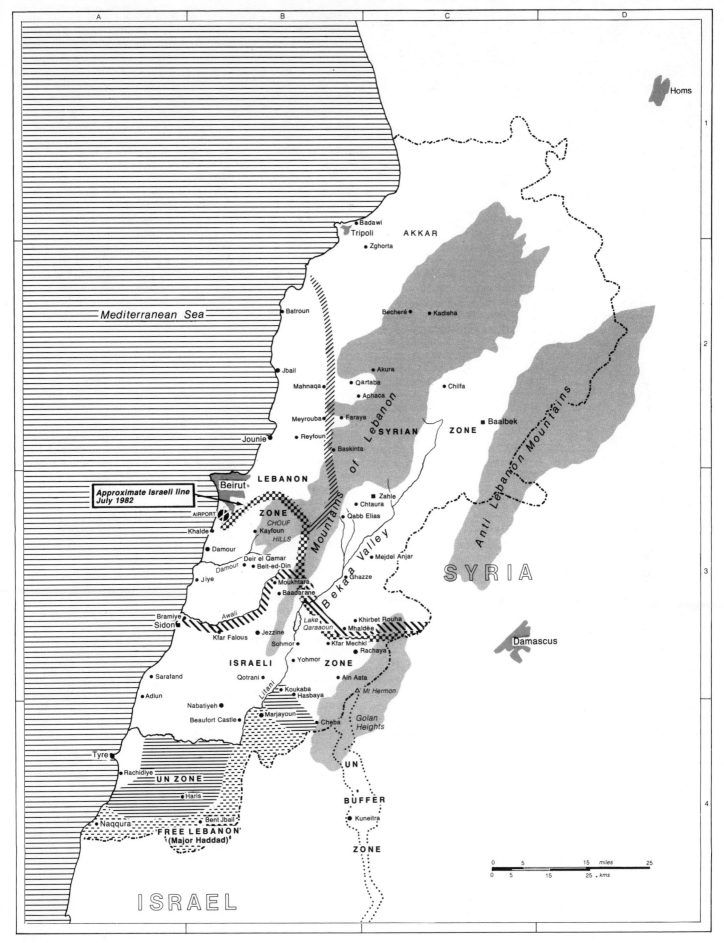

Homs

A · B · C · D

1

Mediterranean Sea

• Badawi
Tripoli
AKKAR
• Zghorta

• Batroun

Becheré • • Kadisha

2

• Jbail

• Akura
Mahnaqa • • Qartaba
• Aphaca
• Chilfa

Meyrouba • • Faraya
SYRIAN   ZONE
• Baalbek

Jounie • • Reyfoun
• Baskinta

LEBANON

Beirut •
**Approximate Israeli line
July 1982**

Zahle ■
• Chtaura

AIRPORT
ZONE
CHOUF
• Qabb Elias

Khalde •
• Kayfoun
HILLS

• Damour
• Mejdel Anjar

Deir el Qamar •
Damour   • Beit-ed-Din

• Jiye
• Moukhtara
• Ghazze

• Baadarane

Bramiye •
Awali

Sidon •
*Lake
Qaraaoun*
• Khirbet Rouha
• Mhaldée

Kfar Falous •   • Jezzine
Sohmor •
• Kfar Mechkl
• Rachaya

ISRAELI • Yohmor **ZONE**

• Sarafand
Qotrani •
• Ain Aata

• Adlun
• Koukaba
Hasbaya •
△ *Mt Hermon*

Nabatiyeh •
Litani

Beaufort Castle •
• Marjayoun
Cheba •
*Golan
Heights*

Tyre •

UN

• Rachidiye
UN ZONE
• Haris

BUFFER

• Naqqura
• Bent Jbail
• Kuneitra

**'FREE LEBANON'
(Major Haddad)**

ZONE

SYRIA

Anti Lebanon Mountains

Damascus •

Mountains of Lebanon

Bekaa Valley

ISRAEL

miles
0   5   15   25
0   5   15   25 kms

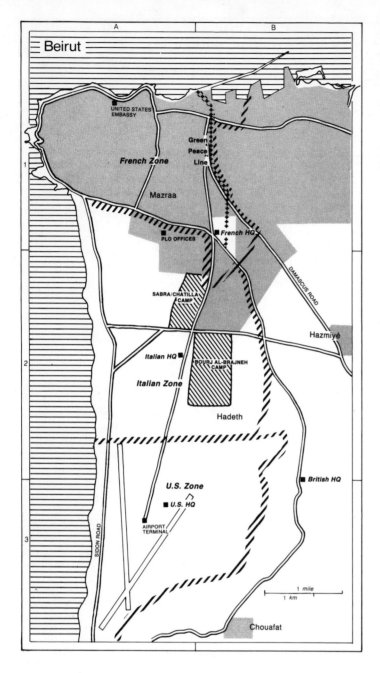

Beirut

United States Embassy
French Zone
Green Peace Line
Mazraa
PLO Offices
French HQ
Sabra/Chatilla Camp
Damascus Road
Hazmiyé
Italian HQ
Bourj Al-Brajneh Camp
Italian Zone
Hadeth
U.S. Zone
British HQ
U.S. HQ
Airport Terminal
Sidon Road
1 mile
1 km
Chouafat

27 June   First clashes between Israeli and Syrian jets since 1974. At least 4 planes shot down.

1980

Intermittent fighting continued throughout the year. During the first 9 months about 1800 people were killed and a further 1700 wounded.

1981

In Israeli attacks on Beirut and clashes between Syrian ADF troops and right-wing Phalangist Christian irregulars about 2100 people were killed during the year.

In the summer of 1981 Israel began planning her latest and most devastating incursion into the Lebanon, finally launched in June, 1982, and described in the *Christian Science Monitor* as 'an attempt to bait the Palestinians into provoking a confrontation in S. Lebanon'; but once the Israeli juggernaut had been set in motion no one seemed able, or willing, to stop it. Estimates of the opposing strengths vary. The *Jerusalem Post* (7 June, 1982) said: 'PLO forces in S. Lebanon number 6000 armed men, about half the PLO's total strength in Lebanon.' Israeli military sources estimated that the PLO had about 35 T-34 Soviet tanks of Second World War vintage 'and a large number of artillery pieces, including 130 mm cannon, 160 mm mortars and 'Stalin-organ' multiple Katushya launchers, anti-aircraft guns and ground-to-air Sam-7 missiles.' Of course, the PLO had no air force and no naval craft. In a despatch from Beirut on 23 June *Associated Press* estimated that Israel had deployed '9 armoured divisions with 90,000 soldiers. In addition Israel has 1300 tanks, 12,000 troop and supply trucks, 1300 armoured personnel carriers, 350 ambulances and 300 buses to carry prisoners.' The main events of the campaign were as follows:

June	Israel invades Lebanon (6th); takes Tyre (7th); Sidon (8th); Damour (9th); cease-fire (11th–13th); Israel's encirclement of Beirut complete (14th).
July	Israel cuts off water and electricity supplies to W. Beirut (4th); gives the 6000 Palestinians in W. Beirut 30 days to leave (17th).
August	Israelis enter Central Beirut (2nd); Seige of Beirut ends after heaviest bombardment of the war (12th); PLO evacuation from Beirut starts (22nd); Bashir Gemayel elected President of Lebanon (23rd).
September	Gemayel assassinated (14th); Israeli troops move into W. Beirut (15th); massacre of Palestinian men, women and children in Sabra and Chatila refugee camps (16th–18th); Gemayel's brother, Amin, elected President (21st); American forces supervise PLO evacuation to Syria; French and Italian troops take up positions in Beirut, Israelis leave Beirut (28th); Yasser Arafat leaves Beirut (30th).

The massacres in the Sabra–Chatila refugee camps, carried out by members of the Phalange militia, aroused violent worldwide condemnation. Michael Jansen in *The Battle of Beirut* says: 'At a rough estimate perhaps a thousand people in all were slaughtered in Sabra-Chatila. But over 900 other people mostly women and children, are known to have been put on trucks and driven away; nothing has been heard of them since.' Summing up the war as a whole, she gives the following figures: 12,000 killed – 40,000 wounded – 300,000 homeless – 100,000 without shelter and several hundreds of thousands destitute.

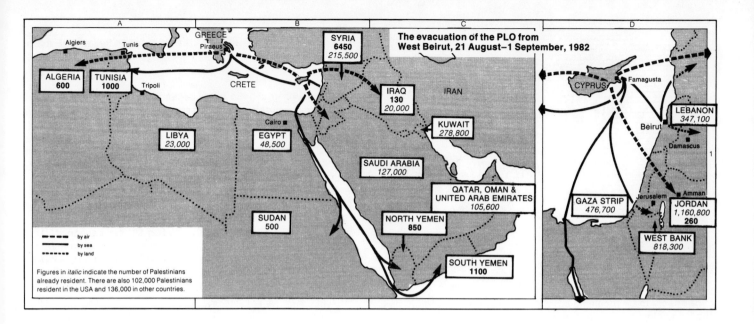

Figures in *italic* indicate the number of Palestinians already resident. There are also 102,000 Palestinians resident in the USA and 136,000 in other countries.

The PLO Diaspora August–September 1982

Until 1964 the handling of the Palestine question had been the preserve of the Arab League, in which the Palestinian Arabs were not directly represented. The Arab summit meeting of that year led to the foundation of the Palestine Liberation Organisation which now consists of several groups, mostly formed since that date. They are: *Al Fatah*, founded about the same time as the PLO and deriving its name from a reversal of the Arabic initials for the Palestine National Liberation Movement, and led by Yassir Arafat. Fatah means conquest. Between 1968 and 1969 Arafat also took over the leadership of the PLO, ousting its founder and first chairman, Ahmed Shuqairi; *The Popular Front for the Liberation of Palestine*, founded in 1967 by George Habash, a Marxist body committed to the total extinction of Israel; *The Popular Front for the Liberation of Palestine*

– *General Command* split from the PFLP in 1968 and led by Ahmed Jibril; *The Democratic Front for the Liberation of Palestine*, split from the PFLP in 1969, led by Naif Hawatmeh; *De Saiga Movement* formed in 1969 led by Issam Lalqaddi; *The Arab Liberation Front*, part of the Ba'athist movement. Various terrorist bodies also claim affiliation with the PLO, the best known being *Black September*, which was responsible for the seizure and deaths of 11 Israeli athletes at the 1972 Munich Olympic Games.

Israel succeeded, by her invasion of Lebanon in September, 1982, in achieving the dispersal of the PLO, the details of which are shown in the accompanying map. Though they left Beirut as self-styled heroes, the reception accorded them by most of the host countries did not reflect the same attitude.

Lebanon 1984

Sadly, the evacuation of the PLO provided no answer to the problems of the Lebanon and within weeks of the cease-fire artillery duels began between the Druze and the Christian Phalange militia in the Chouf Mountains. Plans to organize a joint withdrawal of the 60,000 Syrian troops holding the northern and eastern parts of the country and the 36,000 Israeli troops in the south came to nothing, largely thanks to the unwillingness of President Hafez Assad of Syria to negotiate. When, in September, 1983, the Israelis withdrew from the Chouf Mountains to the Awali Line without enforcing a cease-fire the fighting escalated from sectarian rivalry to an all-out Druze show of force involving the bombardment of the city of Beirut, the airport and posts held by the 'peacekeeping' troops, and the expulsion of all Maronite Catholics from the Chouf and the destruction of their villages. At the same time as the Israelis withdrew, the Shi'ite Amal faction began fighting the Lebanese Army in Beirut. On 8 September 2 US Marines were killed and American warships began shelling Druze positions in the Chouf. On 9 September the Druzes captured Bhamdoun and surrounded the Phalange-held village of Souk-el-Gharb. The Lebanese Army then came to the aid of the Phalangists and the Americans to the aid of the Lebanese Army. On 26 September Saudi Arabian mediators arranged a cease-

fire which commanded token observation until 6.20 am on Sunday, 23 October, when suicide squads drove lorries packed with high explosive into the barracks of the American and French contingents of the Multinational Force. 223 US Marines and 58 French soldiers were killed in the ensuing explosions.

On 3 November fighting broke out between the pro-Arafat and pro-Syrian factions of the PLO in Tripoli, culminating in the evacuation of Arafat and 4000 of his faithful by ship on 20 December. Meanwhile American ships off the Lebanese coast bombarded Syrian positions in Lebanon, but with what ultimate objective was unclear: "each of the *New Jersey's* shells weighs as much as a small car". By the beginning of February if had become apparent that the multinational force was achieving nothing and President Reagan, fearful of pointless loss of life in an election year, decided to "redeploy" the marines. Britain and Italy followed suit and the British contingent was evacuated on 8 February. On 6 February militiamen of Nabih Berri's Shia Amal movement took over West Beirut and President Gemayel's position looked very shaky, but on 5 March he agreed with President Assad of Syria to revoke the 17 May, 1983, military withdrawal agreement with Israel, thereby buying time for himself but dealing a serius blow to American and Israeli policy in Lebanon.

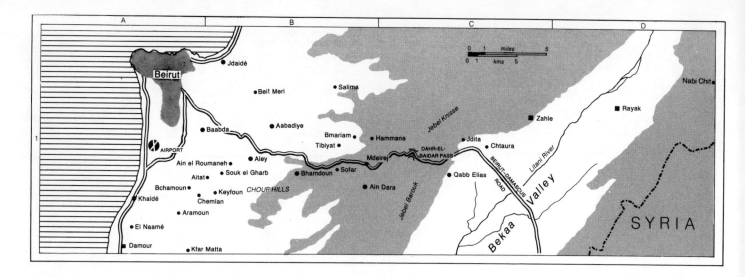

Syria seems to be regaining control over much of the territory that she held before the British Mandate.

Who's Who in the Lebanon

The Druzes are an esoteric sect who call themselves Muslims but are regarded by most Muslims as heretics. Founded in the 11th century, they now number about 500,000, almost equally divided between Syria and Lebanon. The name probably derives from Ismail Durzi, their first apostle in Syria. The fighting element of the Druze community, the Progressive Socialist Party (PSP), was founded by Kamal Jumblatt who led the left-wing side in the civil war of 1975–6. He was assassinated in 1977, whereon the leadership of the community passed to his son, Walid. The Druzes are supported and supplied by the Syrians.

The Shia militia, Amal (meaning 'hope'), was formed by the late Imam Musa Sadr who vanished mysteriously in Libya in 1978. He was an Iranian and a friend of Ayatollah Khomeini. The present leader of Amal is Nabih Berri. Shia and Sunni Muslims recognize different lines of descent from the Prophet Mahomet. About 90% of the world's Muslims are Sunni. Of the remaining 10% about 95% are Shia. The balance is made up by small sects such as the Druzes, the

Alawites and the Ismailis. The Shias are Lebanon's biggest single community and were traditionally the underdogs, but are now asserting themselves. The Druzes and the Shias are sympathetic to each other.

The Phalange or Kataib is a Lebanese nationalist Christian party founded by Pierre Gemayel, father of the present President, in 1936, after a visit to Germany, and so, ironically for a movement which enjoys Israeli support, was originally Nazi-inspired. The Phalange is predominantly Maronite but includes some Orthodox Christians. The Maronites belong to an Eastern Church founded before 423 by the Syrian St Maro. Since 1216 they have been steadfast Catholics. They have been the dominant community since independence, providing both the President and the army commander.

The Lebanese Army, recently retrained by the Americans, is officially neutral but was increasingly drawn into the latest fighting on the Phalangist side. It is regarded by many Druzes and Muslims as an instrument of Maronite domination, for, though 60% of its soldiers are Muslims, almost all Shias, 60% of its officers are Christians, almost all Maronites. It is commanded by General Ibrahim Tannous, reputedly a Phalangist sympathiser.

PART III
The Gulf

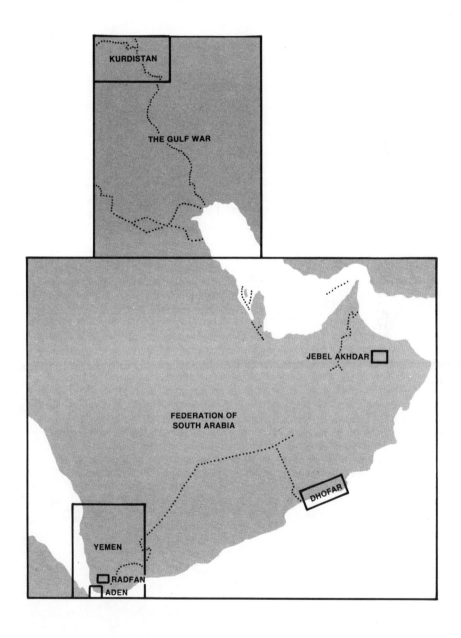

KURDISTAN

THE GULF WAR

JEBEL AKHDAR

FEDERATION OF
SOUTH ARABIA

DHOFAR

YEMEN

RADFAN
ADEN

The Federation of South Arabia

Aden became a British possession in 1839 and was later developed as a coal depot and supply station for ships. It was administered from India until 1937, when it became a Crown Colony. The hinterland, divided into two areas known as the Eastern Protectorate and the Western Protectorate, was populated by tribes whose rulers gradually entered into treaties with Britain which gave them protection in return for an undertaking not to enter into dealings with any other foreign power. During and after the Second World War ten states in the Western Protectorate signed advisory treaties with Britain, binding them to accept the advice of the Governor of Aden and in February, 1959, the Federation of Amirates of the South was inaugurated. On 18 January, 1963, when Aden joined the Federation, it was renamed the Federation of South Arabia. In 1967 the country became the People's Republic of South Yemen, the name being changed to the People's Democratic Republic of the Yemen (PDRY) on 30 November, 1970.

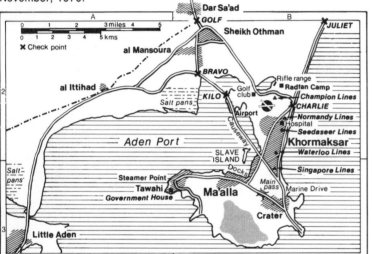

THE RADFAN

During the Emergency in Southern Arabia between 1964 and 1967, two distinct campaigns were fought by the British and Local Security Forces – one against terrorists in Aden State, the other against dissident tribesmen in the mountains of the Federation, supported and supplied by Egyptian and Yemeni nationalist agents. The main area of activity in the latter campaign was the Radfan, a hot, arid, mountainous district covering some 400 sq miles to the east of the Dhala road, the ancient caravan route to the Yemen, travellers along which had for centuries been obliged to pay 'tolls' to the Quteibi tribe. As the number of incidents on the Dhala road mounted, the Federal rulers demanded action; further impetus was added when, on 10 December, 1963, a bomb was thrown at the High Commissioner, Sir Kennedy Trevaskis, injuring him and 52 others, and killing his assistant, following which a State of Emergency was declared. The first operation in the Radfan, in January, 1964, was codenamed 'Nutcracker' and resulted in the building of a road through the Rabwa Pass to the Wadi Taym, but as soon as the troops withdrew, the dissidents destroyed the road. 'Radforce', in May, 1964, was more effective and achieved its objective of showing that dissident activity would not go unpunished. Nevertheless fighting continued, but on a much reduced scale, until the British withdrew in 1967. The map shows the main area of fighting in the Radfan.

ADEN

Britain's aim in the 1950s was to lay the foundations whereon Aden and her associated protectorates could establish a firmly-based framework, leading to eventual self-government. Unhappily the sheikhs and sultans, fearing domination by the Adeni townsmen, favoured a continuing association with Britain, while the trade union movement in Aden wanted to discard the colonial yoke altogether. In July, 1964, the British Government announced that it aimed to grant independence to S. Arabia not later than 1968 but would continue to maintain a military base in Aden. This gave the rival factions 4 years in which to fight it out, while Britain tried vainly to keep the peace. The main contenders were the South Arabian League (SAL), formed in 1951, backed by Egypt; the People's Socialist Party (PSP), the political wing of the Aden TUC, formed in 1962 (these two merged in 1963 to form the Organization for the Liberation of the Occupied South (OLOS)); and the National Liberation Front (NLF), the most militant and left-wing party, to which Egypt transferred her support. In January, 1966, OLOS joined the NLF to form the Front for the Liberation of Occupied Yemen (FLOSY), whereupon the more conservative SAL broke away. In February, 1966, the British Government announced that a military presence would no longer be maintained in Aden after independence, thereby removing any lingering hope of a peaceful solution. In November, 1966, NLF and FLOSY split up and started fighting each other. NLF emerged victorious and in 1967 gained control of the S. Arabian principalities. Britain withdrew in November, 1967, transferring power to NLF which formed the single-party government of the new People's Republic of South Yemen.

CASUALTIES IN ADEN*

	1964 (36)†		1965 (286)		1966 (510)		1967 (approx 2,900)		Total	
	Killed	Wounded	Killed	Wounded	Killed	Wounded	Killed	Wounded	Killed	Wounded
British Forces	2	25	6	83	5	218	44	325	57	651
Local Forces	1	—	9	7	2	8	5	43	17	58
British Civilians	1	5	2	28	6	19	9	31	18	83
Local Nationals	—	2	18	86	32	283	240	551	290	922
Total	4	32	35	204	45	528	298	950	382	1714

† Figures in brackets show annual number of terrorist incidents.

*From *Last Post* by Julian Paget, Faber and Faber 1969.

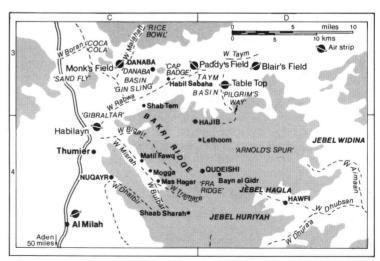

22

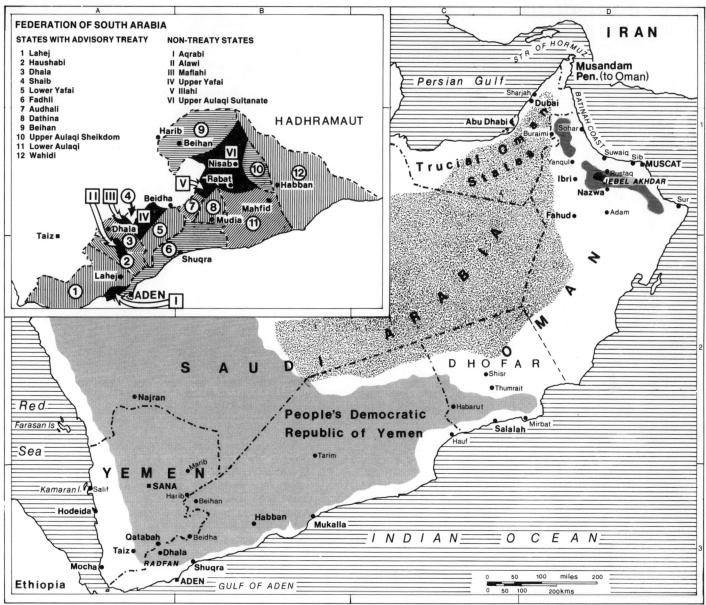

THE WAR IN THE JEBEL AKHDAR 1955–59

The Sultanate of Oman is the largest state in the Persian Gulf. (Though frequently referred to as Muscat and Oman, strictly speaking Muscat is the capital and port, and Oman the hinterland). By the Treaty of Sib in 1920 the Sultan's paramountcy over all Oman was recognized, but the tribal chiefs of the Interior were granted the right to elect their own Imam (religious leader). In 1952 Saudi Arabia occupied the desert oasis of Buraimi. In the three years which elapsed before they were ejected by the Trucial Oman Scouts they managed to turn the weak Imam, Ghalib bin Ali, into a Saudi puppet. In 1955 Ghalib's brother, Talib bin Ali, the Wali (Governor) of Rustaq, raised the Beni Hina tribe in revolt against the Sultan, Said bin Taimur, and managed to take the towns of Nazwa, Bahla and Izki without firing a shot. The Sultan asked for British assistance and the rebels were driven into the mountainous region known as the Jebel Akhdar, from whence they were finally flushed by the SAS in January, 1959. Talib and Ghalib managed to esape to Saudi Arabia.

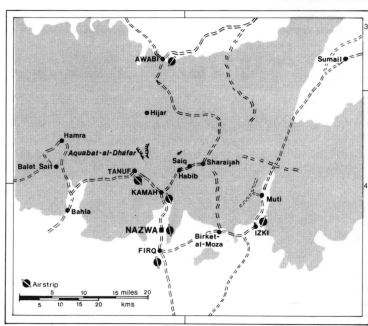

THE WAR IN THE YEMEN 1962–69

Yemen is a small, independent country of little commercial, but considerable strategic interest, as it commands the tanker route from the Persian Gulf to the Suez Canal. From 1904 to 1948 Yemen was ruled by the Imam Yahya who established himself as a national hero by expelling the Turks in 1918; thereafter he excluded all foreigners from his country. Yahya was assassinated in 1948 and was succeeded by his son, the Imam Ahmed, who maintained his rule by terror but did try to bring Yemen into the 20th century. He sent his son, the Crown Prince Mohamed al Badr, to Cairo, where Badr arranged for an Egyptian military mission to train the Yemeni armed forces, thus giving President Nasser the chance to introduce the agents who later organized the revolution. On 18 September, 1962, the Imam Ahmed died and was succeeded by his son. On 26 September al Badr was attacked in his palace in Sana, narrowly escaped with his life and fled to the north to rally his Royalist supporters, while Brigadier Abdullah Sallal, the man behind the coup, proclaimed himself President of the new Republic. Egyptian occupation began almost at once and by April, 1963, there were some 30,000 Egyptian troops in the Yemen. Roughly, the Egyptians/Republicans controlled the coastal plains, most of S Yemen and the main towns on the roads from Sana to Sada and to Harib. The Royalists controlled the mountains of northern, central and eastern Yemen. The Egyptians had total air control and bombed civilian villages indiscriminately, often using poison gas. At one time they had 70,000 troops in the Yemen. Their equipment was supplied by Russia. Royalist arms came from Saudi Arabia. After the Six Day War Nasser withdrew most of his troops from the Yemen. In November, 1967, Sallal was overthrown but the military stalemate continued. Finally, in 1969, King Feisal of Saudia Arabia arranged a conference at Jeddah which resulted in the formation of a coalition government basically pro-Western in its outlook.

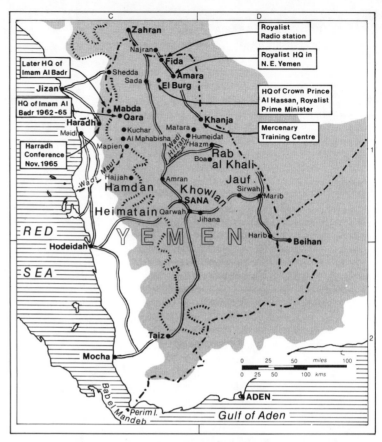

Liberation Front (DAF) and was later absorbed into the People's Front for the Liberation of the Occupied Arabian Gulf (PFLOAG), a Communist organization run from the PDRY, indoctrinated by Russian and Chinese agents and supplied by them with arms and money. By 1970 PFLOAG controlled virtually all of Dhofar except Salalah, Taqa and Mirbat. On 23 July, 1970, Sultan Said bin Taimur was deposed by his son, Qaboos, who took immediate steps to strengthen the SAF, employing British officers and troops from Jordan, Iran, India and Pakistan. Nevertheless, it was not until 11 December, 1975, that the war was officially declared over. The Sultan's success can be ascribed to four main factors: (1) the resistance of Islam to Marxist indoctrination; (2) the strength of tribal loyalties; (3) SAF control of the air and use of helicopters; (4) the enemy's reliance on a single supply line.

THE WAR IN DHOFAR 1965–75

Dhofar is the southern province of the Sultanate of Oman. The war in Dhofar lasted from 1965 until 1975 and was fought between the Sultan's Armed Forces (SAF) and dissident Dhofaris who wanted to 'liberate' the country from the feudal rule of the Sultan. The rebel party called itself the Dhofar

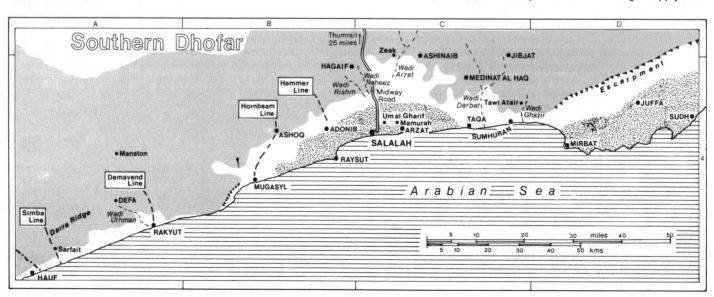

Kurds in the way 1961–79

The Kurds are a semi-nomadic people of Indo-European origin spread over five countries and numbering about 8·5m. In 1920 they were guaranteed self-determination by the Treaty of Sevres but this was superseded by the Treaty of Lausanne in 1923 and thereafter the governments concerned chose to ignore the problem. In 1942 the leader of the Democratic Party of Kurdistan (DPK), Mullah Mustafa Barzani, forced the Iraqi Government to recognize the Kurds' right to autonomy, and, when this agreement was broken, led a rising which lasted for two years. Barzani fled to Persia, then to Russia, from whence he was allowed to return in 1958 after the assassination of King Faisal II and the formation of a new government under Brigadier Kassem. But relations between Kassem and Barzani soon deteriorated and by September, 1961, the Kurdish rebels (the *Pesh Merga* – "Forward to Death") held 250 miles along the Turkish and Iranian frontiers from Zakho to Sulaymaniyah and the Iraqi army was forced to launch a full-scale offensive. On 10 October Kassem announced that military operations were over and that the army was in full control, but in fact the rebels still held the border. In the fighting 270 villages were destroyed, 3,000 Kurds killed and 120,000 made homeless. On 8 February, 1963, Kassem was shot and the new régime, under Colonel Aref, came to an agreement with the Kurds on the matter of autonomy inside Iraq. But the new Government showed little inclination to honour its pledges and military operations were resumed on 10 June, 4 divisions being committed to the battle. Kurdish forces were estimated at between 15–20,000 men. The ensuing campaign was said to be "far more brutal and cold-blooded than anything Kassem ever waged". Barzani's HQ alleged on 30 June that 167 villages had been wiped out and 1943 of their civilian inhabitants killed, 137 of them children under three. But the rebels fought back bravely and in November it was the Government which made overtures for peace. Talks began on 31 January, 1964, and a cease-fire was signed on 10 February in which it was stated that Kurdish national rights would be recognized and a general amnesty granted. But Kurdish aspirations remained unfulfilled and fighting began again in earnest on 3 April, 1965, when 40–50,000 Government troops opened an offensive along a 250-mile front from Khanaquin to Zakho. As usual, the Kurds withdrew into the mountains as the Government forces advanced and hit back with ambushes, night raids and attacks on lines of communications. Heavy fighting took place in January, 1966, for the village of Penjwin in which the Kurds claimed to have killed 2000 Government troops. Another big offensive started on 4 May involving two Iraqi divisions, but failed to achieve its objectives. On 29 June peace terms were proposed by the Government yet again and accepted by Barzani the same day. But, as before, the Government failed to implement the agreement and unrest among the Kurds continued. On 17 July, 1968, the Government was overthrown in a bloodless coup, General Bakr became President and in August entered into fresh negotiations with the Kurds; these came to nothing and in October fighting started again. On 3 January, 1969, 60,000 troops took the offensive on a 200-mile front. On 1 March the insurgents launched a counter-offensive which opened with the shelling of the Iraq Petroleum Co's

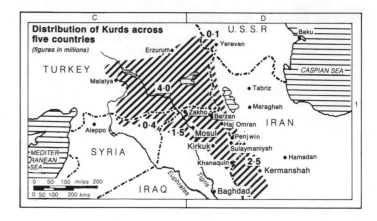

Distribution of Kurds across five countries (figures in millions)

installations at Kirkuk. In June the rebels claimed to have taken Penjwin and Qala Diza and to have killed 1,000 Government troops. They also alleged that Government planes had dropped napalm and nitric acid bombs on 57 villages, killing 730 civilians. In August the Iraqi Army committed four divisions to the offensive. In September 200,000 civilians were forced to take refuge in the mountains following aerial attacks on 120 villages. Peace talks began again in January, 1970, and ended on 11 March, the Government once more guaranteeing Kurdish antonomy. A number of the clauses in this agreement were indeed put into effect during the next 12 months, but the more important provisions, including the controversial question of whether the Kirkuk area was to be Arab or Kurdish, were not implemented. On 12 December 1973, the Government put forward proposals for Kurdish antonomy based on a census carried out in 1957. These were met with counter-proposals by the DPK which the Government found unacceptable. Fighting resumed on 12 March, 1974, in the Turkish border area, spreading by the end of the month to the Arbil, Kirkuk and Sulaymaniyah areas. By 18 April the *Pesh Merga* had come out of the hills and were operating in the plains only 70 miles from Baghdad. On 24 April Iraqi planes destroyed the town of Qala Diza and by July the rebels had been driven back into the mountains. In August the Government launched the biggest offensive since the war began in 1961 – 300 tanks were used in attacks on Ranya and Qala Diza. About 130,000 Kurds, mostly women, children and old men, fled to Iran to escape the war. On 7 March, 1975, a new Iraqi offensive coincided with an agreement between Iran and Iraq, signed in Algiers, which deprived the DPK of Iranian support and led to the collapse of rebel resistance. Iraq announced that in the last year of the war casualties had been 1640 killed and 7903 wounded. *Pesh Merga* casualties are thought to have been about the same. On 3 May Barzani said, "The struggle for Kurdish antonomy has ended and will never be resumed." He was wrong. In May–June, 1976, the fighting began again, the main reason being the Government's policy of compulsory resettlement of Kurdish refugees returned from Iran in the south of Iraq in order to reduce the density of Kurds in the north. Sporadic outbreaks of fighting continued throughout the year, the action intensifying after a major Iraqi offensive on 17 March, 1977. That summer several international organizations accused the Iraqi Government of "atrocities against the Kurdish population". The fall of the Shah in 1979 and the withdrawal of Iranian troops from the border led to renewed activity among the Iraqi Kurds. Iran's importance to the *Pesh Merga* had grown after Iraq and Turkey signed an agreement on 20 April, 1979, which put an end to supplies reaching the Kurds from Turkey. In June, 1979, the Government launched an attack on a number of Kurdish villages inside Iran. In July Masoud Barzani returned to Iraq following the death of his father, Mullah Mustafa Barzani, in the U.S. aged 79. Masoud vowed that he would "rescue the Kurdish people from persecution", but since September, 1980, the Kurdish problem has been largely overshadowed by the full-scale war waged between Iran and Iraq.

Main lines of Iraqi offensive August 1974

The Gulf War

In 1918 the British drove the Turks out of Iraq, which for nearly four centuries had been part of the Ottoman Empire. Thereafter the country was under British mandate from 1919 to 1932. It was an independent kingdom from 1932 until 14 July, 1958, when King Faisal II was assassinated and a republic was set up. The present President, Saddam Hussain, came to power in July, 1979.

Iran, known until 1935 as Persia, was ruled by shahs of the Qajar dynasty from the late 18th century until 1925 when Sultan Ahmed Shah was deposed and Reza Khan, the Prime Minister, was elected in his place. Though he certainly feathered his own nest, Reza Shah did try to bring Iran, at least superficially, into the 20th century. In 1941 he abdicated in favour of his son, Mohammed Reza Shah Pahlavi, who ruled the country with fluctuating degrees of autocracy until he was obliged by public opinion to flee the country on 16 January, 1979. On 1 February Ayatollah Khomeini, spiritual leader of the Shi'a Muslims, returned from exile and, following a referendum, on 1 April Iran was declared an Islamic Republic, of which Khomeini became the virtual dictator.

Relations between Iran and Iraq, always unstable, had been further unbalanced in 1969 when the Shah decided to ignore a 1937 Treaty which had given control of the Shatt-al-Arab, the waterway which connects Abadan with the Persian Gulf, to Iraq, the frontier being defined as the eastern bank of the waterway. Border incidents ensued and diplomatic relations were severed. Then in 1971 the Shah annexed the tiny but strategically important islands of Abu Musa and Greater and Lesser Tunb at the mouth of the Persian Gulf. In 1975 the Treaty of Algiers decreed that the deep-water channel of the Shatt-al-Arab should be the boundary between the two countries and superficial harmony was restored, but Iraq still sought to regain control of the entire waterway. These, though contributory factors, were only background excuses for the war which was to follow. After the fall of the Shah, the increasing fundamentalism of Khomeini's régime and the threat posed by the spread of his Islamic revolution to other Shi'a communities greatly disturbed the leaders of neighbouring Arab states, not least Saddam Hussain who feared the effect this would have on Iraq's Shi'a population and who also nursed a bitter and warmly reciprocated hatred for Khomeini, the latter having spent 14 years in exile in Iraq under virtual house arrest. A declaration by Ayatollah Hossein Ali Montazeri in February, 1980, that the revolution should be exported, followed by actual Iranian intervention among Shi'a communities in Iraq, Kuwait and Bahrain, showed that these fears were well-founded. In early September Iraq presented four demands to Iran: 1) evacuate the islands at the mouth of the Gulf; 2) renegotiate the Treaty of Algiers; 3) grant autonomy to the Iranian Arabs of Khuzestan; 4) stop interfering with the internal affairs of other Arab states. These demands were rejected and on 12 September Iraqi troops invaded Iran. Saddam Hussain had expected Iranian resistance to crumble and the civilian population to turn against the Government. Instead the invasion united the Iranians and, after three years of fighting, the stalemate shows no sign of being broken.

Both sides invariably exaggerate outrageously any success they achieve, so reports of the fighting cannot be taken too literally.

The following main events of the war do, however, seem to have been objectively reported:

1980

12 September Iraqi troops enter Kordestan

22 September Iraqi troops invade Khuzestan. The Iraqi Army made a 3-pronged push in the south, the main thrust being towards Khorramshahr, with subsidiary moves towards Ahwaz and Dezful. Only Khorramshahr fell entirely under Iraqi control.

Each side began bombing the other's oil installations, so endanger-ing its own, and Iran's Abadan refinery and the loading terminal at Kharg Island were soon put out of action.

1981

January   Iranians push back Iraqis around Ahwaz.

June   Iranians advance near Susangerd.

September   Iraqis abandon their bridgehead east of the Karun River near Abadan.

December   New Iranian offensive round Qasr-e-Shirin. Iranians claim to have broken through Iraqi lines near Susangerd.

By the end of the year the tide of war had definitely turned in Iran's favour.

1982

March   Iraqi forces in Khuzestan driven back.

April   Iranian bridgehead established west of the Karun River.

May   Iraqi troops leave Khorramshahr.

June/July   Iranian invasion of S. Iraq towards Basra beaten off with heavy losses.

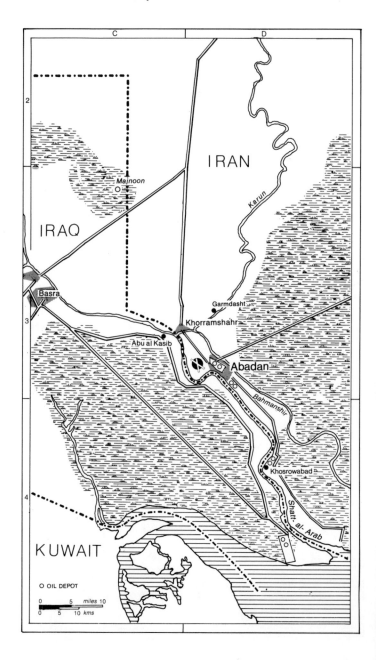

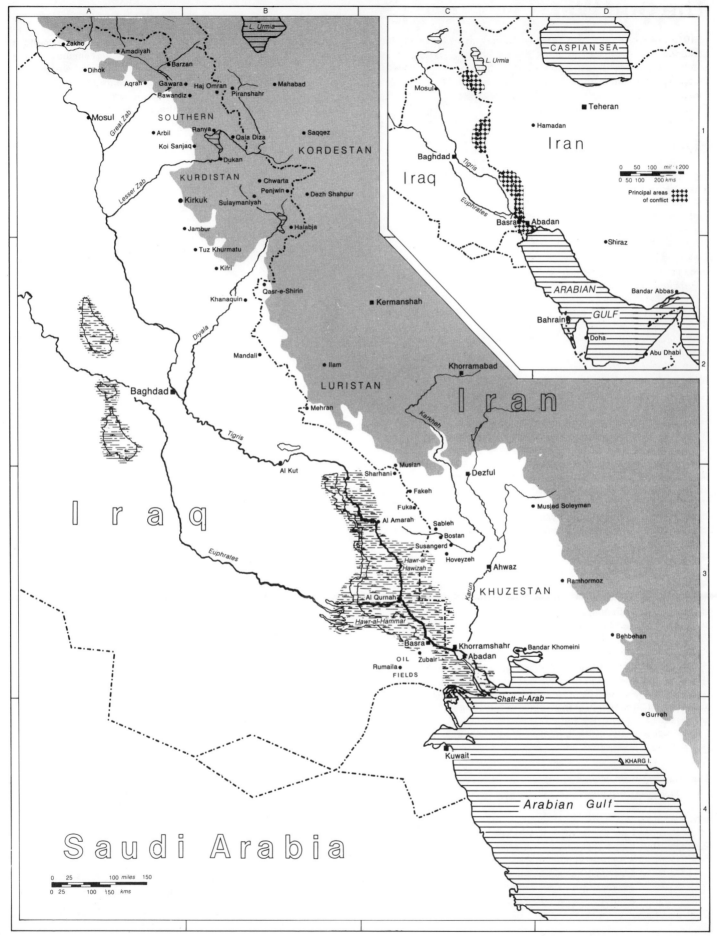

A

Zakho
Amadiyah
Dihok
Barzan
Aqrah
Gawara
Haj Omran
Rawandiz
Piranshahr
Mosul
Arbil
Ranya
Qala Diza
Saqqez
Koi Sanjaq
Dukan
KURDISTAN
Chwarta
Penjwin
Dezh Shahpur
Kirkuk
Sulaymaniyah
Jambur
Halabja
Tuz Khurmatu
Kifri
Qasr-e-Shirin
Khanaquin
Kermanshah
Mandali
Baghdad
Ilam
LURISTAN
Khorramabad
Mehran

B

L. Urmia
SOUTHERN
Mahabad
KORDESTAN

C

Mosul
Baghdad
Tigris
Euphrates
Basra
Abadan

L. Urmia
Teheran
Hamadan
Iran

0 50 100 mil s 200
0 50 100   200 kms

Principal areas
of conflict

D

CASPIAN SEA
Iran
Shiraz
ARABIAN
Bandar Abbas
Bahrain
GULF
Doha
Abu Dhabi

Iraq

I r a n

Muslan
Sharhani
Fakeh
Fukae
Al Kut
Al Amarah
Sableh
Bostan
Susangerd
Hawr-al-Hawizah
Hoveyzeh
Ahwaz
Euphrates
Al Qurnah
Tigris
Hawr-al-Hammar
Basra
Khorramshahr
Zubair
Abadan
OIL
Rumaila
FIELDS
Shatt-al-Arab
Kuwait
KHARG I.

I r a q

Dezful
Musjed Soleyman
KHUZESTAN
Ramhormoz
Karkheh
Karun
Behbehan
Bandar Khomeini
Gurreh

Arabian Gulf

S a u d i   A r a b i a

0   25   100 *miles* 150
0   25   100 150   *kms*

27

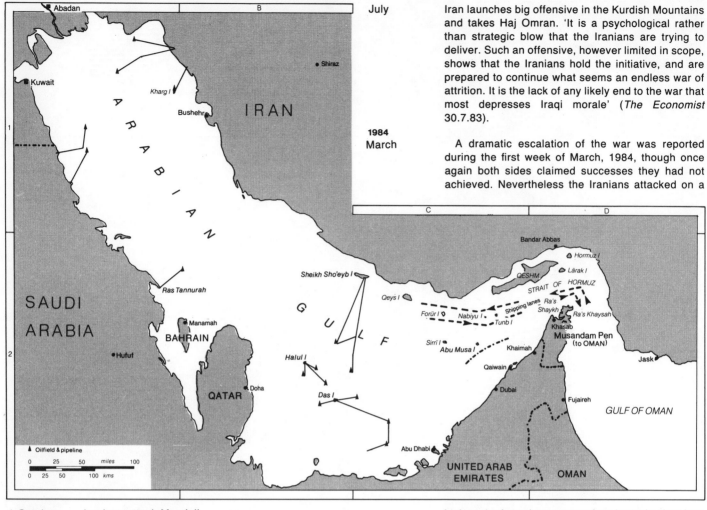

July — Iran launches big offensive in the Kurdish Mountains and takes Haj Omran. 'It is a psychological rather than strategic blow that the Iranians are trying to deliver. Such an offensive, however limited in scope, shows that the Iranians hold the initiative, and are prepared to continue what seems an endless war of attrition. It is the lack of any likely end to the war that most depresses Iraqi morale' (*The Economist* 30.7.83).

1984
March — A dramatic escalation of the war was reported during the first week of March, 1984, though once again both sides claimed successes they had not achieved. Nevertheless the Iranians attacked on a far broader front than any previous incursion into Iraq and were said to be using suicide squads of teenage conscripts to clear minefields. The intensified fighting gave rise to renewed fears that the Iraquis, who are desperate to end the war but not on Iran's punitive terms, might raise the stakes by bombing the Iranian oil installations on Kharg Island, in which event Iran has threatened to close the Strait of Hormuz, which President Reagan is committed to keeping open. In that event he would expect the support of Britain and France.

1 October	Iranians attack Mandali.
November	Iranian thrust into Iraq near Al Amarah repulsed.
1983	
February	Iranian attack in the vicinity of Fakeh makes small gains at heavy cost.
February/ March	Iranian oil wells, damaged by Iraqi gunfire, cause huge oil slick in the Persian Gulf.
April	Iran launches offensive between Musian and Fakeh, but Iraqis break the attack.

"The combined total of killed, wounded and taken prisoner on both sides is now estimated in the West to be about half a million. The number of tanks lost is put at approaching 1,400, which is nearly twice as many tanks as the British Army of the Rhine has in Germany." (*The Times* 7.4.83)

PART IV
Africa

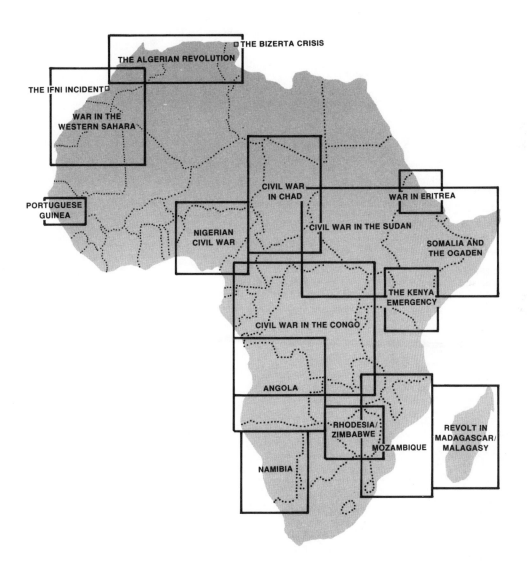

THE BIZERTA CRISIS

THE ALGERIAN REVOLUTION

THE IFNI INCIDENT

WAR IN THE
WESTERN SAHARA

PORTUGUESE
GUINEA

NIGERIAN
CIVIL WAR

CIVIL WAR
IN CHAD

WAR IN ERITREA

CIVIL WAR IN THE SUDAN

SOMALIA AND
THE OGADEN

THE KENYA
EMERGENCY

CIVIL WAR IN THE CONGO

ANGOLA

RHODESIA/
ZIMBABWE

MOZAMBIQUE

REVOLT IN
MADAGASCAR/
MALAGASY

NAMIBIA

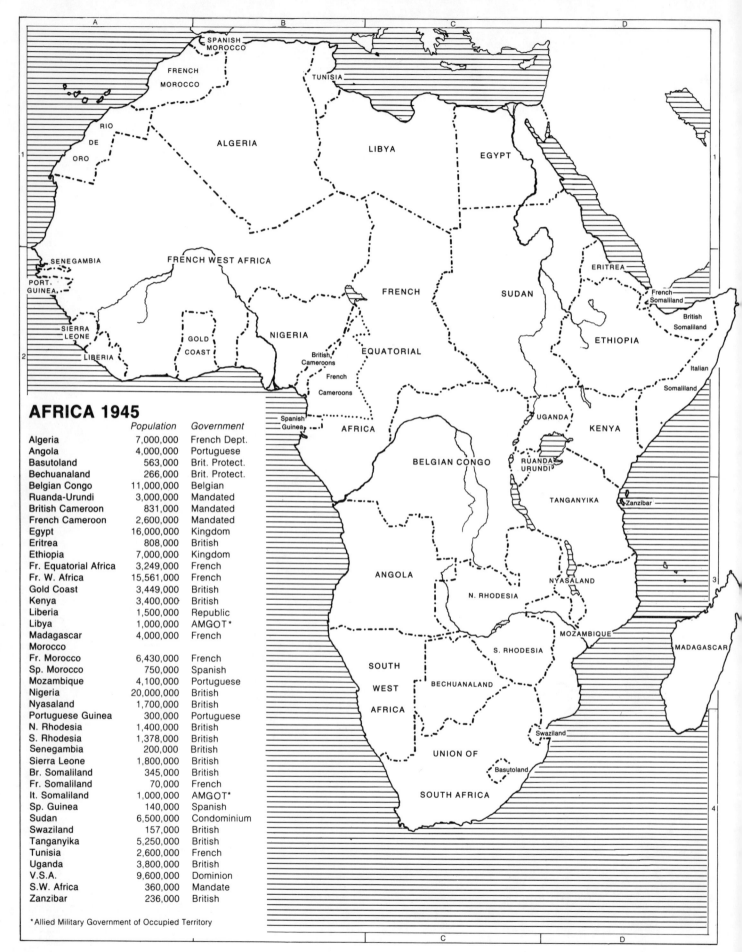

AFRICA 1945

	Population	Government
Algeria	7,000,000	French Dept.
Angola	4,000,000	Portuguese
Basutoland	563,000	Brit. Protect.
Bechuanaland	266,000	Brit. Protect.
Belgian Congo	11,000,000	Belgian
Ruanda-Urundi	3,000,000	Mandated
British Cameroon	831,000	Mandated
French Cameroon	2,600,000	Mandated
Egypt	16,000,000	Kingdom
Eritrea	808,000	British
Ethiopia	7,000,000	Kingdom
Fr. Equatorial Africa	3,249,000	French
Fr. W. Africa	15,561,000	French
Gold Coast	3,449,000	British
Kenya	3,400,000	British
Liberia	1,500,000	Republic
Libya	1,000,000	AMGOT*
Madagascar	4,000,000	French
Morocco		
Fr. Morocco	6,430,000	French
Sp. Morocco	750,000	Spanish
Mozambique	4,100,000	Portuguese
Nigeria	20,000,000	British
Nyasaland	1,700,000	British
Portuguese Guinea	300,000	Portuguese
N. Rhodesia	1,400,000	British
S. Rhodesia	1,378,000	British
Senegambia	200,000	British
Sierra Leone	1,800,000	British
Br. Somaliland	345,000	British
Fr. Somaliland	70,000	French
It. Somaliland	1,000,000	AMGOT*
Sp. Guinea	140,000	Spanish
Sudan	6,500,000	Condominium
Swaziland	157,000	British
Tanganyika	5,250,000	British
Tunisia	2,600,000	French
Uganda	3,800,000	British
V.S.A.	9,600,000	Dominion
S.W. Africa	360,000	Mandate
Zanzibar	236,000	British

*Allied Military Government of Occupied Territory

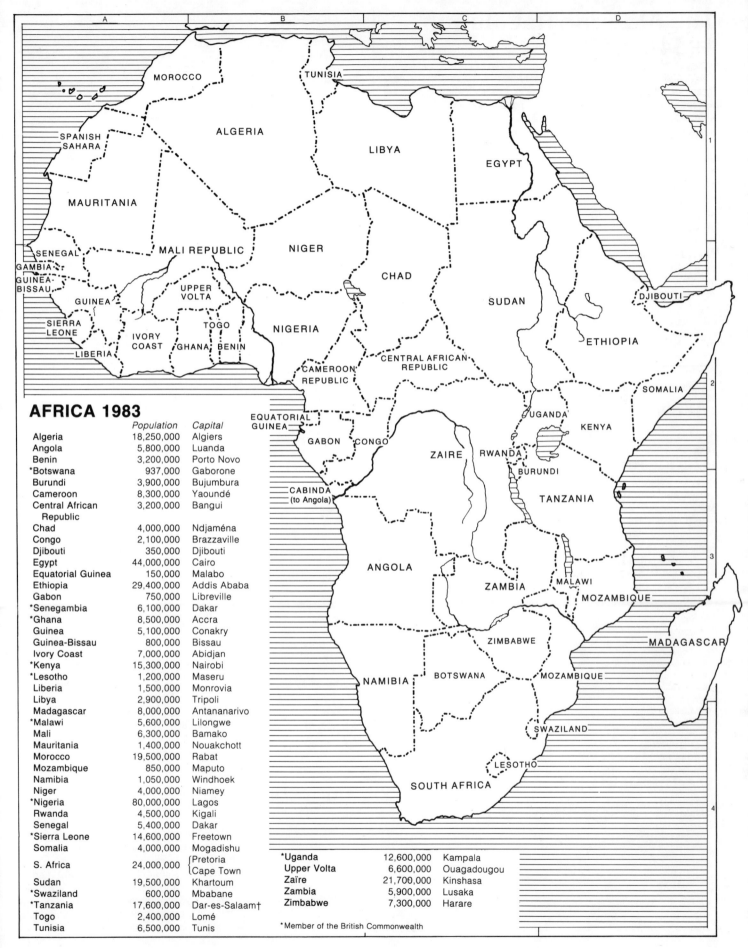

AFRICA 1983

	Population	Capital
Algeria	18,250,000	Algiers
Angola	5,800,000	Luanda
Benin	3,200,000	Porto Novo
*Botswana	937,000	Gaborone
Burundi	3,900,000	Bujumbura
Cameroon	8,300,000	Yaoundé
Central African Republic	3,200,000	Bangui
Chad	4,000,000	Ndjaména
Congo	2,100,000	Brazzaville
Djibouti	350,000	Djibouti
Egypt	44,000,000	Cairo
Equatorial Guinea	150,000	Malabo
Ethiopia	29,400,000	Addis Ababa
Gabon	750,000	Libreville
*Senegambia	6,100,000	Dakar
*Ghana	8,500,000	Accra
Guinea	5,100,000	Conakry
Guinea-Bissau	800,000	Bissau
Ivory Coast	7,000,000	Abidjan
*Kenya	15,300,000	Nairobi
*Lesotho	1,200,000	Maseru
Liberia	1,500,000	Monrovia
Libya	2,900,000	Tripoli
Madagascar	8,000,000	Antananarivo
*Malawi	5,600,000	Lilongwe
Mali	6,300,000	Bamako
Mauritania	1,400,000	Nouakchott
Morocco	19,500,000	Rabat
Mozambique	850,000	Maputo
Namibia	1,050,000	Windhoek
Niger	4,000,000	Niamey
*Nigeria	80,000,000	Lagos
Rwanda	4,500,000	Kigali
Senegal	5,400,000	Dakar
*Sierra Leone	14,600,000	Freetown
Somalia	4,000,000	Mogadishu
S. Africa	24,000,000	Pretoria / Cape Town
Sudan	19,500,000	Khartoum
*Swaziland	600,000	Mbabane
*Tanzania	17,600,000	Dar-es-Salaam†
Togo	2,400,000	Lomé
Tunisia	6,500,000	Tunis
*Uganda	12,600,000	Kampala
Upper Volta	6,600,000	Ouagadougou
Zaïre	21,700,000	Kinshasa
Zambia	5,900,000	Lusaka
Zimbabwe	7,300,000	Harare

*Member of the British Commonwealth

31

The Algerian Revolution 1954–1962

The Algerian Revolution is complicated by the fact that there were three, at times four, contestants – the French Government, the European settlers in Algeria (the *colons* or *pieds noirs*), the Algerian nationalists and, at times, parts of the French Army. In 1848, after 17 years of resistance, Algeria became an integral part of metropolitan France, a situation which led to grave complications. Resistance to French rule started after the First World War and sprang up again as soon as France was liberated in 1944. At Sétif on VE Day, 8 May, 1945, Muslim extremists killed 103 Europeans. In retaliation the Army killed 500 Muslims and the *pieds noirs* are thought to have killed a further 6000. By 1954, of the various Muslim resistance groups, the *Front de la Libération Nationale* (FLN) was dominant, run by a committee of which the most influential members were Ahmed Ben Bella and Belkacem Krim. For political and military purposes the FLN divided the country into six regions known as *Wilayas*. The aim of the FLN was to create an independent Islamic Algeria. The aim of the *colons* was to keep Algeria part of France and the Muslims firmly in their place. The French Army had the unenviable role of referee. The revolution proper is generally regarded as having started on 1 November, 1954.

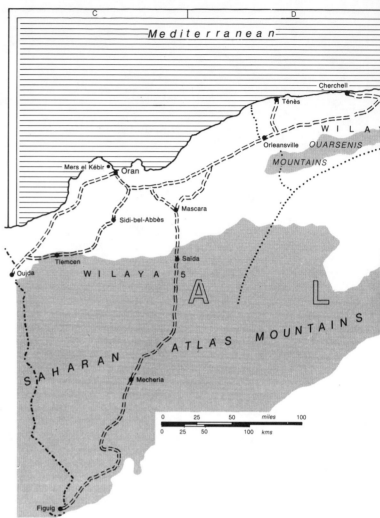

MAIN EVENTS IN THE ALGERIAN REVOLUTION

1954

1 November | FLN attacks on selected French and *pied noir* targets, particularly in area of Aurès mountains. Easily dealt with by French authorities.

1955

20 August | FLN kill and multilate *pieds noirs* in villages round Philippeville. *Pied noir* vigilante groups kill c. 12,000 Muslims in reprisal.

1956

March | Morocco and Tunisia become independent, providing safe bases for FLN troops.

April | Ferhat Abbas allies his UDMA (*Union Démocratique pour le Manifeste Algérien*) to FLN.

August | Soummam Valley Conference commits FLN to hard-line policy. Guerrilla gangs restructured to form the *Armée de Libération Nationale* (ALN).

1957

 | Construction of the Morice Line, a wire fence electrified at 5000 volts, along the length of the Tunisian border.

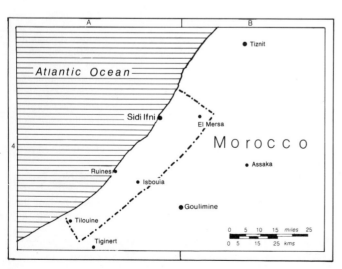

January | General Jacques Massu's paratroopers smash general strike in Algiers but alienate public opinion in France.

18 September | Massu suppresses second general strike of Europeans in Algiers.

1958

January | French reconnaissance plane shot down by machine-gun fire from Tunisian village of Sakiet.

11 February | French Air Force bombs Sakiet, killing 80 civilians.

9 May | FLN execute 3 French soldiers; *pieds noirs* occupy government offices in Algiers.

13 May | General Massu sets up Committee of Public Safety, protesting against political leadership in the war.

1 June | General de Gaulle resumes governance of France.

3 October | de Gaulle announces 5-year industrial plan for Algeria in speech at Constantine. FLN respond by forming *Gouvernement Provisoire de la République*

THE IFNI INCIDENT 1957

1957

23 November | 1200 well-armed Moroccan nationalists attack Spanish enclave of Ifni in S. Morocco. The Moroccan Government disclaims all responsibility.
Spanish garrison raised from 2000 to 10,000 men. 3 Spanish cruisers sent to Ifni.

8 December | Bulletin from Madrid says order now restored. Spanish casualties 61 killed, 128 wounded. Moroccan casualties estimated at several hundred.

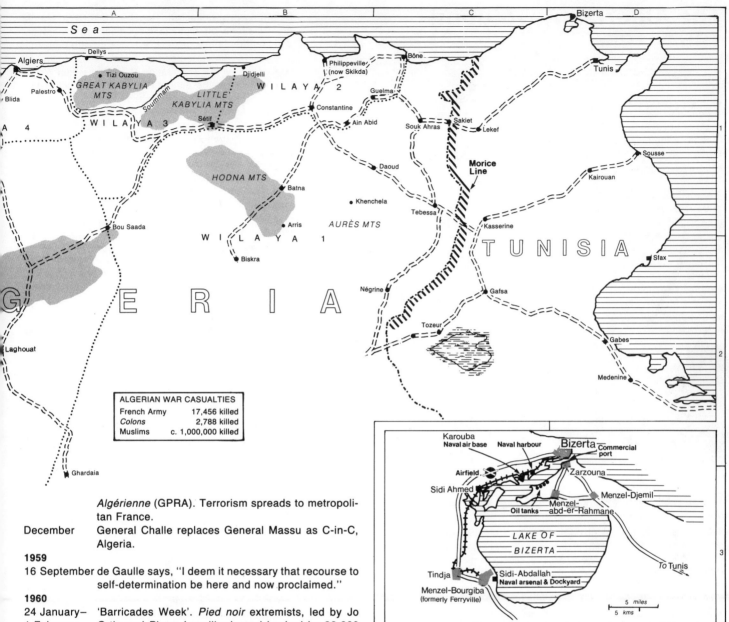

ALGERIAN WAR CASUALTIES

French Army	17,456 killed
Colons	2,788 killed
Muslims	c. 1,000,000 killed

Algérienne (GPRA). Terrorism spreads to metropolitan France.

| December | General Challe replaces General Massu as C-in-C, Algeria. |

1959

| 16 September | de Gaulle says, "I deem it necessary that recourse to self-determination be here and now proclaimed." |

1960

24 January– 1 February	'Barricades Week'. *Pied noir* extremists, led by Jo Ortiz and Pierre Lagaillarde and backed by 30,000 demonstrators, erect barricades in Algiers. Challe reluctant to fire on fellow Frenchmen but rain finally disperses rioters.
April	General Crépin replaces Challe.
25–29 June	Talks between GPRA and French at Mélun end in deadlock.
4 November	de Gaulle, in broadcast speech, talks of Algerian Republic.

1961

| 22–26 April | Generals Challe and Salan head French military revolt; supported by dissident paras, they hold Algiers for 5 days; but majority of troops remain loyal to de Gaulle and mutiny peters out. Salan forms *Organisation Armée Secrète* (OAS). War now mainly between OAS and FLN. |
| May | Peace talks begin at Evian-les-Bains. |

1962

| 18 March | Ceasefire. Algeria granted complete independence under GPRA. *Colons* flock from Algeria. Ahmed Ben Bella becomes premier. |

1965

| 19 June | Ben Bella ousted by Houari Boumedienne. |

THE BIZERTA CRISIS 1961

The Tunisian Government first demanded the evacuation of the French Naval Base at Bizerta on 8 February, 1958, after the bombing of Sakiet, but it was later agreed to suspend negotiations until the Algerian War was over. In July, 1961, Tunisia's attitude changed when President Bourgiba sent a note to General de Gaulle protesting at the extension of the runway at the French airbase at Bizerta.

17 July	Bourgiba announces blockade of French Naval Base.
19 July	French Government sends reinforcements.
19-22 July	Pitched battle rages in Bizerta between French and Tunisian troops. French occupy greater part of the town. 1300 Tunisians killed, mostly civilians; 21 French soldiers killed.
29 September	Agreement signed for the progressive withdrawal of French troops, which began on 1 October.

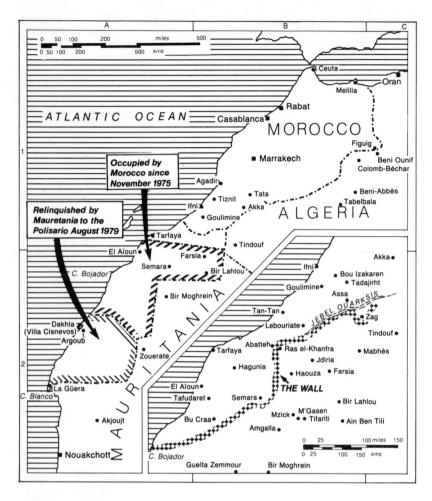

On the map:

- ATLANTIC OCEAN
- Ceuta
- Oran
- Melilla
- Rabat
- Casablanca
- MOROCCO
- Figuig
- Marrakech
- Beni Ounif
- Colomb-Béchar
- **Occupied by Morocco since November 1975**
- Agadir
- Tata
- Beni-Abbès
- Tiznit
- Akka
- Tabelbala
- Ifni
- ALGERIA
- Goulimine
- **Relinquished by Mauretania to the Polisario August 1979**
- Tarfaya
- Tindouf
- El Aïoun
- Farsia
- C. Bojador
- Semara
- Ifni
- Akka
- Bir Lahlou
- Bou Izakaren
- Bir Moghrein
- Goulimine
- Tadajirht
- Assa
- JEBEL OUARKSIS
- Tan-Tan
- Zag
- Dakhla (Villa Cisnevos)
- Lebouriate
- Tindouf
- Argoub
- Zouerate
- Abatteh
- Ras el-Khanfra
- Mabhès
- Tarfaya
- Jdiria
- Hagunia
- Haouza
- Farsia
- **THE WALL**
- C. Blanco
- La Güera
- El Aïoun
- Tafudaret
- Semara
- Bir Lahlou
- Akjoujt
- Bu Craa
- Mzick
- M'Gasen
- Tifariti
- Ain Ben Tili
- Amgalla
- MAURITANIA
- Nouakchott
- C. Bojador
- Guelta Zemmour
- Bir Moghrein

The War in the Western Sahara

Spanish Sahara was colonized by Spain in 1884, but, after the decolonization of most of Africa in the 1950s and 60s, it was claimed by both Morocco and Mauritania. Its other neighbour, Algeria, favoured the creation of an independent state and to this end supported the Popular Front for the Liberation of Saguia el Hamra and Rio de Oro, usually referred to as the Polisario Front, the most powerful of the Spanish Saharan Liberation movements. Moroccan aspirations were initially voiced through the Liberation and Unity Front (FLU), while Spain supported the Sahrawi National United Party (PUNS), a moderate, autonomous movement led by the Chiefs of the indigenous Sahrawi people. Morocco feared that the proposed referendum under U.N. auspices would result in complete independence which would place outside her influence the phosphate seam at Bu Craa, reputedly the longest in the world. Spain, which also ruled the enclaves of Ceuta and Melilla on the Mediterranean coast of Morocco, was faced with an awkward problem: to grant independence to Spanish Sahara would anger Morocco; to hand over the territory to Morocco would anger Algeria and Mauritania, as well as the European consortium working the phosphates. From the autumn of 1974 violent incidents occurred regularly in Spanish Sahara and in the enclaves, mainly the work of Polisario guerrillas. In May, 1975, the U.N. sent a fact-finding commission to the area which recommended that 'the people of Spanish Sahara should be able to determine their own future in complete freedom'. On 23 May the Spanish Cabinet announced that the Government was ready to 'transfer the sovereignty of the Spanish Sahara in the shortest possible period'. On 16 October the International Court of Justice delivered a 'negative advisory opinion', saying that neither Morocco nor Mauritania had any historic claim over the territory, again recommending a referendum. On 6 November King Hassan of Morocco organized a peace march of 350,000 civilians over the border into Spanish Sahara. The march was ordered back by the King three days later. On 14 November Spain undertook to hand over the territory to joint Moroccan-Mauritanian control by the end of February, 1976, and on the 26th of that month the last Spaniards left Spanish Sahara and the Polisario Front proclaimed the

Saharan Arab Democratic Republic (SADR). In March Algeria broke off diplomatic relations with Morocco and Mauritania in a gesture of solidarity with Polisario and on 14 April Morocco and Mauritania signed a convention on the delimitation of borders within Western Sahara, as the district had become known since the withdrawal of the Spaniards. The war was now between Morocco and Mauritania, on the one hand, and the Polisario Front with Algerian backing, on the other. On 7 June Polisario launched an attack on the Mauritanian capital, Nouakchott. In April, 1977, Polisario claimed that in the last 18 months it had killed 14,200 Moroccan and Mauritanian troops and shot down 32 aircraft for the loss of 200 men; Polisario claims have never failed to display Olympian feats of imagination. On 5 June the more modest Moroccan Minister of Information said that, since February, 1976, Moroccan troops had taken 5–600 Algerian prisoners and killed 1,500 Polisario guerrillas, losing only 70 of their own men. In July, 1977, Polisario again attacked Nouakchott and at the end of the year the conflict intensified when French aircraft came to the aid of Mauritania, while relationships between Morocco and Algeria deteriorated sharply. On 10 July, 1978, the President of Mauritania, Moktar Ould Daddah, was overthrown in a bloodless coup and his successors, benefiting from a unilateral Polisario ceasefire, entered into negotiations with the guerrillas; a year later, on 5 August, 1979, a peace treaty was signed between Mauritania and the Polisario Front, leaving Morocco to continue the struggle on her own. Meanwhile Polisario had stepped up its activities, attacking Tan-Tan inside Morocco on 28 January, 1979. After the Mauritanian withdrawal Morocco occupied Dakhla despite determined Polisario efforts to take it. On 24 August they took and briefly held Lebouriate. In November 'The King despatched what military experts called the strongest desert fighting force since the days of Montgomery and Rommel with the aim of pushing all Polisario units out of the country,' but in fact both diplomatically and militarily Hassan lost ground during 1979. In 1980 Polisario also achieved some spectacular successes in S. Morocco: in the Zag and Assa regions in March, at Tan-Tan in September and around Akka in August and September. In July, 1980, at an OAU Conference in Freetown there was, for the first time, a majority (26–24) in favour of the admission of the SADR but the move was frustrated by a Moroccan threat of withdrawal. In March, 1981, Mauritania broke off relations with Morocco and thereafter Polisario was able to operate freely from bases in the former. On 13 October the biggest battle of the war took place at Guelta Zemmour, near the Mauritanian border, when a garrison of 200 Moroccans was overwhelmed by a force of 3000 Polisario equipped with tanks. But diplomatically Polisario lost ground in 1981, its OAU support dwindling to 8 at Nairobi in June. Between the autumn of 1980 and May, 1982, the Moroccans built a 'Berlin Wall' from the Jebel Ouarksis to Cap Bojador, some 200 miles, sealing off the agricultural and phosphate-bearing areas from the desert, which they proposed to abandon to the enemy. During December, 1982, and January, 1983, successive artillery attacks were launched by Polisario forces against Moroccan positions, particulary near Bu Craa. On 15 January, 1983, Moroccan Navy ships bombarded the port of La Güera. At present no end to the fighting seems to be in sight.

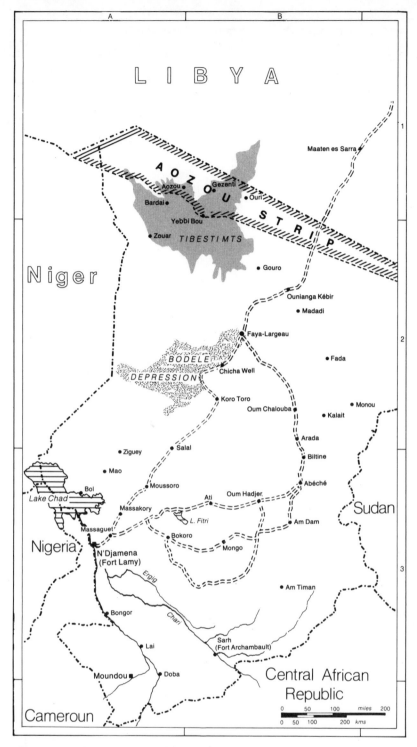

Civil War in Chad

France proclaimed a protectorate in Chad on 5 September, 1900, and in July, 1908, the territory was incorporated into French Equatorial Africa. On 1 January, 1959, it became an autonomous republic within the French Community and achieved full independence on 11 August, 1960. In 1966–7 border disputes with Sudan led to the death of over 200 people. In August, 1968, the Government asked for French military support for Chadian troops besieged by rebels from the northern regions. Air cover was provided but no French troops were directly involved. Most of the guerrillas, styled the Chad National Liberation Front (FROLINAT), were Arabs who opposed the domination of Chad by black men from the south. In March, 1969, President François Tombalbaye again had to call for French assistance and French troops now became directly engaged in

the maintenance of civil order. By the end of 1969 there were about 2500 French troops in the country. These 'policing' operations, which cost the lives of several French soldiers, gave rise to vociferous protest in metropolitan France and the number of troops serving in Chad was temporarily reduced. French intervention was officially ended on 1 September, 1972, though some 2500 French personnel remained in the country. The three years of the so-called intervention had cost the lives of 50 French soldiers and more than 3000 Chadians. On 13 April, 1975, President Tombalbaye was deposed and assassinated after 15 years in office. In May a provisional government was formed by Brigadier General Félix Malloum. In 1977 the Libyan Government cited an agreement made in 1935 between France and Italy, but disavowed in 1938, to justify its occupation of the Aozou Strip. Libya appeared to regard the new frontier as fixed and now started giving aid to the Toubou rebels who, in July, 1977, took the town of Bardai. In January, 1978, a ceasefire agreement with the Toubou rebels was signed in Khartoum and, though the fighting continued, on 29 August Hussein Habré, former leader of the rebels, was appointed Premier. But in February, 1979, a quarrel between Habré and President Malloum, followed by an attack by the national police on Habré's house, led to violent fighting in N'Djamena between the Chad National Army (ANT) and Habré's Armed Forces of the North (FAN). The trouble soon spread to the countryside, where FROLINAT, though itself divided, held three-quarters of the nation. French paratroops intervened and a truce between FAN and ANT was signed, the French now supporting Habré. In March, 1979, an accord was signed in Lagos between no less than eleven warring factions and in November a Transitional Government of National Unity (GUNT) was formed under the presidency of Goukouni Oueddei. Civil war started again on 22 March, 1980, and for most of the year the northern two-thirds of the country saw fighting between Habré's FAN and Goukouni's Popular Armed Forces (FAP). In the south the forces of Colonel Wadal Kamougue, vice-president of GUNT, established a separate capital at Moundou. An estimated 70,000 refugees fled to Cameroon. In May French troops were once again withdrawn. In June Habré's forces won control of Faya-Largeau and Goukouni signed a treaty with Libya. In December Libyan troops began a push towards N'Djamena and the capital was taken in Goukouni's name in mid-December. The fall of Habré's stronghold at Abéché was announced a few days later. In November, 1981, the Libyan troops were withdrawn at Goukouni's request. In the same month, men of Habré's FAN, who had retreated into the Sudan in December, 1980, occupied all the important towns in eastern Chad. In January, 1982, they took Faya-Largeau, in May Massakory, Mao and Ati, Massaguet on 5 June and N'Djamena on 7 June, whereupon Goukouni retired to the Tibesti mountains and became the rebel, while Habré became head of the official Government. In June, 1983, the fighting intensified to an unprecedented pitch, Colonel Gadaffi of Libya giving unstinting aid to the rebels while France and the United States continued to try and shore up Habré's unsteady régime. On 24 June Faya-Largeau fell to the rebels; on 1 August Habré's men retook it, but on 10 August it fell to the rebels again.

The French have tried to impose a no-go area, or *zone rouge*, south of Faya-Largeau and north of Salal, between the rival armies, but the fighting goes on. There were an estimated 3000 French troops in Chad in March, 1984.

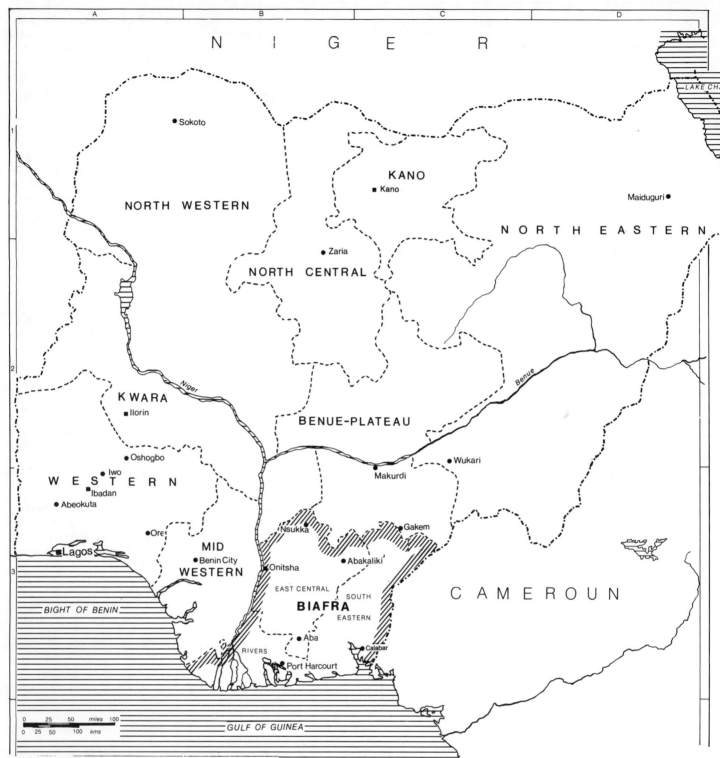

The Nigerian Civil War 1966–70

Nigeria came gradually under British administration between 1861, when Lagos was bought from a native chief, and 1900, when the Northern Nigeria Protectorate was brought under government control. The country was granted full independence in 1960 and became a Federal Republic in 1963. It was regarded as one of the most stable of the new African nations, until, in January, 1966, a *coup d'état* by young army officers led to the overthrow of the government and the setting up of a military régime under General Ironsi. On 29 July elements of the army in Northern Nigeria staged a counter-coup which resulted in the assassination of Ironsi and the emergence of General

Gowon as Supreme Commander and Head of the Military Government. Both coups were followed, particularly in the North, by the indiscriminate slaughter of thousands of Ibos, who were held to have more than their fair share of plum government jobs, and the return of thousands more to their homeland in the Eastern Region. The Federation was then divided into four regions: Northern, Western, Midwestern and Eastern. On 27 May, 1967, Gowon announced the redivision of the country into twelve states, whereupon Lt-Colonel Ojukwu announced that the Eastern Region, of which he was Military Governor, "shall henceforth be an independent and sovereign state of

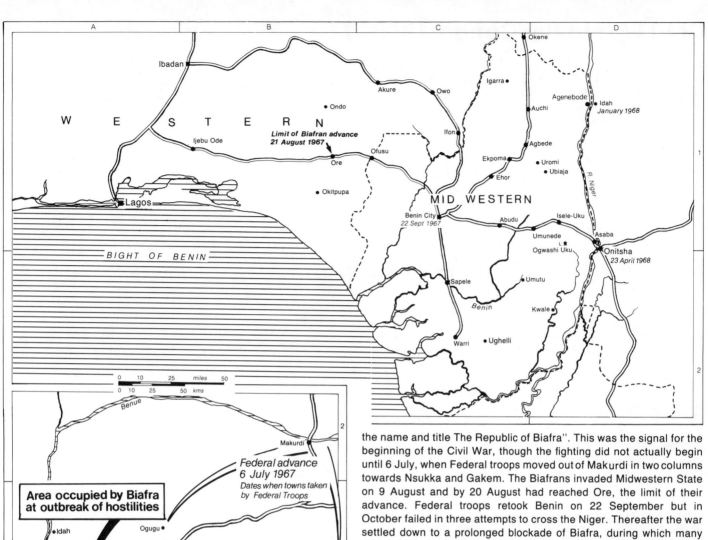

the name and title The Republic of Biafra''. This was the signal for the beginning of the Civil War, though the fighting did not actually begin until 6 July, when Federal troops moved out of Makurdi in two columns towards Nsukka and Gakem. The Biafrans invaded Midwestern State on 9 August and by 20 August had reached Ore, the limit of their advance. Federal troops retook Benin on 22 September but in October failed in three attempts to cross the Niger. Thereafter the war settled down to a prolonged blockade of Biafra, during which many thousands of Biafrans, mostly children, died of starvation. The Federals were thought by many to be prolonging the war as a deliberate act of genocide and Biafran propaganda certainly made the most of the Ibos' plight. The involvement or detachment of other countries aroused bitter passions worldwide. The British supplied limited arms to the Federal side; the Russians were more generous. France supported Biafra, while America remained officially neutral, though public opinion was strongly pro-Biafran, particularly among Jews. The Federals maintained that the war was a purely domestic affair and objected vehemently to the intervention of numerous relief agencies in Biafra.

The war ended with the fall of Owerri on 9 January, 1970. Eastern Region, now divided into three states, remains part of Nigeria.

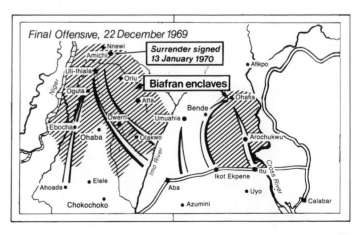

Civil War in the Congo 1960–71

From 1908 until it was granted independence in 1960 the Congo was an absolute monarchy under the King of Belgium, but the educational facilities offered to the Congolese had been so restricted that independence was followed by total anarchy. In a population of 4 million, 17 held university degrees.

1960

30 June	Belgium grants independence to the Congo. Joseph Kasavubu is made President and Patrice Lumumba Prime Minister. Civil unrest begins at once, the Army mutinies and thousands of whites flee the country, the loss of their skills further aggravating the situation. 10,000 Belgian troops remain, mostly in Katanga province.
11 July	Moise Tshombe, Katangan premier, secedes from Congo, hires white mercenaries to assist Katangan forces. Lumumba appeals to U.N. for military aid.
14 July	Establishment of U.N. Security Force in Congo approved by Security Council.
31 July	Most Belgian troops withdrawn at U.N. request. Garrison remains at Katanga.
14 September	Lumumba overthrown by Colonel Joseph Mobutu, Army Chief of Staff, and placed under house arrest. Lumumba's supporters continue to receive Soviet aid.
14 December	Antoine Gizenga, Lumumba's vice-premier, establishes pro-communist régime in Stanleyville.

1961

17 January	Lumumba is sent to 'more secure' prison in Katanga where he is killed (9 Feb.) on Tshombe's orders.
24 February	Gizenga's rebel forces seize Luluabourg, capital of Kasai province.
17 April	President Kasavubu signs U.N.–Congo agreement authorizing U.N. troops to use force if necessary to prevent civil war in the Congo.
1 August	Cyrille Adoula becomes Prime Minister.
18 September	Dag Hammarskjöld, U.N. Secretary General, killed in plane crash at Ndola on his way to meet Tshombe.
August–December	U.N. actions in Katanga lead to eventual (18 Dec.) capture of most of Elisabethville. Tshombe agrees to re-unification of Congo but fails to keep his word and retains control of Katanga.

1962–3

January	Gizenga taken prisoner by Adoula and sent into exile.
29 December–15 January	Katangese forces defeated by U.N. troops. Tshombe flees; secession of Katanga ends.

1963–4

	U.N. troops gradually withdrawn, mainly due to lack of funds, while civil unrest continues. Last U.N. troops leave on 30 June, 1964.
9 July	Tshombe, returned from exile, is named Prime Minister of the Congo, and hires white mercenaries to deal with rebels, now backed by Red China.
30 August	Congolese Army retakes Albertville from rebels
24 November	Belgian paratroops, hired by Tshombe retake Stanleyville and release 1800 white hostages.

1965

March	Major 'Mad Mike' Hoare's mercenaries take Mahaji, Arua, Aba, Faradje and Watsa from rebels.
25 November	Tshombe ousted by Mobutu. Tshombe leaves country for good and dies 'of a heart attack' in an Algerian prison in 1969.

1966

July	Katangese gendarmes revolt in Stanleyville; Mobutu suppresses trouble and thereafter his rule is unchallenged.

1971 Mobutu changes country's name to Republic of Zaire.

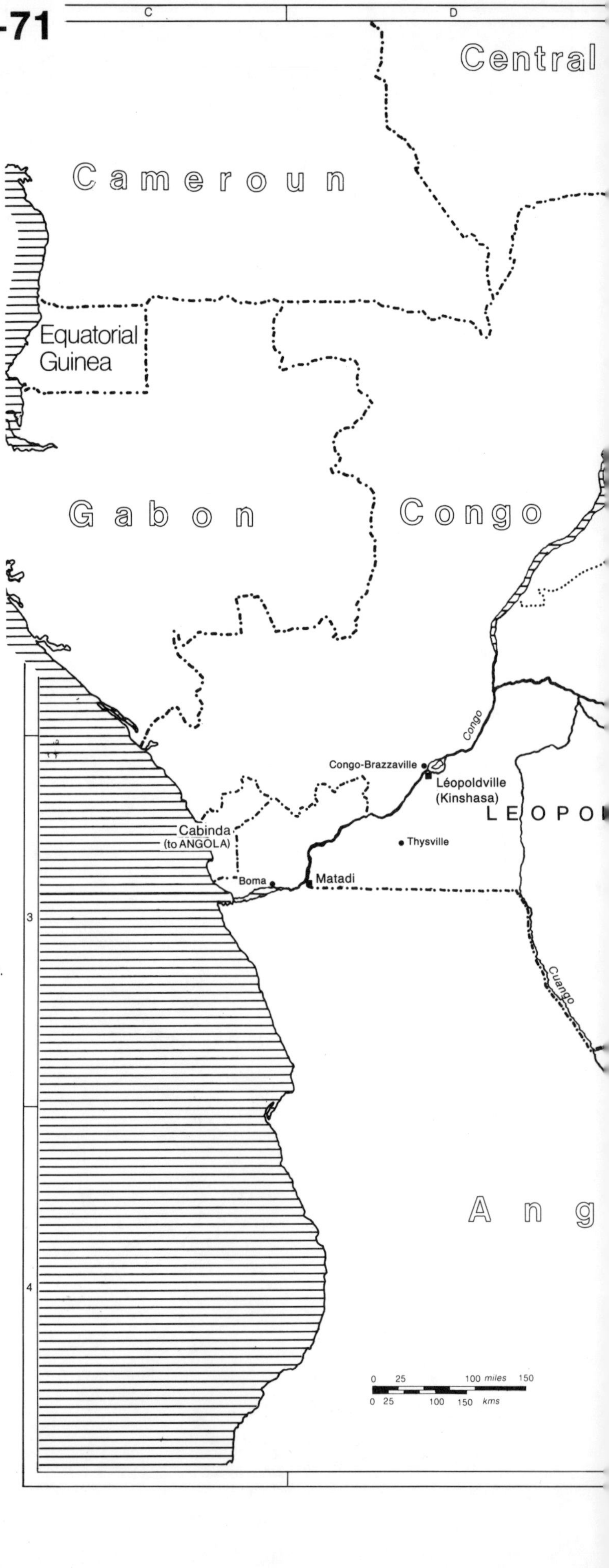

Central

Cameroun

Equatorial Guinea

Gabon   Congo

Congo-Brazzaville
Léopoldville (Kinshasa)

Cabinda (to ANGOLA)   • Thysville

LEOPO

Boma   Matadi

Cuango

Ang

0   25   100 *miles* 150
0   25   100   150 *kms*

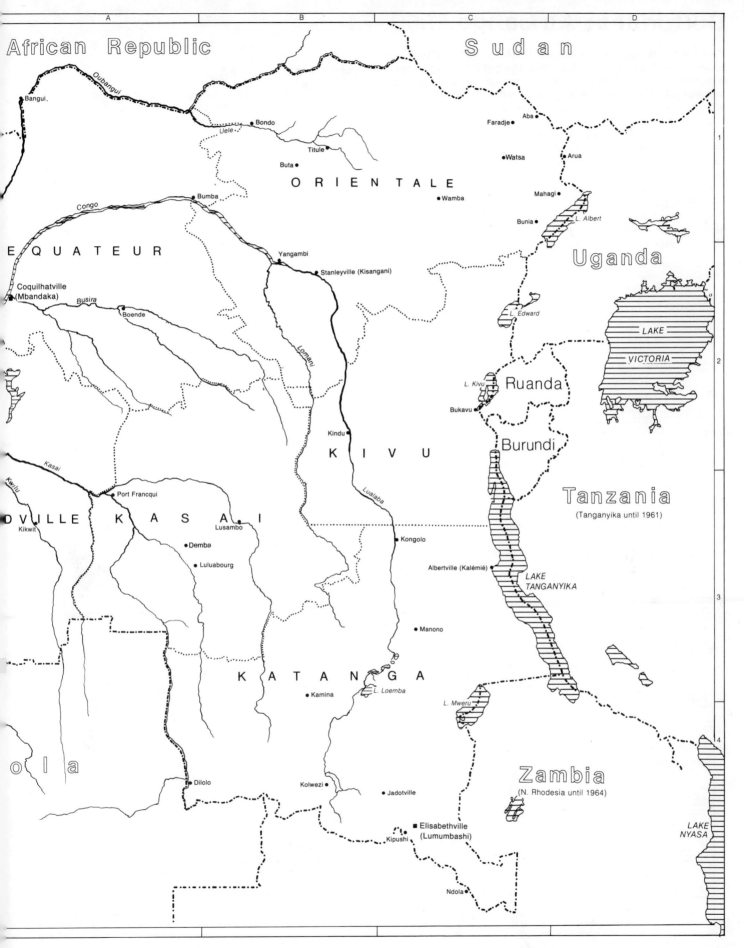

Portuguese Africa

Portugal was the first European power to stake colonial claims on the continent of Africa and the last to leave. The first Portuguese contact with Guinea dates from 1446 but its frontiers were not officially demarcated until 1886. The Portuguese arrived in Angola in 1482 when Diogo Cão discovered the mouth of the River Congo; the boundaries were defined in the 1880s and '90s. Contact with Mozambique dates from the arrival of Vasco da Gama at the mouth of the River Zambesi in 1498; the frontiers were delimited by 1891. In each case the departure of the Portuguese from their African colonies was preceded by a war of independence and in each case has been followed by a state of affairs infinitely more oppressive for the majority of the inhabitants than anything that went before. The final stages of decolonization were much accelerated by the military coup which occurred in Portugal on 25 April, 1974, as a result of which General Sinola replaced Dr Caetano as President.

ANGOLA 1961–75

The road to independence in Angola was complicated by the four-sided struggle that preceded it: the Portuguese Army on one side and three Angolan independence movements on the other. The latter consisted of:

1. The MPLA (Popular Movement for the Liberation of Angola), led by Agostinho Neto, an orthodox Maoist trained at Coimbra University.
2. The UPA (Union of the Population of Angola) which in 1962 became the FNLA (National Front for the Liberation of Angola), led by Holden Roberto, brother-in-law of President Mobutu of Zaïre.
3. From 1966, UNITA (National Union for the Total Independence of Angola), led by Dr Jonas Savimbi, a Protestant graduate of Freiburg and Lausanne Universities.

1961

3 February — Africans attack prison in Luanda where MPLA suspects were held.

15 March — UPA guerrillas massacre 7000 Africans and several hundred whites in Uigé district round Carmona. In the massive retribution which followed, carried out by local whites and blacks whose relations had been killed by the rebels, an estimated 30,000 people died. 300,000 fled from the area to Luanda or to Zaïre.

There followed 14 years of sporadic fighting in which the guerrillas mostly fought the Portuguese, but sometimes each other. Russia supported the MPLA, America the FNLA, while UNITA initially received some support from the Chinese. At the height of the trouble, in 1972, the Portuguese had 50,000 white and 10,000 black soldiers in Angola. The outstanding counter-insurgent commander of the war was General José Bettancourt Rodriguez.

1975

5 January — Neto, Roberto and Savimbi agree at a meeting in Mombasa, Kenya, to work together to achieve independence.

15 January — Portugal agrees to grant Angola independence on 11 September, 1975.

April — Russian advisers and Cuban troops start arriving in Luanda in support of MPLA.

7 August — FNLA withdraws from transitional coalition and UNITA follows suit two days later, leaving Angola virtually ungoverned.

11 November — Independence is declared: over 300,000 whites leave Angola.

Approximate casualties: Portuguese 4,000; insurgents 25,000; civilians 50,000.

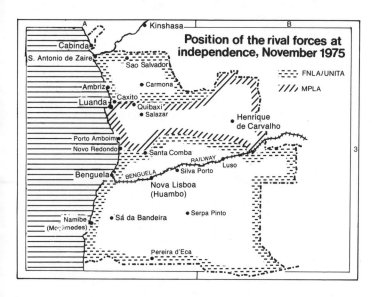

Position of the rival forces at independence, November 1975

The Angolan Civil War

Civil war was already under way when the Portuguese left Angola. The MPLA were supported by about 12,000 Cuban troops, by Russian arms, supplies and advisers. The FNLA was supported by Zaïre and about 300 mainly British mercenaries. UNITA was backed by South Africa. US support for UNITA and FNLA was cleverly exploited by Russian propaganda and on 27 January, 1976, President Ford, bowing to public pressure, announced the end of all US aid to Angola. Soon after, the defeated remnants of FNLA fled to Zaïre. UNITA alone still carries on the fight.

1976

11 February — The Organization of African Unity (OAU) recognizes the MPLA as the rightful government of Angola.

March — Estimated 20,000 Cuban troops now in Angola, with whose aid MPLA hold 90% of the country.

1979

10 September — Agostinho Neto dies in Moscow and is succeeded by José Eduardo dos Santos, who still holds the post in 1984.

Angola's problems were, and remain, complicated by the presence in S. Angola of SWAPO (South-West African People's Organization) troops fighting for the liberation of S.W. Africa (Namibia) from S. Africa, and of S. African troops opposed to them. On 20 September, 1982, Colonel Juan Bock, South African adviser to Dr Jonas Savimbi, claimed that in the last 12 months UNITA guerrillas had killed 1,500 Cubans and 3,000 MPLA soldiers. He estimated that there were still 15–20,000 Cuban troops in Angola. In August, 1983, the MPLA garrison of Cangamba fell to UNITA after an 11-day siege in which more than 1000 MPLA defenders were killed, making it by far the biggest battle so far in the Angolan Civil War. In the first week of September UNITA took Calulo, only 100 miles from Luanda. 'UNITA . . . now appears to be winning the war. It is a turn of events that poses an acute problem for the Angolan government's Soviet and Cuban allies. . . . Angola is beginning to look like the Soviet empire's Vietnam' (*The Spectator* 17.9.83).

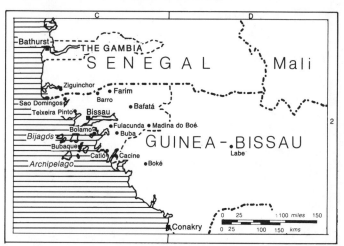

PORTUGUESE GUINEA

PAIGC (Guinea and Cape Verde African Independence Party) was started in 1952 under the leadership of Amilcar Cabral. It was originally an urban movement. The start of the fight for independence in Portuguese Guinea is dated from 'Revolution Day', 3 August, 1959, when 50 strikers were killed by the Portuguese in the shipyards in Bissau.

1960 — Cabral moves to the Republic of Guinea to start reorganizing PAIGC as a rural guerrilla movement on Maoist lines.

From 1961 PAIGC followed Maoist strategy; in 1963 Guinea was described as 'a prison in which the Portuguese have sought shelter'.

1968

May — Antonio de Spinola is appointed Governor and Commander-in-Chief of Portuguese Guinea.

1973

January — Cabral murdered by PAIGC extremists.

23 March — PAIGC shoot down two Portuguese Fiat G91 aircraft with Soviet-made SAM-7 ground-to-air missiles.

August — Spinola returns to Portugal to hero's welcome.

24 September — PAIGC declares Guinea independent.

1974

10 September — Portugal formally recognizes Guinea's independence. Louis Cabral, brother of Amilcar, becomes first President of Guinea-Bissau. PAIGC celebrate independence by shooting several hundred people.

1980

November — Cabral ousted in a coup led by General João Bernado Vieira.

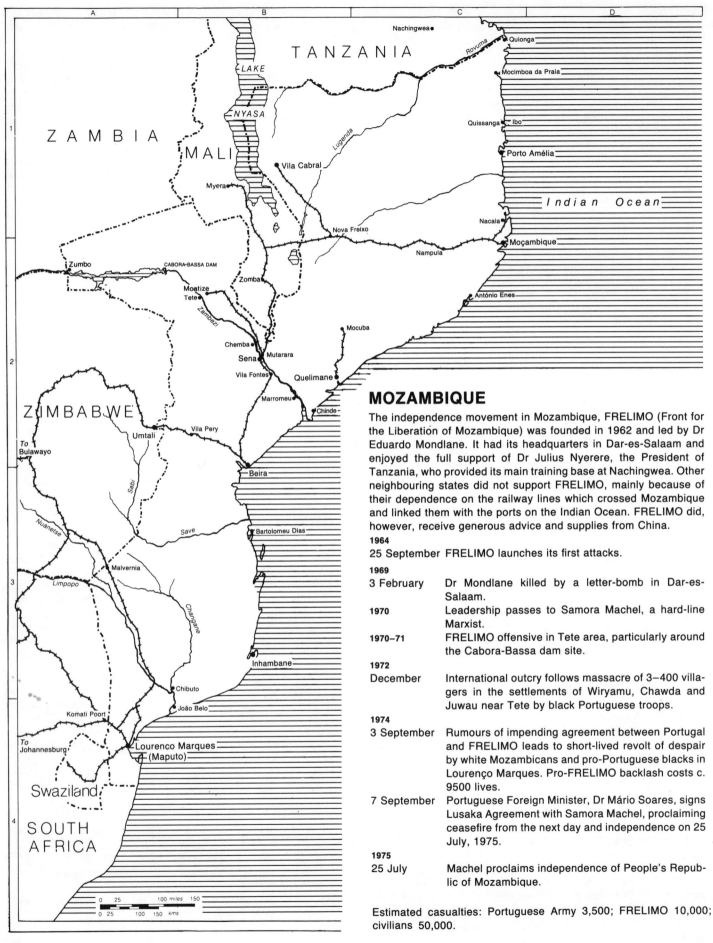

MOZAMBIQUE

The independence movement in Mozambique, FRELIMO (Front for the Liberation of Mozambique) was founded in 1962 and led by Dr Eduardo Mondlane. It had its headquarters in Dar-es-Salaam and enjoyed the full support of Dr Julius Nyerere, the President of Tanzania, who provided its main training base at Nachingwea. Other neighbouring states did not support FRELIMO, mainly because of their dependence on the railway lines which crossed Mozambique and linked them with the ports on the Indian Ocean. FRELIMO did, however, receive generous advice and supplies from China.

1964

25 September FRELIMO launches its first attacks.

1969

3 February   Dr Mondlane killed by a letter-bomb in Dar-es-Salaam.

1970   Leadership passes to Samora Machel, a hard-line Marxist.

1970–71   FRELIMO offensive in Tete area, particularly around the Cabora-Bassa dam site.

1972

December   International outcry follows massacre of 3–400 villagers in the settlements of Wiryamu, Chawda and Juwau near Tete by black Portuguese troops.

1974

3 September Rumours of impending agreement between Portugal and FRELIMO leads to short-lived revolt of despair by white Mozambicans and pro-Portuguese blacks in Lourenço Marques. Pro-FRELIMO backlash costs c. 9500 lives.

7 September Portuguese Foreign Minister, Dr Mário Soares, signs Lusaka Agreement with Samora Machel, proclaiming ceasefire from the next day and independence on 25 July, 1975.

1975

25 July   Machel proclaims independence of People's Republic of Mozambique.

Estimated casualties: Portuguese Army 3,500; FRELIMO 10,000; civilians 50,000.

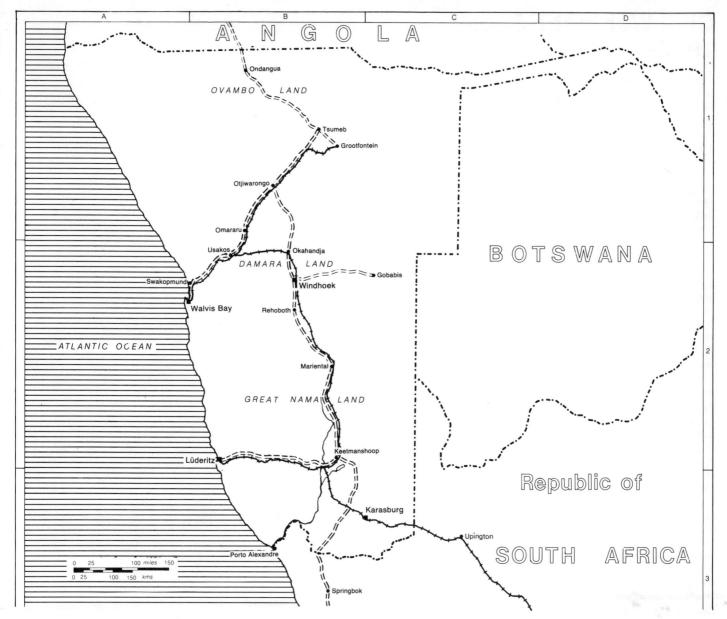

South-West Africa (Namibia)

South-West Africa was first colonized in 1884–90 as German South-West Africa, but was conquered by South African troops in 1915 and subsequently administered by South Africa as a mandated territory on behalf of the League of Nations. Upon the formal dissolution of the League in 1946, South Africa, after failing to win UN approval for the incorporation of the territory, refused to put it under the UN trusteeship system. Since then the status and future of S.W. Africa have been in dispute between South Africa and the UN. In international politics the country has been referred to as Namibia since 1968. In 1960 Sam Nujoma founded SWAPO (South West African People's Organization), dedicated to achieving independence for Namibia and backed by Angola and the Soviet Union. In 1966 SWAPO guerrillas started fighting South African units in the Damaraland bush country. In 1971 the UN General Assembly recognized SWAPO as 'the sole legitimate representative of the Namibian people'. South Africa has made repeated military incursions, sanitized by the euphemism 'hot pursuits', into Southern Angola, allegedly in pursuit of SWAPO guerrillas, but, in Angolan eyes, in an attempt to destabilize the country and create a buffer zone in Southern Angola which would facilitate

guerrilla operations by the pro-Western UNITA (see p. 40) and inhibit infiltration of SWAPO troops into Namibia. In 1981 it was estimated that there were about 600 SWAPO guerrillas in Namibia and a further 6–8,000 inside Angola. The two most recent major operations were Operation Protea (24.8–4.9.81) and Operation Daisy (1–20.11.81). During Protea S. African planes bombed Chibemba, Xangongo and the medical post at Cahama. 130,000 people were forced to flee the area and S. Africa claimed 1000 SWAPO guerrillas dead. S. Africa also captured one Soviet officer and killed four others. During Daisy S. Africa destroyed SWAPO bases at Chitequeta and claimed 71 SWAPO dead. S. Africa refuses to leave Namibia, or to consider its independence, until the Cubans leave Angola. The Angolans, who need a settlement far more than do the South Africans, do not wish to be seen to lose face by bowing publicly before South African demands. The S. Africans could spin out the guerrilla war against SWAPO for years. So the stalemate remains.

43

Civil War in the Sudan 1955–1972

After the defeat of the Khalifa at the battles of Atbara and Omdurman in 1898 an Anglo-Egyptian agreement was signed on 19 January, 1899, whereby the Sudan was jointly governed by those two countries on a condominium basis and from then until 1956 it was known as the Anglo-Egyptian Sudan. In 1953 the country was granted self-government and on 1 January, 1956, a Republic was proclaimed, fighting between North and South having started in the previous July. This marked the beginning of a struggle which dragged on until 1972 and is sometimes referred to as the Sixteen Years' War or the Long War. Its origins can be traced back to the deliberate British policy, at least until 1946, of keeping the Arab Northerners apart from the Negro Southerners, and to the Northerners' traditional contempt for the Southerners, the latter having for centuries been used as slaves by the former, who still frequently referred to them as such (*abeed*). In the 'Sudanization' that followed self-government the more backward and inexperienced Southerners were given only 6 out of 800 senior government posts in the replacement of British officials. Rioting broke out in Yambio on 25 July, 1955, and in Nzara the next day 8 people were killed when 2 Northern merchants fired into a crowd of Southern workmen. On 18 August Southern troops mutinied at Torit and during the month 259 Northerners were murdered in Equatoria. The retribution exacted by the North was prolonged and brutal in the extreme. The horrifying details can be read in Chapter 4 of Cecil Eprile's book *War and Peace in the Sudan* (David & Charles 1974). It is not for the squeamish. The worst period was during the military régime of General Ibrahim Abboud from November, 1958, to October, 1964. In 1963 the Southerners in the bush united to form the *Anya-Nya* guerrilla force (*Anya-Nya* means 'the venom of the viper') under the leadership of General Joseph Lagu. In 1964 the North shocked the Christian world by expelling all foreign Christian missionaries from the South on the wholly unjustified grounds that they were interfering in the political situation. Most of them were Italians belonging to the Verona Fathers. On 25 May, 1969, Gaafer Mohamed Nimery was elected President after a military coup and thereafter Soviet influence began to be increasingly felt in the Sudan. Russian bombers flown by Russian pilots bombed *Anya-Nya* strongholds and Russian helicopters carried Sudanese troops in pursuit of *Anya-Nya* squads. The Sudanese claimed that the Russians were only concerned with civil air transport but the evidence does not support this claim. The fighting was finally brought to an end in March, 1972, largely thanks to the intervention of the Emperor Haile Selassie of Ethiopia and the World Council of Churches. The integration of North and South succeeded better than anyone had dared to hope, particularly the absorption of the *Anya-Nya* into the Sudanese Army. But President Nimery's imposition of Islamic law in September, 1983, was much resented in the largely Christian or pagan south and guerrilla bands are operating once again in the Upper Nile and Bahr el Bhazal regions. One group, styling itself *Anya-Nya II*, is said to number 5000 men.

Somalia and the Ogaden War

The Somali Democratic Republic, consisting of the former Italian trust territory of Somalia and the former British Somaliland Protectorate, was established on 1 July, 1960. British rule in Somaliland had lasted since 1884, except for a short period in 1940/41 when the Protectorate was occupied by Italian troops. Somalia Italiana was colonized in 1886, occupied by British forces in 1941 and replaced under Italian trusteeship by the UN in 1950. From the moment of its birth the new republic's prime object has been to secure the accession to it of French Somaliland (now Djibouti) and the adjacent areas of Kenya and Ethiopia inhabited by Somalis. The British had

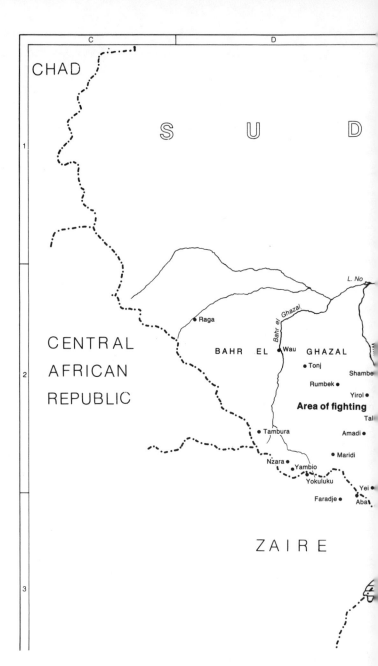

indeed appointed a commission in October, 1962, to ascertain the wishes of the Somali inhabitants of Kenya on the eve of that country's attainment of self-government, and though the vast majority favoured union with Somalia, the British, anxious not to offend the embryo Kenyan administration, ignored the wishes of the Kenyan Somalis, with the result that the Somali Republic broke off relations with Britain in March, 1963, and by the end of that year had already received £18 million in aid from Russia and China. The nomadic Somali peoples in Ethiopia had long been at odds with the Ethiopian Government and, late in 1963, came out in open revolt, the start of a war which has been waged with varying degrees of intensity ever since. Dissident Somali nationalists in Kenya, known as the *Shifta*, continued their desultory war against the Kenyan security forces meanwhile. In 1967 the people of French Somaliland voted to retain their ties with France and President Jomo Kenyatta of Kenya granted an amnesty to the *Shiftas*. In October, 1969, President Shermarke was assassinated and a military-backed Supreme Revolutionary Council assumed power in Somalia, thus ending nearly ten years of democratic government. In 1977 the hitherto sporadic guerrilla campaign erupted into open war between

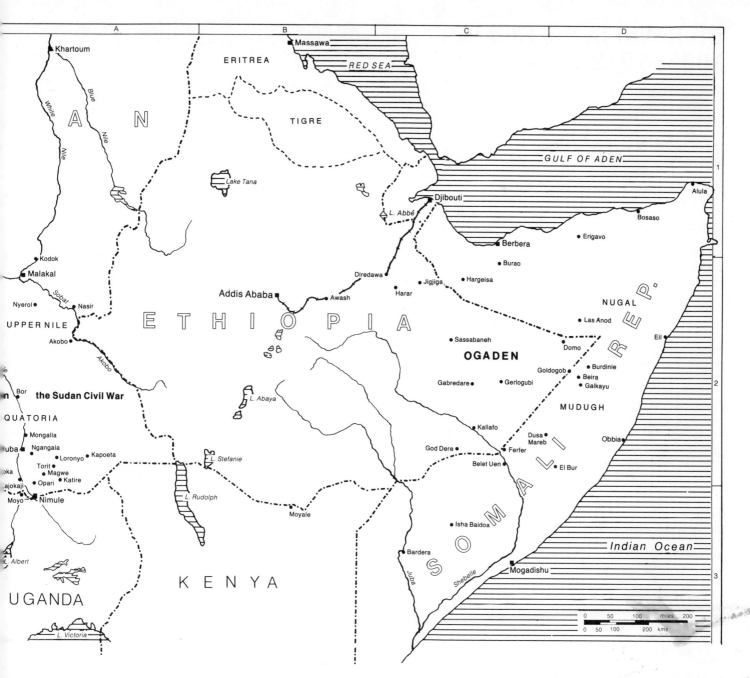

the Ethiopian Army and the 3–6,000-strong Western Somalia Liberation Front (WSLF), a guerrilla movement founded in 1974 whose
avowed aim was to regain all the territory east of a line from Moyale
on the Kenyan border, through Awash, to Lake Abbe, roughly a third
of all Ethiopia. To what extent the Somali Army was involved is
uncertain but certain it is that in May troops crossed the border into
the Ogaden, which, garrisoned only by isolated Ethiopian troops,
was overrun within a week. In July the WSLF cut the Addis Ababa–
Djibouti railway, economically the capital's jugular vein. In September they took Jigjiga and only narrowly failed to take Harar and
Diredawa as well. In November the Somali Government, angered by
the strange state of affairs whereby the Russians were now also
supplying the Ethiopians with arms, ordered all Russians out of the
country and renounced the Soviet–Somali treaty of friendship. At the
same time all Cubans were given 48 hours in which to leave the
country. Meanwhile massive shipments of Soviet arms and Cuban
personnel had enabled the Ethiopians to stabilize the situation and
launch a counter-offensive, which came in February/March and in
anticipation of which on 12 February Somalia publicly committed
Government troops to the Ogaden War, having hitherto claimed that

all the fighting had been conducted by the WSLF. On 4 March the
Ethiopians attacked Jigjiga which fell after two days of fighting, an
estimated 10,000 Cuban troops being involved in the offensive
which was directed by a Russian, General Petrov. On 9 March
Somalia announced its withdrawal from the Ogaden. This defeat was
followed by an influx of refugees into Somalia which by mid-1980
was thought to number in excess of one and a half million and was
described by the UN High Commission for Refugees as "the worst
refugee problem in the world". Despite all this, and the added
problems of drought and famine, the war in the Ogaden went on, as
WSLF continued to fight the Ethiopians and their Cuban supporters.
In July, 1982, serious clashes occurred in the area north-west of
Belet Uen, by which time a new faction, the Somali Democratic
Salvation Front (SDSF), operating from within Ethiopia and dedicated to the overthrow of Said Barre, President of Somalia since
1969, had entered the arena. The Ethiopians accused the SDSF of
having started the trouble but outside observers were of the opinion
that most of the 6–9,000-strong invasion force were Ethiopians. Of
late there has been little news from the Ogaden front, but with the US
now supporting the Somalis, no end to the conflict is in sight.

45

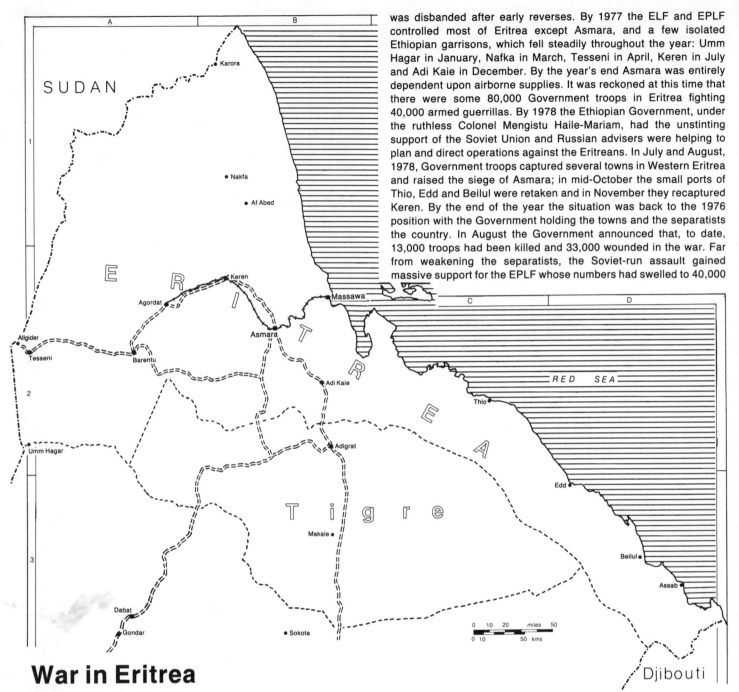

was disbanded after early reverses. By 1977 the ELF and EPLF controlled most of Eritrea except Asmara, and a few isolated Ethiopian garrisons, which fell steadily throughout the year: Umm Hagar in January, Nafka in March, Tesseni in April, Keren in July and Adi Kaie in December. By the year's end Asmara was entirely dependent upon airborne supplies. It was reckoned at this time that there were some 80,000 Government troops in Eritrea fighting 40,000 armed guerrillas. By 1978 the Ethiopian Government, under the ruthless Colonel Mengistu Haile-Mariam, had the unstinting support of the Soviet Union and Russian advisers were helping to plan and direct operations against the Eritreans. In July and August, 1978, Government troops captured several towns in Western Eritrea and raised the siege of Asmara; in mid-October the small ports of Thio, Edd and Beilul were retaken and in November they recaptured Keren. By the end of the year the situation was back to the 1976 position with the Government holding the towns and the separatists the country. In August the Government announced that, to date, 13,000 troops had been killed and 33,000 wounded in the war. Far from weakening the separatists, the Soviet-run assault gained massive support for the EPLF whose numbers had swelled to 40,000

War in Eritrea

Eritrea was first colonized by the Italians in 1882, was occupied by the British in 1941 and remained under British administration until 1952 when it was federated to Ethiopia. Ten years later the Emperor Haile Selassie abolished its autonomous status and it became an integral part of Ethiopia. A year later the Eritrean Liberation Front (ELF) resorted to arms to regain their independence. Over the years various splinter groups broke away from the ELF, in particular the Marxist Eritrean People's Liberation Force (EPLF), the ELF Popular Liberation Forces, the Tigre People's Liberation Front and the Ethiopian Democratic Union (EDU). Though all fighting for Eritrean independence, these factions were otherwise at loggerheads. Had they been united, they might well have succeeded. In December, 1970, martial law was declared in Eritrea after the ELF had assassinated Major-General Teshome Erghetu. In 1974, taking advantage of the confusion which followed the deposition of Haile Selassie and the establishment of a Marxist government in Addis Ababa, the ELF almost succeeded in taking the Eritrean capital, Asmara. In June, 1976, a peasant army levied to fight the separatists

by mid-1979. In March and July Government forces mounted heavy attacks on Nakfa but failed to take the town, and in December the separatists there inflicted a crushing defeat on the Ethiopian troops. For the next six months there was a virtual ceasefire in northern Eritrea, though heavy fighting was reported around Assab in the South. 1980 saw the outbreak of open warfare between the ELF and the EPLF and in 1981 the EPLF established itself as the sole effective separatist force by occupying the territory formerly held by the ELF in Western Eritrea and obliging some 4,000 ELF guerrillas to take refuge in the Sudan. No end to the fighting appears to be in sight and a report in *The Times* on 25 July, 1983, described the EPLF as "one of the most skilled and motivated fighting forces in Africa.... The Front's activities are directed from underground offices equipped with all the trappings of modern African ministries except the bureaucracy and the corruption.... The question remains, how long can the Eritrean people resist an Ethiopian Government supported by both East (arms) and West (food and development aid)?" Only time can tell.

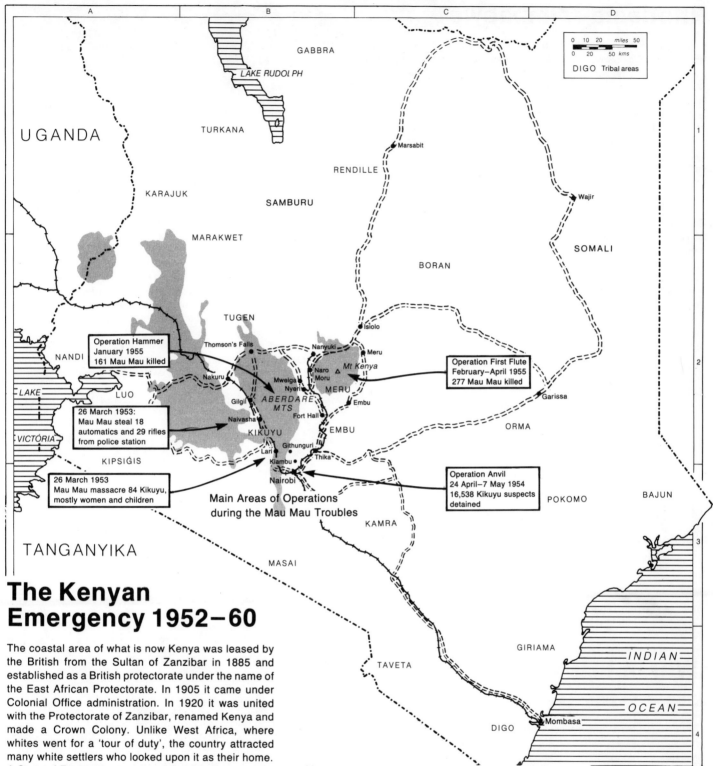

Map labels:

GABBRA

LAKE RUDOLPH

UGANDA

TURKANA

KARAJUK

MARAKWET

SAMBURU

RENDILLE

● Marsabit

● Wajir

SOMALI

BORAN

NANDI

TUGEN

Operation Hammer
January 1955
161 Mau Mau killed

Thomson's Falls

Nanyuki

Isiolo

Meru

Operation First Flute
February–April 1955
277 Mau Mau killed

LUO

Nakuru

Mweiga
Nyeri

Naro
Moru

△ Mt Kenya

MERU

LAKE

VICTORIA

Gilgil

ABERDARE
MTS

Embu

Garissa

26 March 1953:
Mau Mau steal 18
automatics and 29 rifles
from police station

Naivasha

Fort Hall

KIKUYU

EMBU

ORMA

KIPSIGIS

Lari
Kiambu

Githunguri

Thika

26 March 1953
Mau Mau massacre 84 Kikuyu,
mostly women and children

Nairobi

Operation Anvil
24 April–7 May 1954
16,538 Kikuyu suspects
detained

POKOMO

BAJUN

Main Areas of Operations
during the Mau Mau Troubles

KAMRA

TANGANYIKA

MASAI

GIRIAMA

INDIAN

TAVETA

OCEAN

DIGO

● Mombasa

Scale box: 0 10 20 *miles* 50 / 0 20 50 *kms* / DIGO Tribal areas

The Kenyan
Emergency 1952–60

The coastal area of what is now Kenya was leased by the British from the Sultan of Zanzibar in 1885 and established as a British protectorate under the name of the East African Protectorate. In 1905 it came under Colonial Office administration. In 1920 it was united with the Protectorate of Zanzibar, renamed Kenya and made a Crown Colony. Unlike West Africa, where whites went for a 'tour of duty', the country attracted many white settlers who looked upon it as their home. A State of Emergency was proclaimed in Kenya on 20 October 1952 after a period of mounting lawlessness, culminating in the murder on 9 October of Senior Chief Waruhiu, one of Britain's closest allies in the Kikuyu tribe. The situation arose out of Kikuyu dissatisfaction with their standard of living and place in society, those who had fought in the Second World War being particularly aware that they were, at best, second-class citizens in their own country. Terrorist activity was organized through Mau Mau, a loose-knit para-military secret society in which discipline depended largely upon sorcery and peculiarly repulsive oath-taking ceremonies. Nearly all Mau Mau were Kikuyu, though not all Kikuyu were Mau Mau. The meaning of the name Mau Mau has never been established. After early attempts to handle the situation with European tactics had failed, the British adopted the same methods as had proved successful in Malaya in putting down the Mau Mau revolt and by October, 1956, the situation was under control, though the Emergency did not officially end until January, 1960. On 12 December, 1963, Kenya became independent and Jomo Kenyatta, said to have been one of the leaders of Mau Mau, became her first Prime Minister.

CASUALTIES			
		Killed	Wounded
Mau Mau		10527	?
African	C.	1826	918
	S.	534	465
European	C.	32	26
	S.	63	102
Asian	C.	26	12
	S.	3	

C: Civilian
S: Soldiers, Security Forces

Rhodesia–Zimbabwe

Britain's association with Rhodesia dated from 1889 when the British South Africa Company, run by Cecil Rhodes, was granted a charter to develop 'North and South Zambesia'. In 1896 the country was named Rhodesia and in 1911 was divided into Northern and Southern Rhodesia. In 1922 the European population of S. Rhodesia, in response to an offer made by the British Government, voted for 'responsible government', which meant that, though technically a colony, S. Rhodesia became in practice a quasi-dominion. In this event, which placed effective power firmly in the hands of the white settlers, lies the key to the troubles which lay ahead. There were at the time 35,000 whites and 900,000 Africans in the country, of whom 20,000 and 60 respectively were on the voting register. In 1953 N. and S. Rhodesia were federated with Nyasaland to form the Federation of Rhodesia and Nyasaland; but the reactionary attitude of the whites in S. Rhodesia towards the Africans, among whom nationalist sentiments were hardening, doomed the Federation to failure and it was dissolved in 1963, at which time N. Rhodesia gained independence as Zambia and Nyasaland as Malawi. The tragic history of S. Rhodesia since that time is mainly the story of the attempts of successive British administrations to reach an acceptable settlement with the white settlers and falls outside the scope of this work. The background of guerrilla warfare against which the negotiations were conducted must, however, be considered.

The three contestants in the guerrilla war were: ZAPU, ZANU and the RSF.

ZAPU (Zimbabwe African People's Union); set up by Joshua Nkomo in 1961; army – ZIPRA (Zimbabwe People's Revolutionary Army); troops – mainly from Ndebele-orientated tribes; foreign support – mostly Russian.

ZANU (Zimbabwe African National Union); set up in August, 1963, by Ndabaningi Sithole and Robert Mugabe as breakaway party from ZAPU; army – ZANLA (Zimbabwe National Liberation Army); troops – mainly from Shona-orientated tribes; foreign support – Chinese, Russian arms supplied through OAU.

RSF (Rhodesian Security Forces) included the Rhodesia Regiment (8 bns, all white); the Rhodesian Light Infantry (c. 1000 men, all white); Rhodesian African Rifles (6–700 men, black with white officers); SAS (180 men, ell white); Selous Scouts (c. 1000 men, black and white; trained to operate in small groups).

1964
First guerrilla infiltrations across the Zambesi.

April
Ian Smith becomes Prime Minister; ZAPU and ZANU banned; HQ moved to Zambia.

1965
November
Smith declares Unilateral Declaration of Independence (UDI).

1967
ZAPU forms alliance with South African Nationalist Congress (SANC).

Late 1960's
Increasing friction between ZAPU and ZANU.

1971
Bishop Abel Muzorewa forms African National Council (ANC) theoretically as umbrella organization comprising ZAPU and ZANU.

From **1972**
Intensified campaign of intimidation: 'The wretched tribesmen found themselves in an intolerable situation. If they did not help the Government they were in severe trouble with the authorities; if they did they were liable to be murdered by the guerrillas ... the fear of death and disruption ... was to turn their lives into a nightmare of misery and squalor.'

1975
March
Herbert Chitepo, leader of ZANU in Zambia, assassinated in Lusaka on the orders of his rival Josiah Tongogara. Kenneth Kaunda, President of Zambia, arrests several ZANU leaders and shuts their Lusaka office; ZANU HQ moved to recently independent Mozambique.

1976
ZAPU begins to operate into Rhodesia from Botswana.

August
RSF starts counter-raids across Mozambique border.

September
Nkomo and Mugabe unite to form Patriotic Front.

1978
Internal situation deteriorates further: guerrillas now active throughout entire country.

1979
April
Muzorewa becomes first black Prime Minister of Zimbabwe–Rhodesia.

November
British put forward proposals for ceasefire.

6 December
Lord Soames appointed Governor.

1980
January
12,000 ZANLA and 4000 ZIPRA guerrillas report to prearranged assembly areas run by Commonwealth-manned Monitoring Force. Many ZANLA stay out and atrocities continue.

March
Robert Mugabe becomes first Prime Minister of Zimbabwe.

18 April
Independent Republic of Zimbabwe proclaimed.

The post-independence merger of ZIPRA, ZANLA and the RSF has not been entirely successful. (In February, 1981, fighting broke out between ZIPRA and ZANLA in the Bulawayo area with the loss of 300 lives.) In February, 1983 the Army's notorious 5th Brigade was sent to Matabeleland to deal with dissident ZAPU guerrillas who had taken to rebellion in the bush in protest against Mr Nkomo's exclusion from Mr Mugabe's government. It was reported that at least 1,000 civilians were murdered and many more tortured and beaten. In March Mr Nkomo, fearing for his life, fled to London, but returned to Zimbabwe in August. At the end of July it was stated that the 5th Brigade had been withdrawn from Matabeleland.

This map, taken with kind permission from an article by Thomas Arbuckle which appeared in the December, 1979, issue of the *Royal United Services Institute Journal* shows guerrilla infiltration routes and points of attack in Eastern Rhodesia. Anti-guerrilla operations in this area, known as Operation Thrasher, started in 1976 and are typical of other operations – Hurricane (north-east), Repulse (south-east), Tangent (south-west), Grapple (midlands), Splinter (Lake Kariba) – carried out by the RSF.

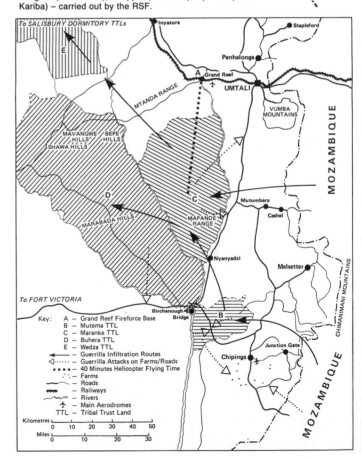

Key:
A — Grand Reef Fireforce Base
B — Mutema TTL
C — Maranke TTL
D — Buhera TTL
E — Wedza TTL
— Guerrilla Infiltration Routes
— Guerrilla Attacks on Farms/Roads
— 40 Minutes Helicopter Flying Time
— Farms
— Roads
— Railways
— Rivers
— Main Aerodromes
TTL — Tribal Trust Land

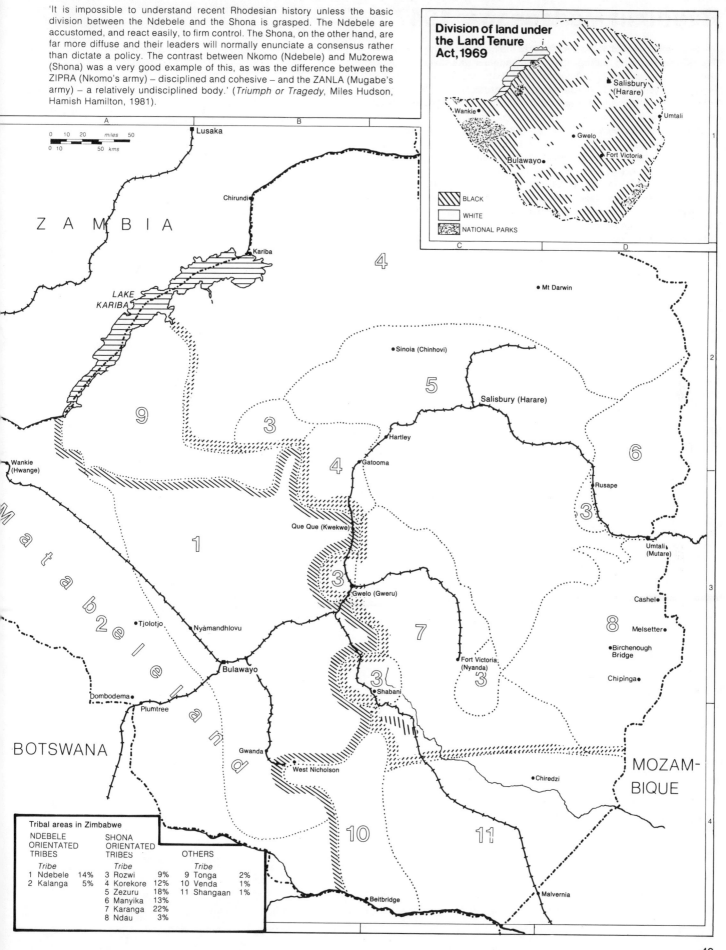

'It is impossible to understand recent Rhodesian history unless the basic division between the Ndebele and the Shona is grasped. The Ndebele are accustomed, and react easily, to firm control. The Shona, on the other hand, are far more diffuse and their leaders will normally enunciate a consensus rather than dictate a policy. The contrast between Nkomo (Ndebele) and Mužorewa (Shona) was a very good example of this, as was the difference between the ZIPRA (Nkomo's army) – disciplined and cohesive – and the ZANLA (Mugabe's army) – a relatively undisciplined body.' (*Triumph or Tragedy*, Miles Hudson, Hamish Hamilton, 1981).

Division of land under the Land Tenure Act, 1969

Wankie · Salisbury (Harare) · Umtali · Gwelo · Bulawayo · Fort Victoria

BLACK
WHITE
NATIONAL PARKS

ZAMBIA

Lusaka

Chirundi

Kariba

LAKE KARIBA

Mt Darwin

Sinoia (Chinhovi)

Salisbury (Harare)

Hartley

Gatooma

Que Que (Kwekwe)

Wankie (Hwange)

Rusape

Umtali (Mutare)

Gwelo (Gweru)

Cashel

Tjolotjo · Nyamandhlovu

Melsetter

Birchenough Bridge

Fort Victoria (Nyanda)

Chipinga

Bulawayo

Shabani

Dombodema

Plumtree

Gwanda

BOTSWANA

West Nicholson

Chiredzi

MOZAM-BIQUE

Beitbridge

Malvernia

Matabeleland

Tribal areas in Zimbabwe

NDEBELE ORIENTATED TRIBES		SHONA ORIENTATED TRIBES		OTHERS	
Tribe		*Tribe*		*Tribe*	
1 Ndebele	14%	3 Rozwi	9%	9 Tonga	2%
2 Kalanga	5%	4 Korekore	12%	10 Venda	1%
		5 Zezuru	18%	11 Shangaan	1%
		6 Manyika	13%		
		7 Karanga	22%		
		8 Ndau	3%		

Revolt in Madagascar 1947

An insurrection aimed at the overthrow of the French administration and the establishment of Madagascan independence was launched on 29 March, 1947, by the *Mouvement Démocratique de la Rénovation Malagache* (MDRM). The most serious outbreak was at Moramanga where some 1200 natives attacked the garrison and killed 20 French and Senegalese troops. Other attacks occurred at Farafangana, Antsirabe and Diego Suarez. On 22 April the insurgents seized an administrative post at Vohilava and on 3 July several thousand natives launched an attack on Antananarivo, but were beaten back. Thereafter the situation came increasingly under the control of the authorities and things were back to normal by the end of July. More than 11,000 lives were lost during the revolt and the leaders of the MDRM were outlawed.

The island, which became a French protectorate in 1895 and a colony in 1896, was granted republican status in 1958 and achieved full independence in 1960.

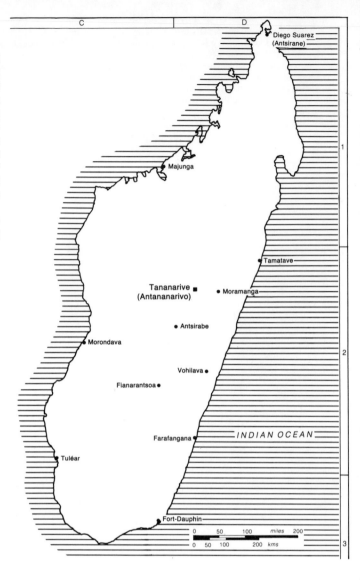

PART V
India

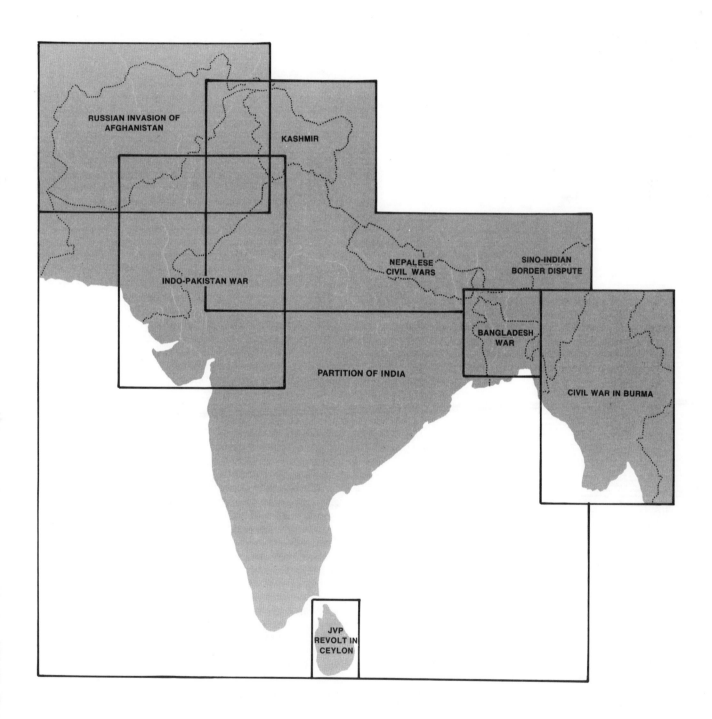

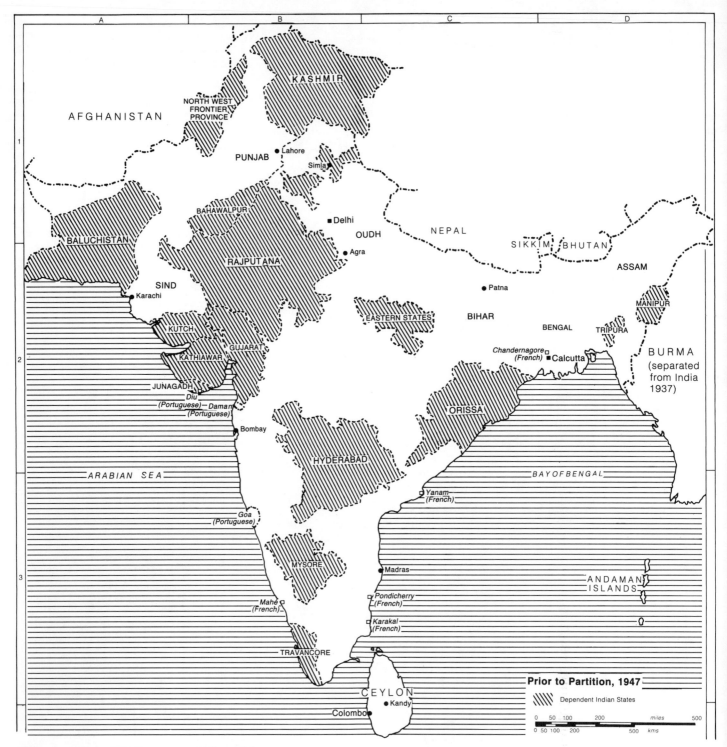

The map is labeled with the following place names:

AFGHANISTAN, KASHMIR, NORTH WEST FRONTIER PROVINCE, PUNJAB, Lahore, Simla, BAHAWALPUR, Delhi, OUDH, Agra, NEPAL, SIKKIM, BHUTAN, ASSAM, BALUCHISTAN, RAJPUTANA, Patna, BIHAR, BENGAL, MANIPUR, SIND, Karachi, EASTERN STATES, TRIPURA, KUTCH, GUJARAT, KATHIAWAR, Chandernagore (French), Calcutta, BURMA (separated from India 1937), JUNAGADH, Diu (Portuguese), Daman (Portuguese), ORISSA, Bombay, HYDERABAD, ARABIAN SEA, BAY OF BENGAL, Yanam (French), Goa (Portuguese), ANDAMAN ISLANDS, MYSORE, Madras, Mahé (French), Pondicherry (French), Karakal (French), TRAVANCORE, CEYLON, Kandy, Colombo

Prior to Partition, 1947
Dependent Indian States
miles 0 50 100 200 500
kms 0 50 100 200 500

The Partition of India

The subcontinent of India came gradually under British rule during the 18th and 19th centuries and was governed by them with a generally benign if condescending hand until 1947. The term 'British Raj' is applied equally to the period and to the administration. The growth of Indian nationalism and the struggle for self-rule date from the 1880s, though it should be borne in mind that at no time prior to the Raj had *all* the territory administered by the British ever been united under a single ruler. In 1882 Bankim Chandra Chatterji's famous novel *Anandamath*, in which he put forward the idea of the nation as 'Mother India', was published, and in 1885 the Indian National Congress was founded, with the aim of representing Indian interests and grievances to the British. Nevertheless it was not until 1942 that the British Government indicated its intention of relinquishing the administration of India when the Second World War was over. Sadly, the Congress Party, which spoke for the Hindu majority, had by then broken irrevocably with the Muslim League, founded in 1906, and the question of who would rule India when the British left had become insoluble. Mohammed Ali Jinnah, leader of the Muslim League, was convinced that, in an undivided India, the Muslim minority would be ruled and overruled by the Hindu majority, and refused to accept any solution other than the creation of a separate Muslim state of Pakistan, a solution which found no favour in the eyes of Pandit Nehru, the leader of the Congress Party, and even less with Mahatma Gandhi, by then in saintly retirement, but still a man of enormous influence. As if to confirm that partition was indeed

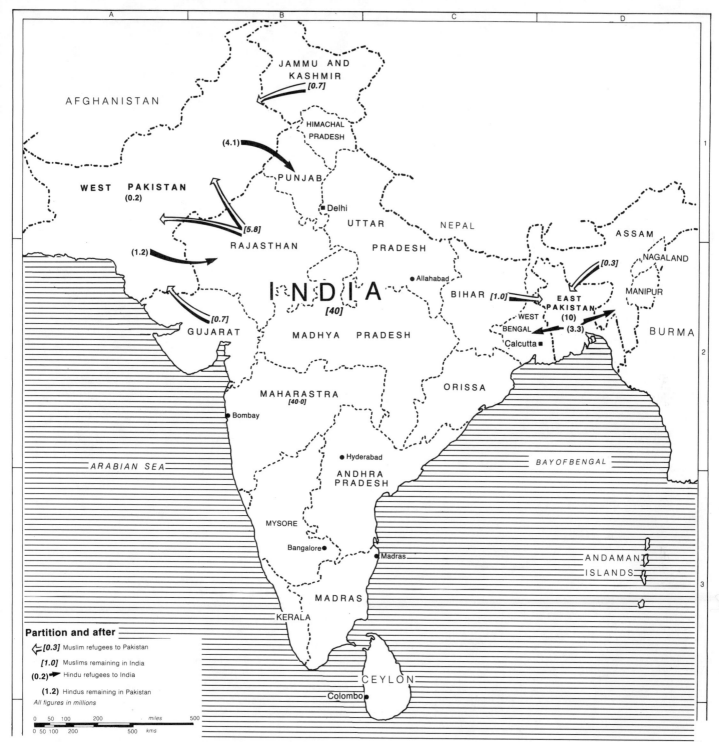

Partition and after

⇐[0.3] Muslim refugees to Pakistan

[1.0] Muslims remaining in India

(0.2)▶ Hindu refugees to India

(1.2) Hindus remaining in Pakistan

All figures in millions

0 50 100   200   miles   500
0 50 100 200   kms   500

inevitable, communal riots broke out in Calcutta in August, 1946, in which at least 4,700 people were killed and thousands more injured. Finally, on 20 February, 1947, Clement Attlee, leader of the post-war British Labour Government, announced that, come what might, the British were leaving India by June, 1948, at the latest and sent Lord Louis Mountbatten to India as Viceroy to implement the final transfer of power. Mountbatten soon came to the conclusion that partition was inevitable and, deciding that delay would only make matters worse, set 15 August, 1947, as Independence Day. Sir Cyril Radcliffe was appointed chairman of both the Punjab and Bengal Boundary Commissions. The Princely States were to be left free to join India or Pakistan or neither, though the last option was strongly discouraged. In the event only three caused problems – Hyderabad, Junagadh and Kashmir. Hyderabad, the largest of the Princely States, was 80% Hindu, but the Nizam was a Muslim and wanted Hyderabad to become an independent sovereignty within the British Commonwealth. Disturbances broke out, Indian troops were sent in, the Nizam capitulated and Hyderabad was integrated in the Indian union. Likewise in Junagadh, the population was 80% Hindu and the ruler a Muslim, who opted for accession to Pakistan. The people revolted; the Nawab fled and Indian troops entered the state and took over the administration. The Kashmir question could not be settled so easily and is here treated separately. The Partition of India was accompanied by an orgy of murder and pillage as millions of refugees trekked to seek safety across the partition lines. No accurate figures exist but it is thought that at least 1,000,000 people were killed or died and upward of 16,000,000 were forced to leave their homes in the biggest mass migration history has ever known.

53

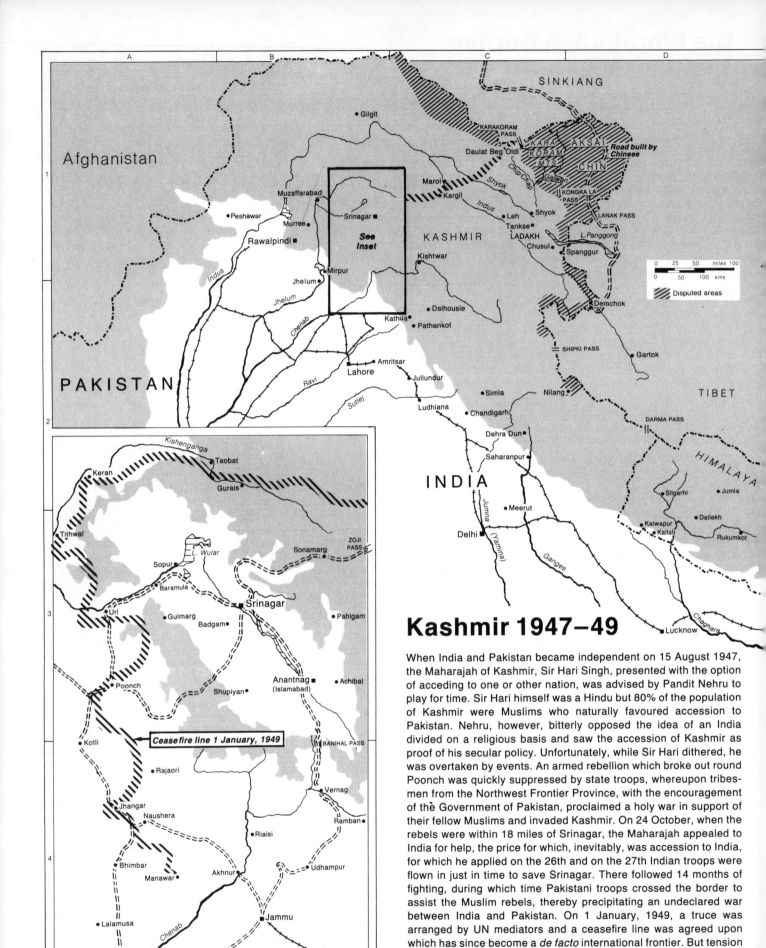

Kashmir 1947–49

When India and Pakistan became independent on 15 August 1947, the Maharajah of Kashmir, Sir Hari Singh, presented with the option of acceding to one or other nation, was advised by Pandit Nehru to play for time. Sir Hari himself was a Hindu but 80% of the population of Kashmir were Muslims who naturally favoured accession to Pakistan. Nehru, however, bitterly opposed the idea of an India divided on a religious basis and saw the accession of Kashmir as proof of his secular policy. Unfortunately, while Sir Hari dithered, he was overtaken by events. An armed rebellion which broke out round Poonch was quickly suppressed by state troops, whereupon tribesmen from the Northwest Frontier Province, with the encouragement of the Government of Pakistan, proclaimed a holy war in support of their fellow Muslims and invaded Kashmir. On 24 October, when the rebels were within 18 miles of Srinagar, the Maharajah appealed to India for help, the price for which, inevitably, was accession to India, for which he applied on the 26th and on the 27th Indian troops were flown in just in time to save Srinagar. There followed 14 months of fighting, during which time Pakistani troops crossed the border to assist the Muslim rebels, thereby precipitating an undeclared war between India and Pakistan. On 1 January, 1949, a truce was arranged by UN mediators and a ceasefire line was agreed upon which has since become a *de facto* international frontier. But tension was not removed and the area was the scene of renewed fighting in the Indo-Pakistan War of 1965 (*qv*).

The Sino-Indian Border Dispute 1962

Owing largely to the hostile nature of the terrain, long stretches of frontier between India and China had never been mutually agreed, so, at the time of Independence, India simply adopted the frontiers which the British had claimed, though China rightly pointed out that she had never signed any treaty delimiting these frontiers. The main areas in dispute were the north-east corner of Kashmir, known as the Aksai Chin, and a part of the North-East Frontier Agency south of Tibet, between Bhutan and Burma, where the Indians claimed the McMahon Line, named after the British representative at a tripartite conference held at Simla in 1913, as the border. In 1951 Chou En-lai, Premier of China, proposed talks between China, India and Nepal to 'stabilize the frontier of Tibet', adding that 'there was no territorial dispute . . . between India and China', but the invitation was not taken up and in 1954 Nehru announced that the boundaries were to be settled unilaterally without negotiation. In 1956/7 the Chinese built a road through the Aksai Chin to link Tibet and Sinkiang. The remoteness of the area can be judged by the fact that the Indians were unaware of the project until the Chinese announced its completion in September, 1957, and issued maps showing much territory claimed by India as part of China. Nehru protested politely and Chou replied in like vein but thereafter tension rose steadily, aggravated by Nehru's unashamedly forward policy and fuelled by anti-Chinese feeling in India following the flight of the Dalai Lama. The first armed clashes occurred in August, 1959, when the Indians exchanged fire with Chinese border guards near Longju in the Eastern disputed area and at the Kongka La Pass in the Western sector, where, by late 1961, the Indians had established 40 posts in territory claimed by the Chinese. Indian lines of communication were hopelessly overstretched and were only sustained by the supply of Russian AN12 transport aircraft and helicopters capable of operat-ing at high altitudes. Nehru, however, continued to pursue his forward policy against all the advice of his military commanders. In June, 1962, India protested to China at what it alleged to be constant incursions into Ladakh, while in July China accused India of trespassing into Sinkiang. On 10 July Chinese troops took an Indian post on the Galwan River. On 21 July Indian and Chinese troops clashed in the Chip Chap Valley and near Panggong Lake.

8 September	Chinese troops cross the McMahon Line.
20 October	Chinese stage massive offensives in Eastern and Western sectors. Attacks in N.E.F.A. stretch from Khinzemane to Walong. Indians evacuate Tawang.
26 October	Nehru declares State of Emergency.
29 October	Britain and U.S.A. send arms to India.
31 October	Nehru sacks Minister of Defence V.K. Krishna Menon.
5 November	Indians evacuate Daulat Beg Oldi.
18 November	Chinese take Walong.
19 November	Chinese take Bomdila. Indians evacuate Tezpur.
21 November	China announces cease-fire. Beginning on 1 December they would 'withdraw to positions 12½ miles behind the lines of actual control which existed between China and India on 7 November, 1959'.

In effect China offered to recognize the McMahon Line in exchange for the Ladakh Salient of Kashmir. No Chinese casualty figures were published. Indian casualty figures are inconsistent but seem to have been roughly 1,400 killed, 1,700 wounded and 4,000 captured.

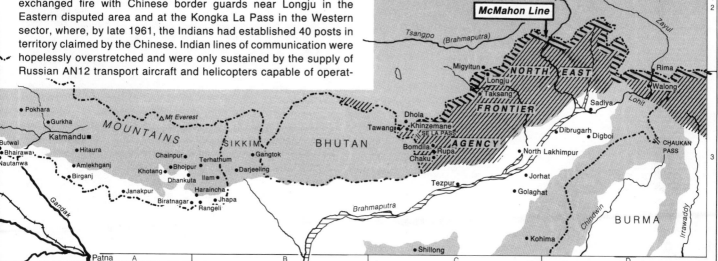

Nepalese Civil Wars

The modern state of Nepal dates from 1769 when the ruler of the Gorkha principality, Prithvi Narayan Shah, from whom the present King is descended, conquered the Nepal Valley and moved his capital to Katmandu. In 1846 political power passed into the hands of the Rana family, the head of which held the hereditary office of Prime Minister. In 1946 the Nepali Congress was formed to unite opposition to the Rana régime. On 11 November, 1950, their supporters rose in revolt, occupied the town of Birganj and set up a provisional government. On 13 November the rebels advanced to Amlekhganj, but by 19 November Government troops had dispersed them and retaken Birganj. To the west rebels had already taken Butwal and Nautanwa on 3 November, and had attacked but failed to take Bhairawa. In the south-east they took Jhapa (15th), Bhojpur, Chainpur, Khotang (18th), Biratnagar (23rd) and Terhathum (30th), while in W. Nepal the town of Kailali was occupied. The revolution succeeded in breaking the power of the Ranas and re-establishing the authority of the royal family. But the introduction in 1959 of a democratic system in a country accustomed to autocracy proved unworkable and in December, 1960, King Mahendra, who had come to the throne in 1955, dismissed the Government, thereby provoking another revolt by the Nepali Congress. Riots in W. Nepal were soon quelled by Government troops but more serious trouble occurred in January, 1962, with peasant uprisings in 9 of the country's 32 districts. On 6 January the rebels took the town of Ilam. On 22 January a bomb was thrown at King Mahendra's car in Janakpur; he was unhurt. Disturbances continued throughout the year until, on 8 November, General Subarna Shamsher, acting president of the Nepali Congress announced that activities would be suspended in view of the Chinese attack on India and the need for national unity. In the same year Mahendra introduced a new partyless constitutional system based on elected councils at village, district and zonal levels. He died in 1972 and was succeeded by his son, Birendra, the present King.

THE INDO-PAKISTAN WAR 1965

The Rann of Kutch is a desolate salt marsh through which the frontier between India and Pakistan was left undefined at the time of partition. Fighting broke out there on 9 April, 1965, when two Indian outposts near Sardar, south of Kanjarkot, were shelled by Pakistani artillery. Sporadic fighting continued until the end of June when the Indian and Pakistani Governments signed a ceasefire agreement negotiated by the British Government providing for a return to the status quo of 1 January, the withdrawal of troops and the setting up of a tribunal to determine the border. The ceasefire took effect from 1 July.

Meanwhile fighting on a much larger scale had broken out further north. On 21 June India complained to the UN that in six days Pakistani forces had committed 40 violations of the 1949 cease-fire line.

5 August	Pakistani irregulars launch 'full-blooded invasion' from 'Azad Kashmir' (that part of Kashmir west of the cease-fire line) into East Kashmir, claims Kashmiri Chief Minister.
9 August	India rushes reinforcements to Kashmir.
14 August	Pakistani regular forces attack near Chhamb.
24 August	Indian forces cross cease-fire line at Uri, Tithwal and Kargil and attack the Uri-Poonch Salient.
28 August	Indians take Haji Pass.
1 September	Pakistan launches massive tank attack in the Chhamb sector.
6 September	Indians launch 3-pronged offensive aimed at Lahore, named Operation *Grand Slam*.
8 September	India spreads conflict to two new areas with attacks near Sialkot and north of Gadra towards Hyderabad.
20 September	UN Security Council demands a cease-fire.
23 September	Fighting ceases, but Pakistani border violations continue.

The war left Pakistan in possession of a large tract of territory in Rajasthan and a salient in Kashmir, while the Indians held a small but strategically important area of Pakistani territory near Sialkot. Indian casualties were officially given as 2,212 killed, 7,636 wounded and 1,500 missing. Pakistani figures were not published but are thought to have been about the same. Both sides lost about 200 tanks, with 150 more damaged but repairable.

The Bangladesh War, December, 1971

The seeds of the war which led to the creation of the state of Bangladesh in 1971 were sown in 1947 when East and West Pakistan were created by the partition of India. United only by adherence to the Muslim faith, they were separated from each other geographically by 1000 miles and immeasurably by race, culture, language and economics. Though the East provided 75% of the foreign earnings and exports, the reins of power were almost exclusively in the hands of West Pakistanis. Initially Pakistan called itself a democracy, but effectively the country was run by the army, the President from 1958 to 1969 being Field-Marshal Ayub Khan. The arrest in 1966 of Sheikh Mujibur Rahman, leader of the Awami League and the outstanding political figure in E. Pakistan, convinced his supporters that limited autonomy was no longer a realistic aim and that total separation was the only answer. In March, 1969, Ayub Khan, having lost all semblance of popular support, gave way to General Yahya Khan, who, in December, 1970, held an election in which the Awami League won a clear majority, whereupon Yahya announced the indefinite postponement of the opening of Parliament. Rioting broke out in E. Pakistan; on 25 March, 1971, the Sheikh was again arrested and the following day the unofficially styled 'Bangladesh' seceded from the Government of Pakistan by unilateral declaration. Yahya then sent Lieut-Gen Tikka Khan to E. Pakistan with orders to 'sort them out'. Thereafter the army went on the rampage and some estimate that as many as a million civilians were murdered. Refugees poured into India and those who remained, having nothing to lose, flocked to join the Awami League's militant resistance organization, the Mukti Bahini, including most of the 70,000 locally recruited members of the armed forces. By August, 6 million refugees had fled to W. Bengal, an intolerable burden for the Indian Government, whose armed forces were now actively preparing to come to the aid of the Mukti Bahini. This was not practicable until November when the monsoon would be over and

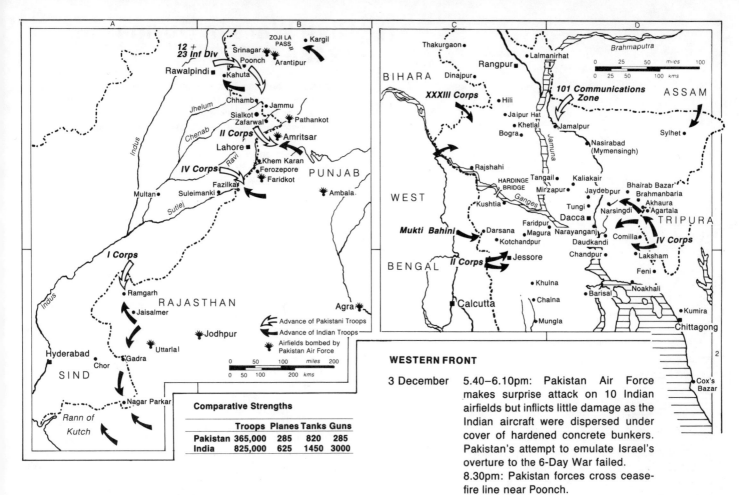

Comparative Strengths

	Troops	Planes	Tanks	Guns
Pakistan	365,000	285	820	285
India	825,000	625	1450	3000

Key:
- Advance of Pakistani Troops
- Advance of Indian Troops
- Airfields bombed by Pakistan Air Force

the ground hard enough to allow large-scale operations, while the onset of winter would close the Sino-Indian frontier and inhibit interference from China. There were several clashes between Indian and Pakistani forces on the E. Pakistani border in October and November, when the latter crossed the frontier in 'hot pursuit' of the Mukti Bahini, finally leading, on 3 December, to the outbreak of open warfare on two fronts.

EASTERN FRONT

3 December	Pakistan Air Force attacks Agartala airfield.
4 December	India launches integrated ground, air and naval offensive. Aircraft from the carrier *Vikrant* bomb airfield at Cox's Bazar. Dacca bombed every ½ hour.
5 December	Indian Army links up with Mukti Bahini and enters E. Pakistan from five directions.
6 December	India announces recognition of independent state of Bangladesh.
5–14 December	Indian troops occupy E. Pakistan towns on dates shown: 5th – Akhaura, Laksham; 6th – Feni; 7th – Sylhet, Jessore; 8th – Magura, Comilla, Brahmanbaria; 9th – Chandpur, Daudkandi; 10th – Bhairab Bazar; 11th – Noakhali, Nasirabad, Kushtia; 12th – Narsingdi; 14th – Bogra.
14 December	Indian artillery starts shelling Dacca. Garrisons now still holding out only at Dacca, Rangpur, Dinajpur, Khulna, Barisal, Chittagong and Mainamati (a fortified cantonment outside Comilla).
15 December	Indian forces close on Dacca from all sides.
16 December	General Niazi signs surrender document for Pakistan, though fighting continues in the Khulna and Sylhet areas until 17 December.

WESTERN FRONT

3 December	5.40–6.10pm: Pakistan Air Force makes surprise attack on 10 Indian airfields but inflicts little damage as the Indian aircraft were dispersed under cover of hardened concrete bunkers. Pakistan's attempt to emulate Israel's overture to the 6-Day War failed. 8.30pm: Pakistan forces cross cease-fire line near Poonch.
4 December	Pakistani forces cross border into Rajasthan but are driven back.
4–6 December	Indian Air Force retaliates. Indian forces take Pakistani posts round Kahuta and the Zoji La Pass. Pakistani attack on Poonch repelled.
5 December	Indian forces enter Pakistan at Gadra, also N. of Jaisalmer and in the Nagar Parkar area of the Rann of Kutch.
6 December	Indians occupy Khem Karan Salient N. of Ferozepore.
7 December	Pakistanis force Indians out of Chhamb.
7–14	Pakistanis lose 3000 men in battle to hold Chhamb.
15–16 December	Indians knock out 45 Pakistani tanks between Zafarwal and Pathankot in what was said to be the longest tank battle since the Second World War.
17 December	Mrs Gandhi announces unilateral ceasefire.

India captured about 2000 square miles of Pakistan's territory in Sind, including a portion of the Rann of Kutch which an international tribunal had awarded to Pakistan in 1966. On the Punjab/Jammu and Kashmir front India gained about 1000 square miles, but lost the 60-square mile tract of Chhamb and a few more square miles on the Punjab border. 10,633 officers and men were killed, wounded or missing. Material losses amounted to 73 tanks and 45 aircraft. Pakistani figures were not released but are estimated at about 17,000 killed, wounded or missing and 10,000 taken prisoner. 94 aircraft and 246 tanks were lost. Sheikh Mujibur Rahman became Prime Minister of the new state of Bangladesh on 12 January, 1972, but was killed in a military coup on 14 August 1974. Except for a period in 1979–81 the country has remained under martial law ever since. Military rule also still prevails in Pakistan where General Zia-ul-Haq assumed power in July, 1977, ousting President Zulfikar Ali Bhutto, whom he had executed in April, 1979.

Civil Wars in Burma
1948–1958

Lower Burma became part of the British Empire in 1853, Upper Burma in 1885. From 1941 to 1945 the country was occupied by the Japanese, who were finally driven out by General Slim's heroic 14th Army. On 4 January, 1948, Burma became a sovereign independent state, no longer 'forming part of His Majesty's dominions nor entitled to His Majesty's protection.' Civil war broke out almost at once. By the end of March the Burma Communist Party and the Communist Party (Burma), known as the White Flag and Red Flag communists, were in open rebellion and in control of much of the country between Mandalay and Rangoon. In August the situation was aggravated by mutinies in the army at Mingaladon and Thayetmyo but these were put down by loyal troops. More serious was the demand of the 2 million-odd Karens for autonomy, a demand hard to realize since they did not inhabit a consolidated area. The rebellion started in August and by the beginning of September the Karens had taken the towns of Thaton and Moulmein. In January, 1949, they took Bassein, Toungoo and Insein, in February Meiktila and Maymyo, and on 12 March Mandalay. But they were numerically incapable of holding such widely separated towns and at the end of May withdrew to concentrate in the Sittang Valley with headquarters at Toungoo, where, on 14 June, they proclaimed the establishment of a separate state. The Left Wing rebels maintained themselves throughout the year in the central Irrawaddy Valley between Magwe and Prome. In May they took the oilfields at Yenangyaung and Prome but were expelled by Government troops in June. In 1950 Government troops took the initiative against the Karens. Pyu was retaken on 5 March and Toungoo on 19 March, but the Karens carried on the fight in the adjoining Salween district and in the Irrawaddy delta. Government troops took Magwe from the Left Wing rebels on 8 April, Pakokku on 29 April, Prome, their capital, on 19 May, and Thayetmyo on 13 October, after the rainy season. In 1952 an effort was made to conciliate the Karens by the establishment of a Karen state, autonomous for purposes of local government, in the eastern hills of Lower Burma. This was inaugurated on 1 June, 1954, but Karen resistance continued and even though Papun, their last stronghold, fell to Government troops in March, 1955, in October of that year it was reckoned that there were still 3000 Karen and 5000 Left Wing rebels under arms. There were large-scale surrenders after the amnesty offer promulgated by the President on 31 July, 1958, and thereafter resistance gradually faded away.

The Russian Invasion of Afghanistan

Afghanistan first emerged as an independent country in 1747 under Ahmed Shah Abdali, who in 1761 beat the Mahrattas at the Battle of Panipat, described as one of the decisive battles of the world. By the 1830s, however, the country was enfeebled and Britain, apprehensive of Russian intentions and concerned about the safety of British India, began to interest herself in Afghan affairs, and from that time until the mid-1950s exercised the predominant external influence over the country's affairs. In 1953 King Amanullah died, his cousin Mohammad Daoud Khan seized power and soon sought and received aid from both Russia and America. But in the early 1960s American aid was cut off and in 1963, in protest at the country's subsequent overdependence on Soviet assistance, Daoud resigned. He returned to power in 1973 but was assassinated in 1978 in a coup from which Nur Mohammad Taraki emerged as President. The new government's efforts to stampede the country into the 20th century,

involving, among other things, drastic land redistribution and unpopular female emancipation, angered the reactionary and fiercely Muslim peasantry and by April, 1979, most of the provinces were in revolt. Concerned by the effect that this Islamic revival, mirrored in neighbouring Iran by the overthrow of the Shah in January, 1979, might have on the Muslim population of Soviet Central Asia, Russia tried to decelerate the pace of reform, but, finding the hardliners intractable, resorted in December, 1979, to armed intervention. The Soviets claimed that the Afghan Government had asked for their help, but this was hardly borne out by the fact that Hafizullah Amin, the Prime Minster, was killed during the invasion. The Afghan Army put up little resistance and half its 80,000 men were said to have deserted shortly after. Most went home but some joined the Muslim freedom fighters [*Mujihadeen*] who today continue to wage war against the Russian invaders. Reports of their success or otherwise

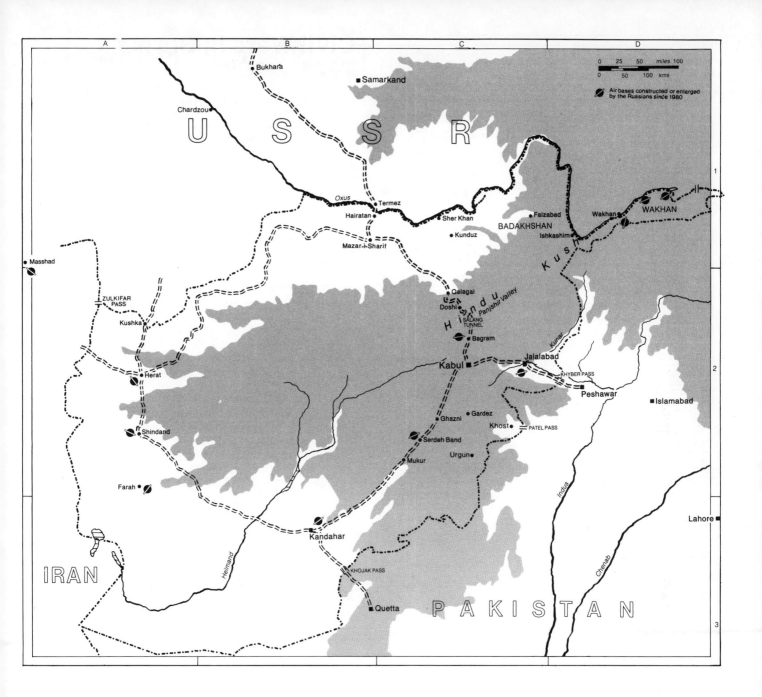

Air bases constructed or enlarged by the Russians since 1980

are contradictory. "Diplomats who have access to information from Kabul said that in the latest fighting the rebels were virtually in complete control of Afghanistan's main western city of Herat", said *The Times* on 13.4.83. But Lt-Col Colin Mitchell, who had recently spent some time with the *Mujihadeen* told the *Sunday Telegraph* (31.7.83) that ultimately they had no hope without practical support from the West. "At present there is something of a stalemate. The success of the guerrillas in dominating the countryside has humiliated the Russians and their puppets, but the *Mujihadeen* can deliver only pinpricks from which the Russians themselves are largely immune. Meanwhile, the Russians are subject to none of the constraints affecting Western governments in prosecuting counter-guerrilla warfare. Young men are shipped off to Russia for indoctrination, crops and livestock destroyed, water supplies cut off, villages attacked until the refugees now occupying them beg the

Mujihadeen to keep away". Gordon Brook-Shepherd, in an earlier article in the same paper (8.8.82) drew attention to the longer-term motives of the invaders: "The Russians are remorselessly building up a vast military infrastructure which ... will enable them to dominate the entire south-east region – Iran, Pakistan, the Indian Ocean and the Persian Gulf included.... Six new Soviet airfields are under construction in the north-eastern province of Badakhshan where the guerrillas do not even operate.... Major military airbases being extended are at Bagram, Shindand, Kandahar and Jalalabad. ... Completely new airfields are either operating or under construction at Farah, at Serdeh Band and at Askargh, near Kandahar."

59

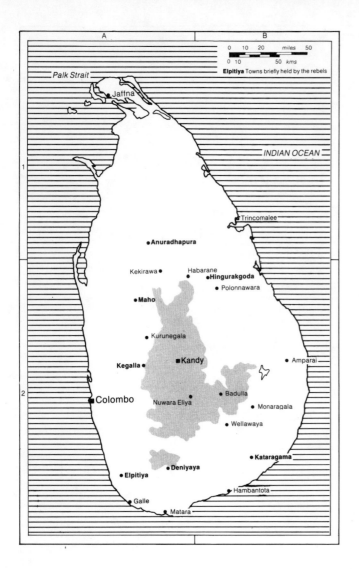

Map labels:

A B

0 10 20 miles 50
0 10 50 kms
Elpitiya Towns briefly held by the rebels

Palk Strait

Jaffna

INDIAN OCEAN

1

Trincomalee

• **Anuradhapura**

Kekirawa • Habarane
•**Hingurakgoda**
• Polonnawara

• **Maho**

• Kurunegala

• **Kandy** Amparai

Kegalla

2 **Colombo** • Badulla
Nuwara Eliya • Monaragala

• Wellawaya

• **Kataragama**
• **Deniyaya**
• **Elpitiya**
Hambantota

Galle
Matara

The JVP Revolt in Ceylon 1971

A State of Emergency was declared in Ceylon on 16 March, 1971, following the disclosure of a plot to overthrow the Government by an armed left-wing organization calling itself the Janatha Kimukthi Peramuna (JVP) or People's Liberation Front, made up mostly of unemployed graduates of under 25, with a strength variously estimated at between 25,000 and 80,000. Led by Rohan Wijeweera, a graduate of the revolutionary Lumumba University in Moscow, they launched an abortive revolt on 5 April with a view to overthrowing the Government, which they regarded as insufficiently left-wing. For a month the rebels controlled considerable rural areas, from which they attacked police stations and cut power lines in different parts of the country. But the Government, which had no proper standing army, received support from Britain, the US, the USSR, China and India and by 23 April over 3000 of the rebels were in custody. Two of the last remaining towns in rebel hands, Elpitaya and Deniyaya, were recaptured by Government forces between 21 and 25 April. On 1 May a 4-day amnesty was announced, during which 3188 rebels surrendered. By the end of the first week in May rebel activity had ceased; at least 1200 people had been killed, 60 of them from the police and security forces. In April, 1972, 13,433 JVP, virtually all aged between 15 and 23, were still in custody undergoing compulsory rehabilitation.

PART VI
China and Korea

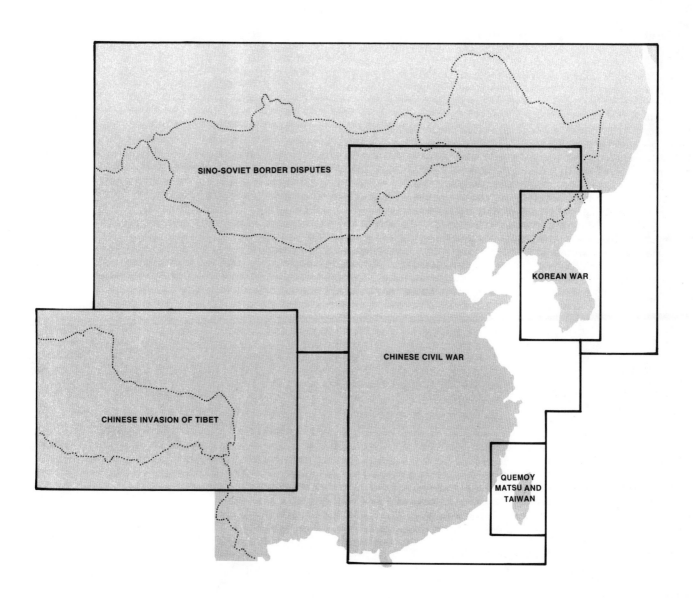

SINO-SOVIET BORDER DISPUTES

KOREAN WAR

CHINESE CIVIL WAR

CHINESE INVASION OF TIBET

QUEMOY MATSU AND TAIWAN

The Chinese Civil War

China became a republic in February, 1912, on the abdication of the 3-year-old Emperor P'u-yi, after an uprising inspired more by anti-dynastic than pro-republican sentiments. The first President of the new Republic of China was Marshal Yuan Shih-k'ai. After his death in 1916 the country degenerated into feudal anarchy as various 'war-lords' fought each other, and the central government grew progressively weaker. By 1925 the Chinese Nationalist Party or Kuomintang (KMT), founded by Dr Sun Yat-sen, had become the dominant political force in China. Sun died in March, 1925, and in June, 1926, Chiang Kai-shek became Chairman of the KMT. In 1927 the Communist element (CCP), led by Mao Tse-tung, rebelled against Chiang and fled to the mountains of western Kiangsi. This marks the beginning of the Chinese Civil War, which was to last for the next 22 years. In 1934, threatened with extermination by Chiang's blockade, Mao and his followers set out on the famous 'Long March' to Yenan, a distance of 6000 miles by the indirect route followed. In January, 1933, Japan had occupied Inner Mongolia and in July, 1937, launched a full-scale invasion of China which led to the formation by the KMT and the CCP of an anti-Japanese 'united front', though in effect this was little more than an armed truce, which the CCP put to good use by expanding and consolidating its control of N.W. China. It also gained a reputation for honesty and sound organization that contrasted sharply with the incompetence and corruption of the Nationalist régime and which was to stand it in good stead when the Civil War burst into even fiercer flames after the surrender of Japan in August, 1945, and the failure of the two sides to reach agreement at the American-inspired Chungking conference which broke up in November, 1945. Thereafter, the Americans committed themselves to the military and economic support of the Nationalist Government. The Communists received no significant help from the Russians. The war involved so many movements of such large bodies of men over such immense distances for so long a period that it would take a whole volume of maps adequately to cover the campaigns. The maps and the text which follow show the main areas of the fighting and give the dates of the major events. In the context of this book both may seem overweighted. In fact the opposite is more likely, since the Chinese Civil War settled the fate of one quarter of the human race.

I am most grateful to Dr Hugh Baker, Head of the Contemporary China Institute of the School of Oriental and African Studies, University of London, for his invaluable advice on the spelling of place-names, but nevertheless take full responsibility for any errors or inconsistencies in the accompanying maps.

MAIN EVENTS
1945

August	Communists move to take over Japanese-held areas of N. China. There were 2m Japanese troops in China at the time of the surrender.
25 August	Nationalists enter Nanking.
August–October	U.S. planes airlift 500,000 Nationalist troops north to stop Communist takeover.
10 September	Nationalists enter Shanghai.
30 September	1st U.S. Marine Division lands at Tientsin.
15 October	Communists destroy 5 Nationalist divisions in Tunliu/Hsiangyuan area.
21 October	Mao announces withdrawal of all Communist troops to N. of Yangtse.
31 October	2 Nationalist armies wiped out in N. Honan.
24 November	Nationalists take Hulutao.
30 November	Communist offensive in Shantung.
1 December	Nationalists reach Tahushan.
13 December	Nationalist troops airlifted to Mukden.
23 December	U.S. General George Marshall arrives as mediator: arranges 6-month truce in all China except Manchuria.

1946

End February	Nationalists occupy Liao Ho valley S. of Mukden.
1 March	Soviet forces begin withdrawal from Manchuria, after dismantling and removing all Japanese machinery: estimated value $858m.
April	Communists take Changchun (15th), Kirin (22nd), Harbin (25th), Tsitsihar (28th).
1 May	Nationalist capital returns from Nankin to Chungking.
May	Nationalists take Ssuping (19th), Kungchuling (21st), Changchun (23rd), Kirin (29th).
5 June	Nationalists take Shuangcheng.
July–November	Nationalist offensive recovers most of Kiangsu and Hopeh from Reds.
July	Nationalists regain control of Kiaochou–Tsinan railroad. Communists encircle Tatung.
28 August	Nationalists take Chengte.
3–8 September	Nationalist 3rd Army destroyed at Tingtao.
27 October	Nationalists take Antung.
October–November	Nationalists drive Reds from Tapieshan.
8 November	Nationalists take Tunghua.

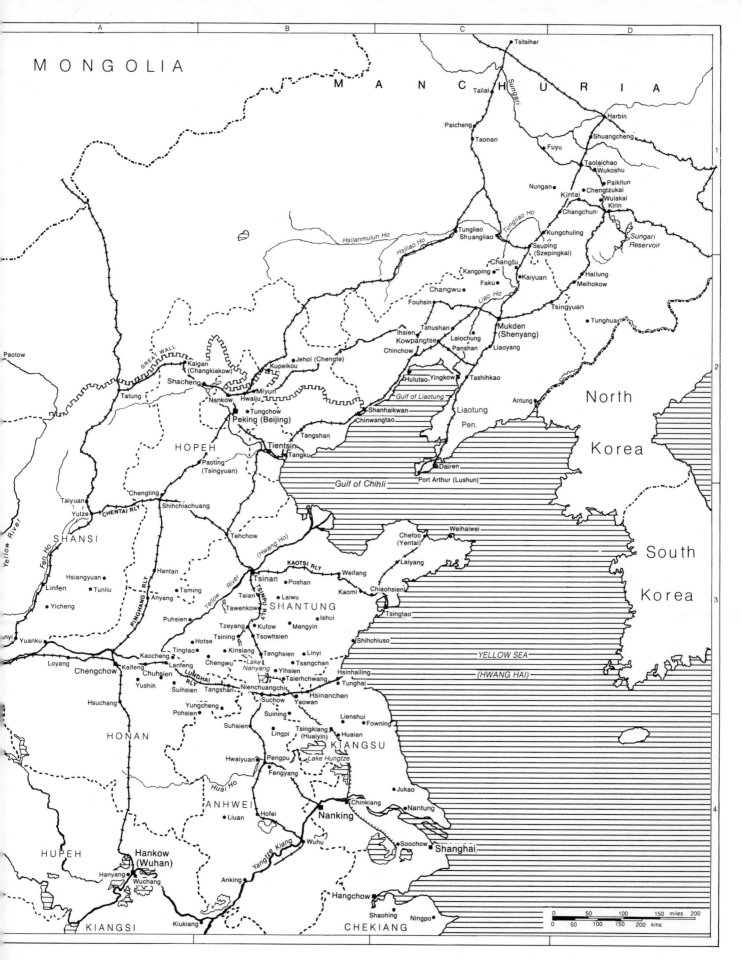

MONGOLIA

MANCHURIA

Tsitsihar

Tailai

Paicheng

Taonan

Fuyu

Harbin

Shuangcheng

Taolaichao
Wukoshu

Nungan

Paikitun

Kintai

Chengtzukai

Wulakai

Kirin

Changchun

Hsilanmulun Ho

Hsiliao Ho

Tungliao

Shuangliao

Tungliao Ho

Kungchuling

Ssuping
(Szepingkai)

Sungari
Reservoir

Changtu

Kangping

Faku

Kaiyuan

Hailung

Meihokow

Changwu

Liao Ho

Tsingyuan

Tunghua

Fouhsin

Paotow

Ihsien

Tahushan

Kowpangtse

Laiochung

Panshan

Mukden
(Shenyang)

Liaoyang

Chinchow

GREAT WALL

Kalgan
(Changkiakow)

Kupeikou

Jehol (Chengte)

Hulutao

Yingkow

Tashihkao

Shacheng

Miyun

Hwaiju

Gulf of Liaotung

Antung

North

Tatung

Nankow

Tungchow

Shanhaikwan

Liaotung
Pen.

Peking (Beijing)

Chinwangtao

Korea

HOPEH

Tientsin

Tangshan

Tangku

Paoting
(Tsingyuan)

Dairen

Port Arthur (Lushun)

Gulf of Chihli

South

Chengting

Chefoo
(Yentai)

Weihaiwei

Taiyuan

Shihchiachuang

Korea

Yutze

CHENTAI RLY

Tehchow

Laiyang

SHANSI

(Hwang Ho)

Hsiangyuan

Hantan

Tsinan

KAOTSI RLY

Weifang

Poshan

Linfen

Tunliu

Taming

Anyang

Taian

Laiwu

Kaomi

Chiaohsien

Yicheng

Puhsien

SHANTUNG

Ishui

Tsingtao

Yellow River

Tawenkow

Kufow

Mengyin

Tzeyang

Tsowhsien

YELLOW SEA

Yuanku

Tingtao

Tsining

Kinsiang

Tenghsien

Linyi

Shihchiuso

(HWANG HAI)

Loyang

Kaocheng

Chengwu

Tsangchan

Kaifeng

Lanfeng

Lake
Nanyang

Yihsien

Hsinhailing

Chengchow

Chuhsien

LUNGHAI

Taierhchwang

Tunghai

Hsuchang

Yushih

Suihsien

Tangshan

Nienchuangchi

Hsinanchen

Yungcheng

Suchow

Yaowan

Pohsien

Suining

Lienshui

Fowning

Suhsien

Lingpi

Tsingkiang
(Huaiyin)

Huaian

HONAN

Hwaiyuan

Pengpu

KIANGSU

Lake Hungtze

Fengyang

Huai Ho

Jukao

ANHWEI

Chinkiang

Nantung

Liuan

Hofei

Nanking

HUPEH

Wuhu

Soochow

Shanghai

Hankow
(Wuhan)

Yangtze Kiang

Hanyang

Wuchang

Anking

Hangchow

KIANGSI

Kiukiang

Shaohing

Ningpo

CHEKIANG

PINGHANG RLY

TSINPU RLY

0   50   100   150   miles 200

0   50   100   150   200   kms

63

1947

7 January — Marshall concedes failure of his mission, returns to US; remaining US Marines in N. China withdrawn.

MANCHURIA

January–March — Lin Piao, Communist commander in Manchuria, launches 3 unsuccessful attacks across the Sungari River.

10 May — Reds launch successful offensive, reaching Faku and Kangping by 24th, encircling Kirin (17th), taking Tunghwa (25th).

June — Reds take Antung (10th), Laioyang (20th). All L'aiotung peninsula now in Red hands: Nationalist counterattack a failure.

July — Campaign halted by rain.

September — 6th Red offensive in Manchuria temporarily cuts Peking–Mukden railway, isolating Manchuria from N. China.

October — Reds take Kungchuling (4th), Changtu and Kaiyuan (5th).

November — Nationalists retake Kungchuling (1st), relieve Kirin (13th).

SHANTUNG

February — Nationalists take Lini (15th), Yihsien (17th), Tenghsien (24th), Tsowhsien (25th), Kufow (28th).

March — Nationalists take Tawenkow (27th).

May — Nationalists routed in Red counterattack near Ishui (16th).

August — Nationalists stage amphibious landings at Shihkinso, Tsingtao and Chefoo.

November — Reds retake Laiyang, Chaiohsien and Kaomi, and push south nearly to Anwhei and Kiangsu. Shantung campaign ends in crushing defeat for Nationalists.

SHENSI – The attack on Yenan

March — Nationalists take Fuhsien (15th), Kanchuan (16th), enter Yenan (19th) to find it empty. Hollow victory proclaimed as great triumph by Chiang Kai-shek.

1948 — At the beginning of the year the comparative strengths of armed forces were: Communists: 700,000 men; Nationalists: 1,250,000 men.

MANCHURIA

5 January — 8th Red offensive launched.

February — Reds take Kowpangtze, Laioyang (4th), Yingkow (27th).

March — Reds take Kirin (9th), Ssuping (13th). Changchun and Mukden now isolated. There was a lull in the fighting during the summer.

12 September — Start of final Communist offensive: Red strength 600,000; Nationalists 300,000.

October — Reds take Chinchow (17th), Changchun (20th). Lin Piao destroys bulk of Mukden garrison as they withdraw to Tahushan. Mukden surrenders (30th).

November — Reds take Yingkow (5th). All Manchuria now in Red hands.

NORTH-WEST CHINA

March — Reds take Ichuan (3rd), Kanchuan (5th), Fuhsien (6th). Nationalists evacuate Yenan.

April — Reds suffer serious defeat in Linyu–Fengsiang–Kienyang triangle. Loyang falls to Reds (7th) after changing hands three times.

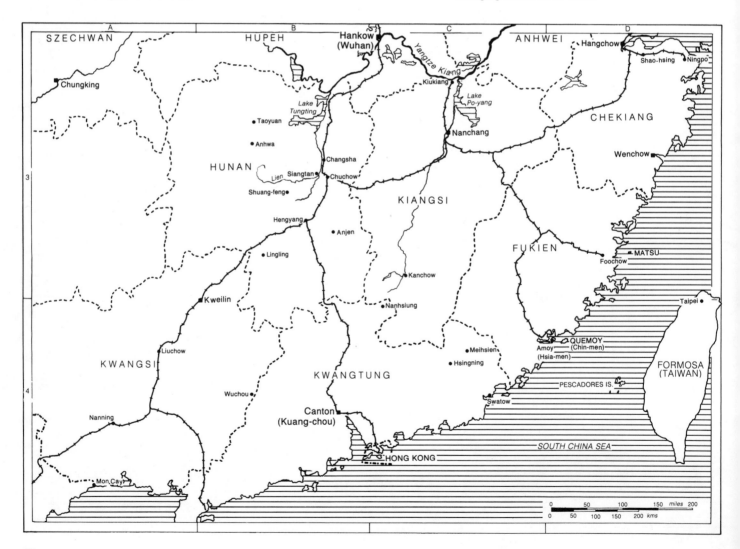

May	Reds take Linfen (17th).
	EASTERN AND CENTRAL CHINA
April	Reds take Weihaiwei (27th). All of Shantung Peninsula but Chefoo now in Red hands.
May	Reds take Taian.
30 May–8 July	Battle of Kaifeng, first positional as opposed to guerrilla-type battle of the Civil War, results in Pyrrhic victory for Nationalists. The Reds were forced to disperse but the Nationalists lost 90,000 men, while the Reds gained much in morale and prestige.
14–25 September	Reds Attack and take Tsinan.
5 November–10 January	Battle of Suchow in which about 1,200,000 men took part ends any hope of Nationalist victory. Reds take 327,000 prisoners.
	NORTH-EAST CHINA
October	Reds take Paoting (23rd).
November	Reds take Chengte (9th), Shanhaikwan (18th).
December	Reds take Kupehow (2nd), Miyun, Huiju (7th), Tangshan (13th), Tungchow (15th).

1949	
January	Reds take Tientsin (15th), Peking (23rd).
	EASTERN CHINA
April	Reds cross the Yangtze and take Nanking (23rd).
May	Reds take Hangchow (3rd), Shaoting (7th), Shanghai (27th).
June	Reds take Tsingtao (2nd).
20 April–30 July	The *Amethyst* Incident. Reds fire on British frigate, taking supplies to the British Embassy at Nanking, at Chinkiang on the Yangtze and hold her prisoner for three months. On 30 July Commander J. S. Kerans makes his famous dash downriver to rejoin the British Fleet; but Reds gain much propaganda value from the incident.
	CENTRAL, WEST AND SOUTHERN CHINA
April	Reds take Taiynan (24th).
May	Reds take Sian (20th), while Nationalists mount brief counterattack in Shensi.
August	Reds take Changsha (4th).
October	Reds take Canton (15th), Swatow and Amoy (17th).
November	Reds take over all of Kweichow and Szechwan Provinces.
December	All Nationalist resistance on the mainland ceases. Chiang Kai-shek sets up Nationalist government on island of Formosa.

Quemoy, Matsu and Taiwan

The island of Formosa was part of the Chinese Manchu Empire from 1683 until 1895 when it was annexed by Japan after the Sino-Japanese war of 1894–5, under the terms of the Treaty of Shimonoseki. It remained under Japanese control until 1945, in September of which year troops loyal to Chiang Kai-shek took over and it reverted to its traditional Chinese name of Taiwan. In 1949 it became the refuge of Chiang Kai-shek's Nationalist forces, the Government of the Republic of Taiwan claiming to be the legitimate government of China. Its representatives sat in the United Nations until 1971 when they were expelled. A mutual defence treaty between Taiwan and the United States was signed in 1954 but was terminated on 1 January, 1979, when the US formally recognized the validity of the People's Republic of China. The territories administered by the Chinese Nationalists include the Pescadores Islands and the offshore islands of Quemoy and Matsu. The Tachen and Nanchi Islands, some 200 miles north of Formosa, were also originally held by the Nationalists but were taken by the Chinese Communists on 18 January, 1955. Meanwhile the islands of Quemoy and Matsu had been heavily garrisoned by the Nationalists with the intention of using them as bases for a future invasion of China. But the Communists brought siege artillery to the nearest points on the mainland and tried to bombard the garrisons into submission. On 3 September, 1954, a heavy bombardment of Quemoy was followed by Nationalist air attacks on gun emplacements and other military targets in and around Amoy. On 23 August, 1958, the Communists began a heavy bombardment of Quemoy and, 5 days later, called on the Nationalist commander of the garrison to surrender, intimating that an invasion was imminent. The incident led to exchanges between Mr Khruschev and President Eisenhower, but both American and Chinese Communist troops were careful to avoid a direct confrontation. The bombardment, suspended on 6 October, was resumed on 20 October but, curiously, on even dates only. It continued sporadically throughout 1959. Both Quemoy and Matsu were heavily bombarded when President Eisenhower visited Taiwan on 18 June, 1960. The shelling ended in 1962, having continued, off and on, for 8 years.

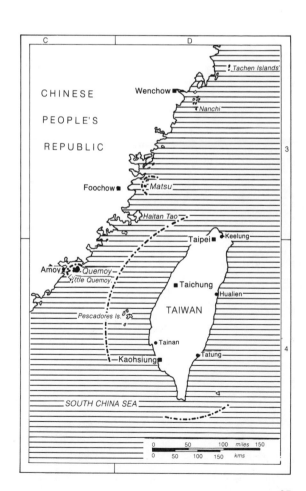

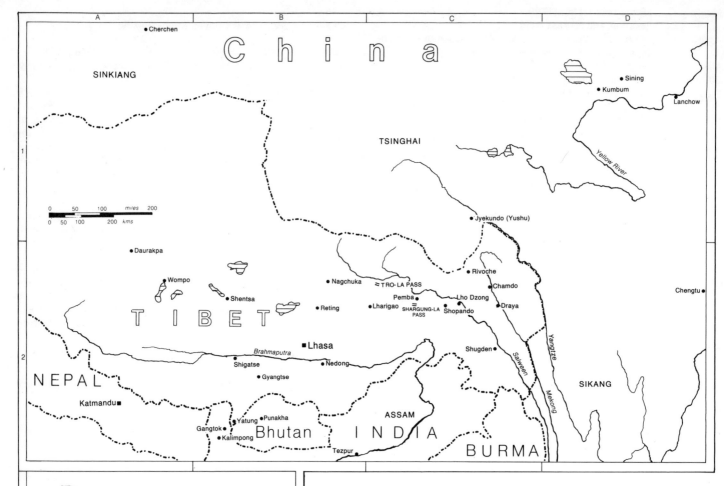

The Chinese Occupation of Tibet 1950–51

On 7 October, 1950, Chinese Communist forces invaded Eastern Tibet and occupied Chamdo. The Tibetan Army was only about 10,000 strong and equipped with a limited quantity of small arms, but the Tibetan plateau with an average elevation of 12,000 ft above sea level, offered great physical difficulties to the invaders who had to negotiate two of the highest passes in the world, Shargung-la (16,700 ft) and Tro-la (17,100 ft). The 15-year-old Dalai Lama, the archpriest of Lamaism, reverenced as the living incarnation of the saviour Avalokitesvara, left Lhasa secretly on 21 December and set up his government at Yatung, near the border with Bhutan. On 17 August, 1951, he was brought back to Lhasa where he remained the puppet of the Chinese. However, it was not until September, 1951, that Chinese Communist troops entered Lhasa, the main occupation force arriving on October 26. Tibetan independence was over. Resentment at the strain on the country's resources imposed by the Chinese presence led, in March, 1956, to a serious rising among the Golok tribesmen of Kham province in Eastern Tibet, who reputedly massacred an entire Chinese garrison of 8–900 men, whereafter Golok villages were bombed in retaliation with heavy civilian casualties. Sporadic revolts occurred during the next three years, culminating in a large-scale rebellion in March, 1959, which led to the flight of the Dalai Lama. The revolt started in Lhasa on 17 March and lasted for several days. By the time it had been quelled by Chinese troops, at least 2,000 Tibetans had been killed, two large monasteries totally destroyed and thousands of monks put in concentration camps or condemned to forced labour. The Dalai Lama fled from Lhasa on 17 March with a retinue of 80 and reached the Indian frontier on 30 March. Tibet is now, in all but name, a province of China and the Dalai Lama remains in exile.

Sino-Soviet Border Disputes

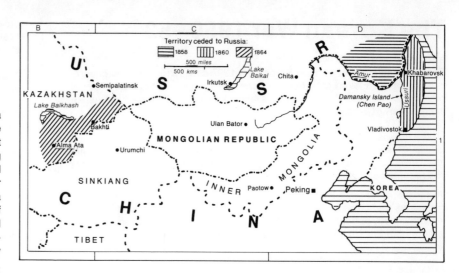

The origins of the border disputes between China and Russia that started in 1969 long antedate the advent of Communism. Under the Tsars about 700,000 square miles of Chinese Territory, including the Amur River Basin, the Maritime Territory and Soviet Central Asia, were annexed by Russia under three 'unequal' treaties in 1858, 1860 and 1864. As a result China and Russia shared a common border of more than 4000 miles from Manchuria to Central Asia. Deteriorating relations between the two countries, arising from ideological differences and rivalry for world communist leadership, led on 2 March, 1969, to fighting at Damansky Island (Chinese – Chen Pao Island), an uninhabited islet on the Ussuri River which forms most of the Manchurian border between Russia and China. In May incidents occurred in the Bakhti area south of Semipalatinsk on the border between Kazakhstan and Sinkiang. A Chinese note of protest on 19 August charged Russia with 429 frontier violations during June and July. On 10 September the Russians hit back, charging the Chinese with 488 frontier violations between June and mid-August. The death of Ho Chi Minh on 3 September brought both Chou En-lai and Aleksei Kosygin to Hanoi and, although they avoided each other there, Kosygin made an unexpected stop at Peking on the way home and held a long conference with Chou at the airport. On 7 October it was announced that the two countries had decided to start negotiations, which opened in Peking on 20 October, but soon reached stalemate. Talks have been resumed intermittently since then but no agreement has been reached, though a limited agreement on navigation on the Amur and Ussuri Rivers was signed in October, 1977. A number of border incidents were reported during 1977–80, but nothing on the scale of the 1969 clashes. On 25 September, 1981, the Soviet Government proposed that border negotiations be resumed in Moscow, but as China reacted with conditional demands, including (1) Russian withdrawal from Afghanistan; (2) withdrawal of Vietnamese troops from Kampuchea; (3) thinning out of Russian forces along the Sino-Soviet border, it seems unlikely that much headway will be made.

The Korean War 1950–53

BACKGROUND

The native dynasty of Yi ruled Korea from 1392 until 1910 when the country was formally annexed to Japan and renamed Chosen. In 1919 an Imperial rescript announced that Korea was henceforward to be regarded as an integral part of Japan.

At the Potsdam Conference in July 1945 it was agreed that, after the defeat of Japan, Russia would disarm the Japanese troops north of the 38th parallel, the United States those south of it, pending the envisaged unification and independence of Korea.

In the North (capital: Pyongyang) were 9 million Koreans and nearly all the industrial resources. The South (capital; Seoul) had a population of 21 million, mostly engaged in agriculture. The Russians refused to recognize the authority of the UN Commission set up in November 1947 to supervise the election of a national assembly.

In August 1948 Syngman Rhee became President of the Republic of Korea (ROK) following elections under UN supervision. In July 1949 the US withdrew their forces.

In September 1948 Kim Il Sung became Premier of the Democratic People's Republic of Korea (DPRK) following Communist-style elections. In December the Russians withdrew their forces.

In June 1950 the North Korean People's Army (NKPA) numbered about 135,000 men; the ROK army numbered 95,000. The NKPA was vastly better equipped.

INVASION

1950

25 June	(Sunday) At 0400 hrs the NKPA cross the 38th parallel.
25 June	At 0930 hrs **Kaesong** taken by NKPA.
27 June	Han River bridge south of Seoul blown prematurely.
28 June	NKPA take **Seoul**: over 40,000 ROK soldiers already missing, captured or dead.
3 July	NKPA take **Inchon**.

THE PUSAN PERIMETER

1 July	First US forces land at **Pusan**.
5 July	NKPA break through US forces at **Konji**.
8 July	General MacArthur appointed C-in-C, UN Command.
9 July	US troops retire to **Kum River**.
14 July	NKPA cross Kum River. All ROK troops placed under General MacArthur's command.
20 July	NKPA take **Taejon**.
24 July	NKPA take **Suchon**.
1 Aug	US and ROK forces consolidate behind **Pusan Perimeter**.

In August UN troops begin to arrive in Korea. By the end of August UN strength (including ROK troops) is about 180,000. NKPA strength about 92,000.

General MacArthur, against all advice, determines to launch the UN counter-attack with an amphibious landing at Inchon, the port of Seoul.

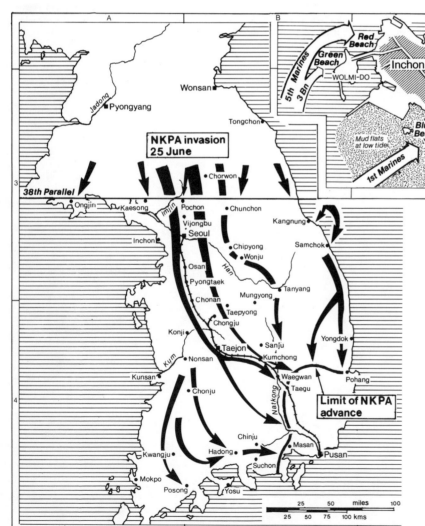

THE INCHON LANDING

15 Sept	0630 hrs 3rd Bn, 5th Marines, land on **Wolmi-do Island**. 1732 hrs 1st Marines land on 'Blue Beach'. 1733 hrs 5th Marines land on 'Red Beach'.
16 Sept	**Inchon** taken.
17 Sept	**Kimpo Airfield** taken. 7th Infantry Div lands at Inchon.
28 Sept	**Seoul** taken.

THE ADVANCE TO THE YALU RIVER

19 Sept	UN troops break out from Pusan Perimeter and cross **Natkong** River.
26 Sept	US 1st Cav Div and 7th Inf Div meet near **Osan**.
1 Oct	ROK troops cross the 38th parallel.
7 Oct	US troops cross the 38th parallel.
10 Oct	ROK troops reach **Wonsan**.
19 Oct	UN troops take **Pyongyang**; 135,000 PoWs taken.
21 Oct	North Korean government moves to Sinuiju.
26 Oct	ROK 6th Div reaches Yalu River at **Chosan**.

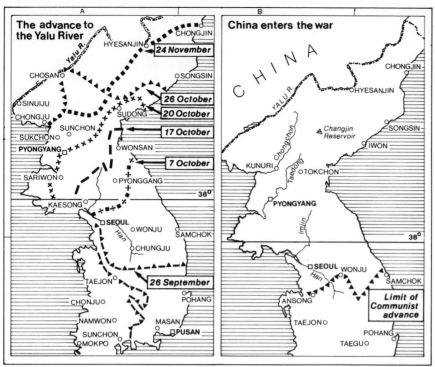

The advance to the Yalu River

CHONGJIN · HYESANJIN
24 November
CHOSAN · SONGSIN
SINUIJU · CHONGJU · SUDONG
26 October
20 October
17 October
SUNCHON · WONSAN
7 October
SUKCHON
PYONGYANG
SARIWON
KAESONG
26 September
SEOUL · WONJU · SAMCHOK
CHUNGJU
TAEJON · POHANG
CHONJU
NAMWON · MASAN
SUNCHON · PUSAN
MOKPO

China enters the war

C H I N A
CHONGJIN
YALU R. · HYESANJIN
Chongchon · SONGSIN
Changjin Reservoir · IWON
KUNURI · TOKCHON
Taedong
PYONGYANG
Imjin
38°
SEOUL · WONJU · SAMCHOK
Han · ANSONG
TAEJON
POHANG
TAEGU
Limit of Communist advance

United Nations counterattack Spring 1951

Iron Triangle
PYONGGANG · KUMHWA · KANSONG
CHORWON
38° · TAEPORI
21 April
31 March
CHUNCHON
MUNSAN
28 February
SEOUL · YANGPANG
25 January
SUWON · WONJU
CHECHON
PYONGTAEK

Chinese counterattack

PYONGGANG
CHORWON · KUMHWA · KANSONG
Line Wyoming · No Name Line
TAEPORI
INJE · Line Kansas
NAEPYONG · 38°
MUNSAN · SABANGUO · OHANGYE
KIMPO · SEOUL · PUNWON
WONJU

CHINA ENTERS THE WAR

During October about 200,000 men of the Chinese People's Volunteer Army (CPVA) secretly enter Korea.

26 Oct — CPVA attacks ROK troops on the **Yalu River**.
2 Nov — CPVA engages UN units
26–7 Nov — CPVA mounts strong offensive round **Tokchon**.
4 Dec — UN troops in retreat; CPVA retake **Pyongyang**.
1951
4 Jan — CPVA retake **Seoul**.
15 Jan — CPVA offensive halted.

UNITED NATIONS COUNTERATTACK, SPRING 1951

7 Feb — CPVA withdraws north of **Han River**.
14 Mar — UN troops retake **Seoul**.
11 Apr — President Truman sacks General MacArthur; General Ridgway replaces him. CPVA withdraw to a prepared defensive line north of the 38th parallel, the main feature of which is the 'Iron Triangle'.

CHINESE COUNTER-ATTACK

22 Apr — CPVA launch counter offensive.
30 Apr — UN forces retire to **No Name Line**.
3 May — CPVA offensive halted.
16–21 May — Second CPVA counter offensive.
21 May–1 Jun — UN counter offensive establishes **Line Kansas**.
13 June — UN forces take **Chorwon** and **Kumhwa**: **Line Wyoming** established.
10 July — Truce talks begin.

Forces deployed at the end of 1951: Communist 1,200,000
United Nations 768,000

After June 1951 the front line stabilized north of the 38th parallel. 'It was trench warfare of 1914–18 all over again.'
Air warfare played an increasingly large part in this phase of the campaign but the US Air Force maintained overall superiority throughout.
After more than two years of negotiations the Ceasefire Agreement was signed on 27 July 1953.

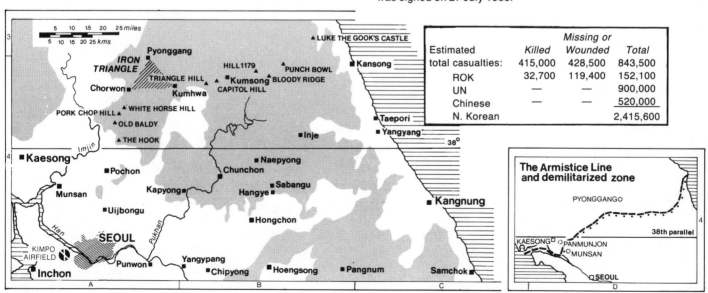

5 10 15 20 25 miles
5 10 15 20 25 kms

LUKE THE GOOK'S CASTLE
Pyonggang
IRON TRIANGLE
HILL 1179 · PUNCH BOWL · Kansong
TRIANGLE HILL · Kumsong · BLOODY RIDGE
Chorwon · Kumhwa · CAPITOL HILL
PORK CHOP HILL · WHITE HORSE HILL
Taepori
OLD BALDY
Yangyang
THE HOOK · Inje
38°
Kaesong · Imjin
Naepyong
Pochon · Chunchon
Munsan · Kapyong · Sabangu
Hangye
Uijongbu · Hongchon · Kangnung
SEOUL · Pukhan
KIMPO AIRFIELD
Punwon · Yangypang
Inchon · Chipyong · Hoengson · Pangnum · Samchok

Estimated total casualties:	Killed	Missing or Wounded	Total
	415,000	428,500	843,500
ROK	32,700	119,400	152,100
UN	—	—	900,000
Chinese	—	—	520,000
N. Korean			2,415,600

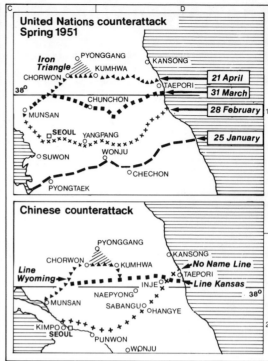

The Armistice Line and demilitarized zone

PYONGGANG
38th parallel
KAESONG · PANMUNJON · MUNSAN
SEOUL

PART VII

South-East Asia

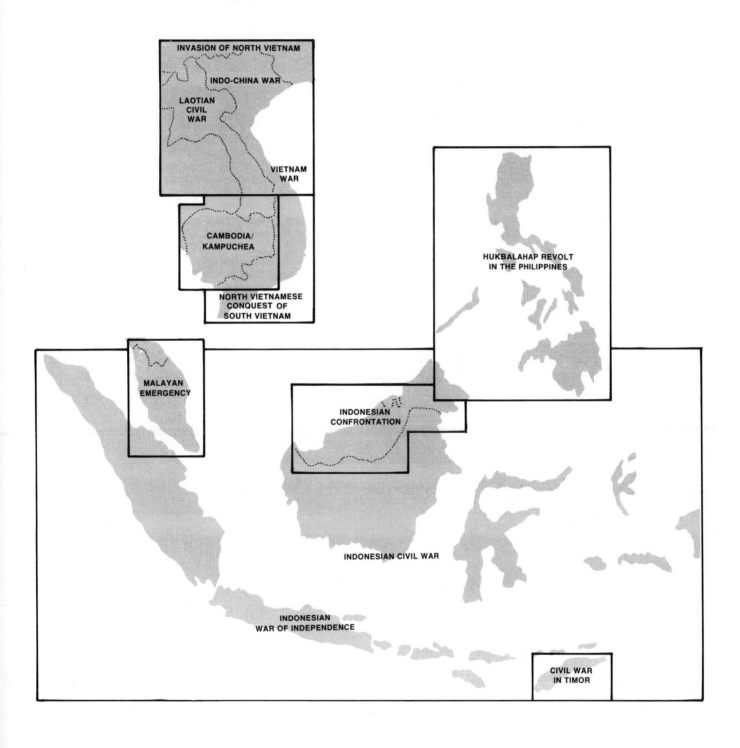

INVASION OF NORTH VIETNAM

INDO-CHINA WAR

LAOTIAN CIVIL WAR

VIETNAM WAR

CAMBODIA/ KAMPUCHEA

NORTH VIETNAMESE CONQUEST OF SOUTH VIETNAM

HUKBALAHAP REVOLT IN THE PHILIPPINES

MALAYAN EMERGENCY

INDONESIAN CONFRONTATION

INDONESIAN CIVIL WAR

INDONESIAN WAR OF INDEPENDENCE

CIVIL WAR IN TIMOR

The Malayan Emergency 1948–60

During their occupation of Malaya in the Second World War the Japanese showed leniency to the Malays but treated the Chinese brutally; many of the latter fled into the jungle to join the Communist-inspired Malayan People's Anti-Japanese Army (MPAJA) which then enjoyed active British support.

In June, 1948, the Malayan Communist Party (MCP), having failed by political means to wreck the Federation Agreement, on which was based the Constitution agreed upon between the British Government and Malay, Chinese and Indian leaders, mobilized the MPAJA Old Comrades' Association

and returned to the jungle and to terrorism, calling themselves the Malayan Races Liberation Army (MRLA).

On 16 June, 1948, a State of Emergency was declared after the murder of three European managers on a rubber estate near Sungei Siput.

In 1948 there were 11 infantry battalions in Malaya, 6 Gurkha, 3 British and 2 Malay.

In April, 1950, at a time when terrorist incidents were running at 400 a month, Lt-Gen. Sir Harold Briggs was appointed Director of Operations. He instituted the 'Briggs Plan', whereby almost all the Chinese rural population was resettled in strongly protected 'new villages'. Gradually contact between the terrorists and the people, without which the terrorists could not survive, was severed.

In February, 1952, General Sir Gerald Templer was appointed High Commissioner and Director of Operations. He brought the Briggs Plan to fruition and under his dynamic leadership the tide was turned. The terrorists thereafter were on the run.

In 1954 there were 22 infantry battalions in Malaya, a total of 45,000 troops.

By 1957 the Emergency was virtually over and on 31 August of that year Malaysia became an independent country within the Commonwealth. The State of Emergency was formally declared to be over on 31 July, 1960.

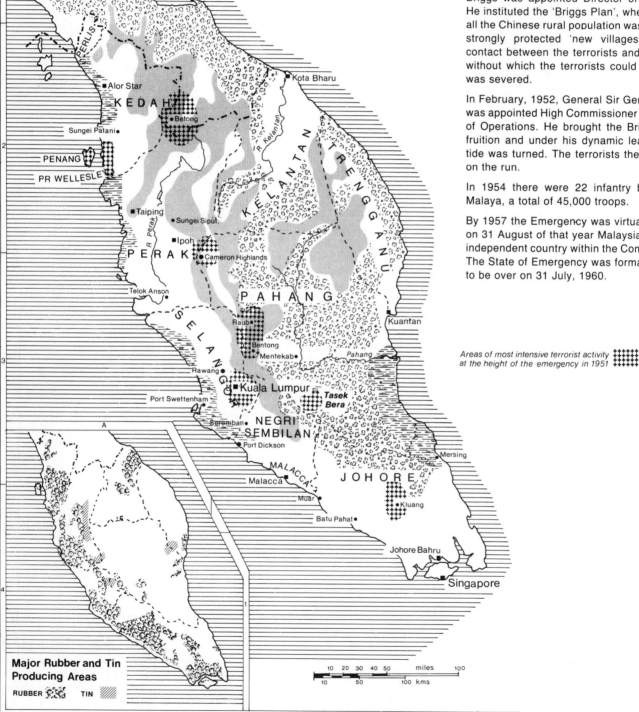

Areas of most intensive terrorist activity at the height of the emergency in 1951

Major Rubber and Tin Producing Areas

RUBBER TIN

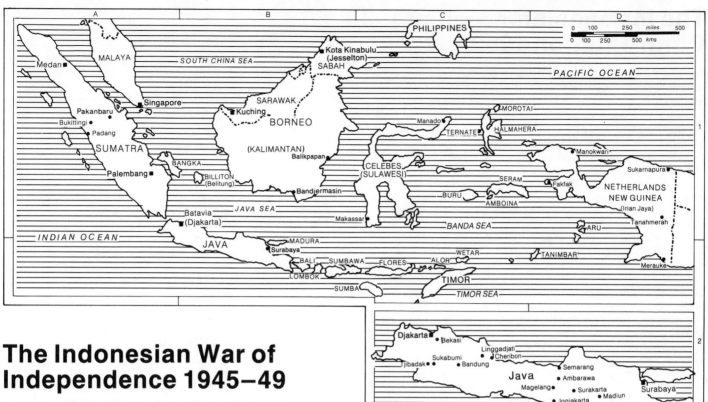

The Indonesian War of Independence 1945–49

Most of the Indonesian Archipelago was ruled by the Netherlands East India Company from 1602 until its dissolution in 1798, whereafter the Netherlands Government ruled the colony until 1941 when it was occupied by the Japanese. When the latter surrendered on 17 August, 1945, Dr Sukarno, who, during the occupation, had headed a puppet régime under the Japanese, unilaterally declared the independence of the colony. British and Indian troops, charged with the task of releasing prisoners, disarming the Japanese and restoring Dutch control, arrived in Batavia on 29 September. The first Dutch troops returned on 3 October, whereupon the more extreme nationalists took up arms and on 13 October the 'Indonesian People's Army' declared war on the Dutch, and implicitly with the British, whom they accused of helping the Dutch. Severe fighting continued for three weeks round Surabaya after armed Indonesians attacked British troops on 28 October and murdered Brigadier Mallaby who had gone to parley with them. Hostilities continued throughout 1946 with daily attacks on convoys and guard posts. During the autumn British troops were gradually withdrawn, the last leaving on 30 November, while Dutch strength was increased to 130,000 men. It was announced on 4 September that from October, 1945, to August, 1946, British casualties had totalled 49 killed and 134 wounded, Indians 507 killed and 1,259 wounded. By the Cheribon Agreement of November, 1946, both sides recognized the Government of the Republic of Indonesia as having authority over Java, Sumatra and Madura, and agreed that the areas occupied by Dutch and Allied troops would eventually be included. But, for differing reasons, opposition to the Agreement grew in strength both in Holland and in the Republic where ceasefire orders were repeatedly violated. On 20 July, 1947, the Dutch Governor-General, Dr van Mook, ordered a resumption of military action and, in what was termed a "police action" against the Republic, Dutch troops reoccupied much of central and eastern Java. The problem was referred to the US Security Council who set up a Committee of Good Offices which, on 17 January, 1948, produced a precarious settlement called the Renville Agreement, which collapsed on 18 December when the Dutch undertook a second "police action" and rapidly occupied the Republic. Dutch aims having been achieved, hostilities ceased in Java on 1 January, 1949, and in Sumatra on 6 January. But this second "police action" aroused worldwide condemnation

and closed Indonesian ranks behind the Republic. At a Round Table Conference at The Hague in August, 1949, the Netherlands finally agreed to transfer sovreignty to an independent United States of Indonesia and on 27 December the reins of government were handed over to Dr Sukarno. Dutch casualties after 4 years of fighting were estimated at 25,000, Indonesian at 80,000.

THE INDONESIAN CIVIL WAR 1950–61

Unity, however, could not easily be imposed upon so scattered and disparate a community and the chain of authority failed to hold the parts together. In N. Sumatra the central government was ignored, while in west and central Java Dar 'ul Islam, a fanatical Muslim sect, terrorized the rural population and defied the government. By 1954 the Muslim insurgent movement had assumed alarming proportions in parts of Sumatra, western Java, central and southern Celebes and Borneo. It was felt that the economic interests of the other islands were sacrificed to those of Java. In March, 1957, 5 military commanders took control of their respective areas, provincial separatist feeling being strengthened by mistrust of Sukarno's leftist policies. On 15 February, 1958, the dissidents proclaimed the Revolutionary Government of the Indonesian Republic at Padang. Government troops under General Nasution rapidly moved against the rebels and took their HQ at Bukittingi on 5 March after the rebel broadcasting station had been bombed and destroyed. On 12 March Pakanbaru was taken, and the rebel capital at Manado in Celebes fell on 26 June. But scattered bands of rebels remained and at the end of 1959 it was reckoned that in certain areas of Sumatra, Java, Celebes and Halmahera there were about 28 rebel battalions at large, 15 belonging to Dar 'ul Islam and 13 to the rebel colonels. By mid-1961, however, it was reckoned that the rebel forces had fallen to 17,000 men, less than half of whom were armed. The rebel leaders were offered a free pardon by Sukarno and between April and August most of them abandoned the struggle.

The Indonesian Confrontation 1962–66

The long-term plan of President Sukarno, who became President of the newly-proclaimed Republic of Indonesia on 15 August, 1950, was to create an Indonesian Empire embracing Malaya, the Philippines and Indonesia (Maphilindo). The British proposal in 1962, earlier voiced by Tunku Abdul Rahman, Prime Minister of Malaya, to unite the then colonies of Sarawak, Sabah and Brunei, which lie along the N.W. coast of the island of Borneo, with the Federation of Malaya to form Malaysia, was an obvious threat to this plan and Sukarno acted swiftly to prevent it coming about. Since it was not in the interest of either side formally to declare war, the four years of jungle fighting which ensued are known by the convenient euphemism of "The Indonesian Confrontation".

The revolt started on 8 December, 1962, when the so-called North Kalimantan Liberation Army (TNKU), led by A. M. Azhari, who was opposed to Brunei joining the Malaysian Federation, seized various strategic points in Brunei. It was quelled after 10 days' fighting by British and Gurkha troops rushed from Singapore. A strong naval force, including two commando carriers, a cruiser and a destroyer, was also sent to British Borneo waters. The following towns were taken by the rebels and recaptured by British troops on the dates shown in brackets: Weston, Miri, Tutong (10th); Seria (11th); Limbang, Kuala Belait, Lawas (12th). The end of the revolt was formally announced by the British Commissioner-General for S.E. Asia on 17 December and British casualties were given as 7 killed and 28 wounded; rebel casualties were estimated at 60–70 killed, 600–700 captured. The *Annual Register* jovially remarked, "For a brisk little war without many casualties or international consequences, Borneo was undoubtedly the place". Both reactions were decidedly premature. The trouble was not over; it merely changed in character. On 19 December Major-General Walter Walker arrived to take command.

1963–6
Campaign settles into raid, patrol and ambush routine. British and Commonwealth troops, making full use of helicopters and river patrol boats, eventually mount ambushes as far as 20,000 yards inside Indonesian territory.

1963
16 September State of Malaysia proclaimed.

1964
17 August   Indonesians launch small unsuccessful raid on mainland of Malaya.

1966
12 March   General Suharto replaces Sukarno.
11 August: Peace agreements signed.

Though a cheap war in human terms (114 British troops, many of them Gurkhas, killed; *c.*600 Indonesians killed) its effect on the future stability of Britain's former colonies in S.E. Asia should not be underrated; nor, indeed, should the decisive part played by General Walter Walker.

THE MASSACRE OF THE INDONESIAN COMMUNISTS 1965/6

On 30 September, 1965, 6 senior army officers were kidnapped and later murdered by a group calling itself the 30 September Movement, which had the support of the Indonesian Communist Party (PKI). The coup failed but led to violent popular demonstrations against suspected communists, especially Chinese, and in the epidemic of slaughter which followed the death toll was thought by western observers to have been in excess of 300,000, some say nearer 500,000. The power of President Sukarno was broken and in March, 1966, General Soharto took over effective control. He became President in March, 1968, and remains in office.

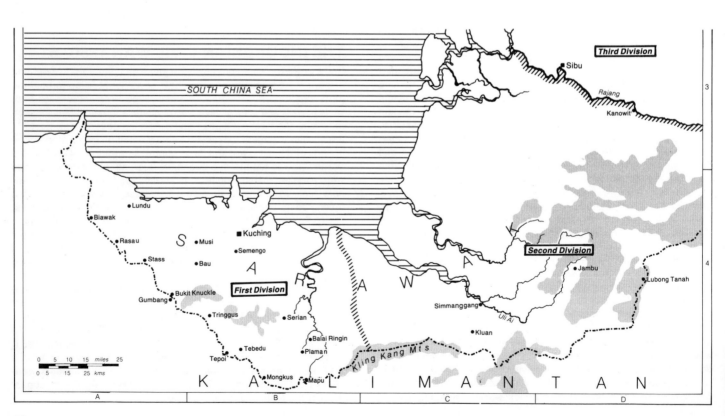

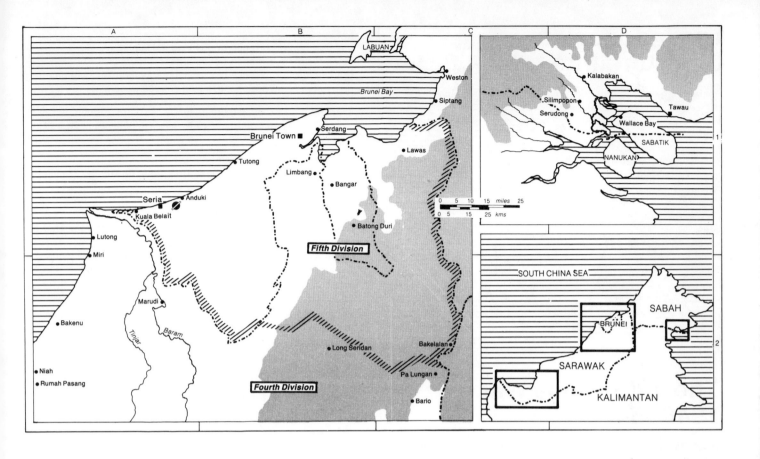

Civil War in Timor 1975

The Portuguese began trading with the islanders of Timor as early as 1520. In 1613 the Dutch established themselves at Kupang and the Portuguese moved to the north and east. Treaties of 1860 and 1914 divided the island between Portugal and The Netherlands and set the boundaries. Dutch Timor became part of Indonesia in 1950 and when Portugal granted independence to her African colonies in 1975 it was clear that there was no chance of her holding on to E. Timor. On 11 August, 1975, the Timor Democratic Union (UDT) attacked the police headquarters in Dili, kidnapped the Chief of Police and demanded immediate independence and the imprisonment of all members of the Revolutionary Front for Independence (FREITLIN), its communist-orientated rival. On 20 August full-scale civil war broke out between, on the one hand, FREITLIN and, on the other, UDT and the Timorese Democratic People's Union (APODETI), which favoured the integration of Timor into Indonesia.

22 August   FREITLIN launch mortar bombardment on Dili.
1 September   FREITLIN claims complete control of E. Timor.
16 September 32,000 refugees estimated to have fled to W. Timor.
25 September FREITLIN launches mortar attack across frontier into W. Timor.
26 September Indonesia warns that retaliation can be expected.
5 October   Refugees now put at 40–50,000.
28 November FREITLIN proclaims Independent Democratic Republic of E. Timor. Francesco Xavier Amaral, a former Jesuit priest, is named President.

7 December   1000 Indonesian paratroopers enter E. Timor, seize Dili and drive FREITLIN troops into the hills. Indonesians take Maubara.
11 December Indonesians take Baucau.
17 December UDT and APODETI form provisional government.
28 December Indonesians take the enclave of Ocussi Ambeno and Ataúro Island, whence the Portuguese Governor had decamped.

In July, 1976, Portuguese Timor was officially integrated into Indonesia.

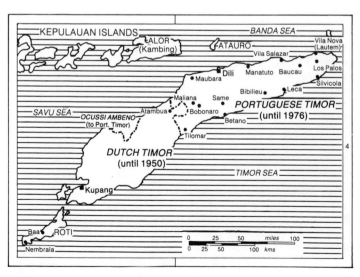

The Indo-China War 1946–54

Before the Second World War Indo-China was geographically divided into the five regions of Tonking, Annam, Laos, Cambodia and Cochin-China, all of which, between 1863 and 1892, had become French Protectorates and were known collectively as French Indo-China. Resistance to French rule, both Nationalist- and Communist-inspired, had begun to crystallize in the 1930s and was well established by the outbreak of the Second World War. When France fell in 1940 the French in Indo-China, deprived of external aid, could offer little resistance to the Japanese, who occupied the country in 1941, in which year the Communist Nguyen Ai Quoc, later famous as Ho Chi Minh (the Enlightened One), set up the League for the Independence of Vietnam (*Vietnam Doc Lap Dong Minh Ho*), later famous as the Viet Minh. During the War the Viet Minh cooperated with the Allies, but the defeat of Japan in August, 1945, found the French unprepared to reestablish their rule over Indo-China, and on 2 September Ho Chi Minh proclaimed the Democratic Republic of Vietnam at Hanoi. In the north the Nationalist Chinese disarmed the Japanese and sold or bartered their equipment to the Viet Minh. South of the parallel British and Indian troops under command of General Gracey flew into Saigon on 12 September. The city was in a state of chaos and Gracey had to use the Japanese troops he was supposed to be disarming to help him restore order. French troops began to return in October, 1945, and soon regained control of the towns, but not of the countryside, as far north as the 16th parallel, beyond which Ho Chi Minh's régime, commanded in the field by Vo Nguyen Giap, was well established under the protection of the Nationalist Chinese. This, briefly, was the background to a war which was to last until 1954.

MAIN EVENTS OF THE INDO-CHINA WAR

1945
October	General Leclerc arrives in Saigon with a division of colonial infantry.
November	Admiral d'Argenlieu arrives in Saigon as High Commissioner of Indo-China.

1946
6 March	French troops land at Haiphong.
16 March	French troops enter Hanoi.
November	French cruiser bombards Indo-Chinese quarter of Haiphong, killing c. 6000 people.

1947–49
	Stalemate: guerrilla warfare; French casualties average 2500 a year, Vietnamese 7500 a year.

1950
February	Viet Minh take Lao Kai.
25 May	Viet Minh take Dong Khe; retaken by French para battalion.
18 September	Viet Minh retake Dong Khe.
3 October	French evacuate Cao Bang.
October	French lose 6000 men in retreat from That Khe and Lang Son.
December	De Lattre de Tassigny takes over as French C-in-C and High Commissioner. Orders construction of 'de Lattre line' to protect the Red River delta.

1951
13–17 January	French repulse attack on Vinh Yen; 6000 Viet Minh killed, 8000 wounded.
23–28 March	French repulse attack on Mao Khe; 3000 Viet Minh killed.
29 May–18 June	French repulse attacks on Phat Diem, Ninh Binh and Phu Ly; 11,000 Viet Minh killed.
3 October	French repulse attack on Nglia Lo.
14 November	French take Hoa Binh.

1952
January	De Lattre dies and is succeeded by General Salan.
22 February	Salan orders withdrawal from Hoa Binh.
17 October	Viet Minh take Nglia Lo.
29 October– 24 November	*Operation Lorraine*: French push towards Phu Yen and Tuyen Quang fails: 1200 casualties.
December	French repulse attack on Na San.

1953
April	Viet Minh invade Laos; French evacuate Sam Neua but establish defensive positions at Luang Prabang, Moung Khoua and on the Plain of Jars. Viet Minh then withdraw.
May	General Navarre replaces General Salan.
December	French set up fortified positions at Dien Bien Phu.

1954
7 May	French capitulate at Dien Bien Phu at cost to Viet Minh of 8,000 killed, to French of 7,184 killed, wounded or missing and 11,000 taken prisoner.
21 July	Geneva Conference ratifies French withdrawal from Indo-China. Ho Chi Minh takes control to north of the 17th parallel, Ngo Dinh Diem to the south.

DIEN BIEN PHU
31 January	French positions come under fire.
10 March	Airstrip hit by artillery fire.
15 March	*Gabrielle* evacuated.
17–18 March	*Anne-Marie* taken by Viet Minh.
1 April	Viet Minh attack *Huguette*.
3 April	Viet Minh attack *Eliane* and *Isabelle*.
4 April	Viet Minh withdraw.
1 May	Viet Minh resume attack.
7 May	French surrender. 11,000 men taken prisoner.

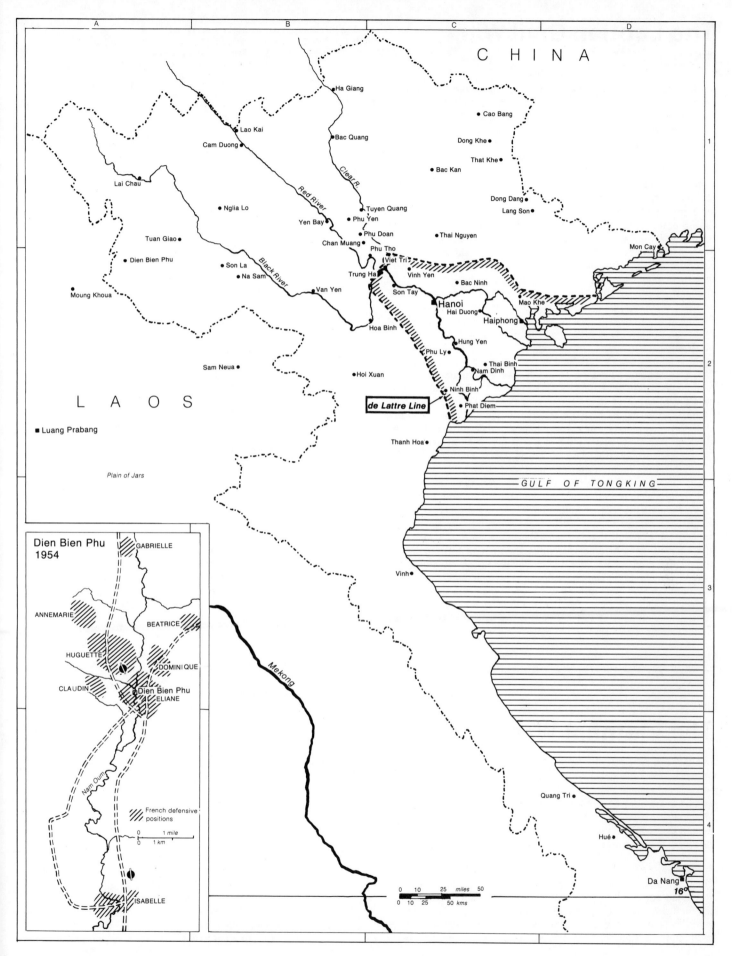

CHINA

● Ha Giang

● Cao Bang

● Lao Kai
Cam Duong ●
● Bac Quang
Dong Khe ●
That Khe ●

Lai Chau

● Bac Kan

● Nglia Lo

Dong Dang ●
Lang Son ●

Tuan Giao ●

Yen Bay ●
● Tuyen Quang
● Phu Yen
● Phu Doan
Chan Muang ●
● Thai Nguyen

Mon Cay ●

● Dien Bien Phu

● Son La
● Na Sam

Phu Tho ●
Viet Tri ■

Moung Khoua ●

Van Yen ●
Trung Ha ■

● Vinh Yen
● Bac Ninh

Son Tay ●

Hanoi ■
Hai Duong ●
Mao Khe ●

Hoa Binh ●

Haiphong ■

● Hung Yen

Sam Neua ●

Phu Ly ●

● Thai Binh
Nam Dinh ●

● Hoi Xuan

de Lattre Line

● Ninh Binh

● Phat Diem

● Luang Prabang

Thanh Hoa ●

L A O S

Red River
Clear R.
Black River

Plain of Jars

GULF OF TONGKING

Vinh ●

Mekong

Dien Bien Phu 1954

GABRIELLE

ANNEMARIE

BEATRICE

HUGUETTE

DOMINIQUE

CLAUDIN

Dien Bien Phu ■
ELIANE

Nam Oum

Quang Tri ●

Hué ●

French defensive positions

0   1 *mile*
0   1 km

ISABELLE

Da Nang ■
16°

0   10   25 *miles* 50
0   10   25   50 kms

The Laotian Civil War 1953–73

Laos, never previously united under a single government, became a French protectorate in 1893 and acquired its present boundaries in 1907. In March, 1945, the Japanese ousted the French from Indo-China and declared Laos independent. When the Japs withdrew, after their surrender, an independence movement known as Lao Issara set up a government which collapsed when the French returned in 1946, and the leaders fled to Thailand. In 1949 Laos became an independent sovereign state within the French Union and most of the Lao Issara leaders came home. A few remained in exile and, under Prince Souphanouvong, formed the Pathet Lao (Lao State) movement in alliance with the Vietminh. In April, 1953, the Vietminh, aided by the Pathet Lao, invaded Laos and, though soon dispersed by French troops, raised the curtain on a civil war which lasted almost continually for the next 20 years. 'There were three main contending parties striving for power: royalist-neutralists, under Prince Souvanna Phouma; communists led by his half-brother, ex-Prince Souphanouvong, and generally known as the Pathet Lao movement, and a succession of army officers, pro-American but with little else in common apart from an inability to seize and retain power convincingly' (*Dictionary of 20th Century History*). Conferences were held in Geneva in 1954 and 1961–2 to find a settlement based on neutrality and independence but the resulting coalition governments were short-lived. Beginning in 1965 the US Air Force carried out bombing raids against areas held by the Pathet Lao. North Vietnamese activity in Laos increased steadily after 1967. In January, 1968, they captured the Government enclave at Nam Bac and, soon after, the military post at Na Khang. Government troops retaliated by taking Xieng Khouang from the communists but in June the NVA took Muong Soui. In September, 1969, Government forces stormed across the Plain of Jars and recovered a wide area that had not been under Government control for 5 years, but the NVA recaptured most of it in February, 1970, and in October retook Muong Soui. In February, 1971, South Viet-namese forces made a large-scale raid across the Ho Chi Minh Trail and caused considerable disruption before withdrawing in late March after very heavy fighting. In December the NVA made an assault on the Bolovens Plateau. Fighting continued throughout 1972 but the NVA was now primarily concerned with operations in Vietnam. Peace talks between the Government and the Pathet Lao started in Vientiane in October and a cease-fire agreement was signed on 21 February, 1973, by which time communist forces

The Ho Chi Minh Trail, which was not a single trail but a network of tracks, initially for men and bicycles but later improved to take trucks and even tanks, was the artery down which supplies and reinforcements were funnelled from Russia and China, through North Viet-nam and Laos, to the Viet Cong fighting in South Vietnam. Between 1967 and 1970, when Prince Sihanouk fell, a second line of communication was the Sihanouk trail by which supplies sent from Russia by ship to Sihanoukville were funnelled through Cambodia.

controlled most of the strategic areas of the country. After the fall of Saigon in 1975 the Pathet Lao assumed complete control and imposed an austere and authoritarian régime on the country. Souphanouvong was made President in December, 1975, which office he still holds.

The Vietnam War 1961–75

The Geneva Agreements, signed on 21 July, 1954, provided for a Demilitarized Zone between North and South Vietnam at the 17th parallel, but stipulated that in July, 1956, a combined election should be held to determine 'the national will of the Vietnamese people'. But on 16 July, 1956, Ngo Dinh Diem, since 26 October, 1955, the Roman Catholic President of S. Vietnam cancelled the reunification elections, claiming that the election in communist N. Vietnam, run by Ho Chi Minh, would not be free. Already, in October, 1954, President Eisenhower had publicly committed the US to supplying direct aid to Diem 'for maintaining a strong, viable state capable of resisting attempted subversion or aggression through military means.' The communist forces in the war with France were called the Viet Minh. In the Vietnam War the Viet Minh of southern origin remaining in the south after the Geneva Agreements are normally referred to as the

Viet Cong (literally Vietnamese Communists). It was to fight the guerrilla forces of the Viet Cong that Diem needed US aid, a process which led from a handful of military advisers in 1954 to an army of 539,400 U.S. troops at the height of the war in 1969.

US TROOPS IN SOUTH VIETNAM 1961–1972*											
61	62	63	64	65	66	67	68	69	70	71	72
950	9000	15,000	16,000	60,000	268,000	449,000	535,000	539,000	415,000	239,000	47,000

*From *War in Peace*, edited by Sir Robert Thompson.

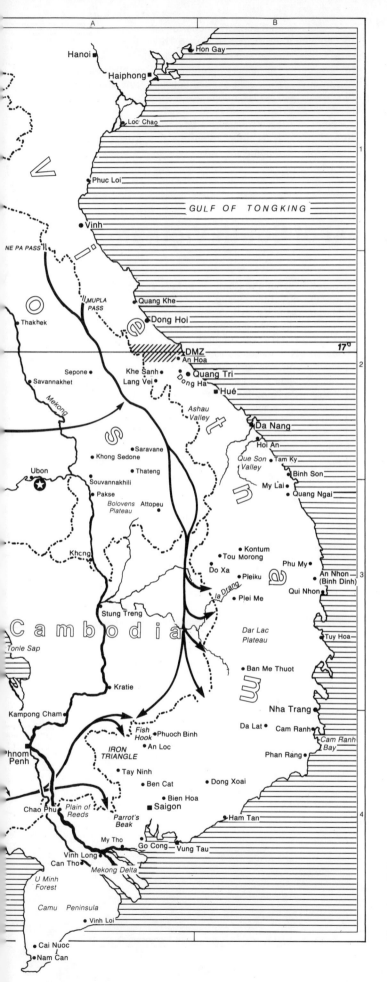

79

1972

30 March	NVN starts conventional invasion of SVN.
5 April–12 June	Siege of An Loc.
28 April	VC take Dong Ha.
1 May	VC take Quang Tri.
10 May	Martial Law declared in SVN.
12 August	Last US ground troops leave SVN; 43,000 air force and support troops remain.
15 September	ARVN retake Quang Tri.

1973

15 January	US military operations against NVN cease.
27 January	Peace agreement between NVN and US signed.
29 March	Last US troops leave SVN.

1975

| 5 March | NVN launches final offensive. |
| 30 April | NVN troops enter Saigon; SVN surrenders unconditionally. |

The North Vietnamese Conquest of South Vietnam, January–April 1975

The ceasefire agreement which marked the end of the Vietnam War (27 January, 1973) brought no end to the agonies of the people of Indo-China. The agreement provided for talks between the Hanoi and Saigon governments on the political future of Vietnam. The talks made no progress, hostilities between the two Vietnamese armies continued intermittently and the talks were broken off in April, 1974. Meanwhile US aid to S. Vietnam was cut back sharply, while Russia's aid to N. Vietnam increased. On 6 January, 1975, the North Vietnamese mounted an assault on Phuoc Long Province and captured the town of Phuoc Binh. The invasion proper started at the beginning of March, the main events being as follows:

4 March	N.V. 968 Div. makes feint attack on Pleiku.
5 March	S.V. 23 Div. sent from Ban Me Thuot to defend Pleiku.
10 March	N.V. 316 Div. takes Ban Me Thuot.
11 March	23 Div. returns from Ban Me Thuot but is cut off.
13 March	23 Div. flees; S.V. planes bomb Ban Me Thuot.
15 March	S.V. Rangers ordered to evacuate Kontum and Pleiku.
17 March	S.V. airborne division withdrawn from Quang Tri to defend Saigon.
18 March	Pleiku and Kontum fall to N.V. troops; An Loc taken.
19 March	N.V. take Quang Tri unopposed.
26 March	Tam Ky and Quang Ngai taken without a fight; Hué occupied unopposed.
28 March	Hoi An taken in north, Bao Loc in south.
29 March	N.V. forces surround Da Nang; General Truong takes to the sea and deserters and refugees mob evacuation planes and ships.
30 March	Da Nang falls, undefended.
1 April	Qui Nhon taken unopposed.
2 April	S.V. surrender Tuy Hoa, Da Lat, Phan Rang and Phan Thiet.
21 April	President Thieu resigns.
30 April	N.V. tanks enter Saigon (now Ho Chi Minh City); 11th hour American evacuation by helicopter from the roof of the US embassy.

By the time Saigon fell over one half of the rural population had fled to the cities and many abroad, 140,000 to the United States. A National Assembly representing the whole of Vietnam was elected on 25 April, 1976, met in Hanoi on 24 June and on 2 July approved the reunification of North and South Vietnam under the name of the Socialist Republic of Vietnam.

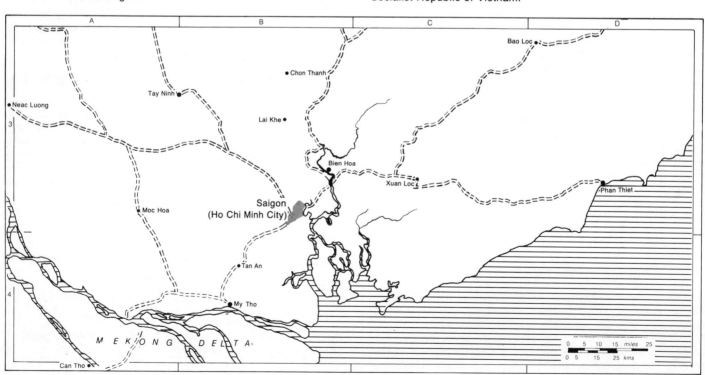

The Chinese Invasion of Vietnam, February–March 1979

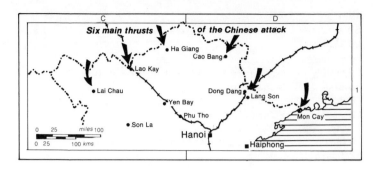

On 17 February, 1979, in retaliation for Hanoi's interference in Cambodia, Chinese troops advanced into Vietnam on a wide front. It was estimated that 200,000 troops had been massed along the border, of which 70–80,000 took part in the initial invasion. They were opposed by about 50,000 regular Vietnamese troops and the same number of local militia. The advance took the form of six main thrusts: towards Lai Chau, Lao Kay, Ha Giang, Cao Bang, Dong Dang and Mon Cay, the two heaviest being those directed against Dong Dang, which fell on the first day, and Lao Kay, which fell on the 19th. Cao Bang and Ha Giang fell on the 22nd. But the Chinese had met with stronger opposition than they expected and already, on the 18th, had halted the advance almost completely along a line about 6 miles south of the border to await reinforcements. By 24 February the invasion force had reached 200,000 and the advance was resumed. There was heavy fighting round Lang Son which Chinese infantry finally entered on 2 March. Then, on 5 March, a Chinese Government statement announced that the Chinese troops, having 'attained the goals set for them', were withdrawing into Chinese territory. As they retreated, the Chinese were harassed by Vietnamese troops and heavy fighting was still going on round Lang Son on 7 March. On 17 March Hua Guofeng, the Chinese Prime Minister, said that all Chinese troops had left Vietnam. On 19 March the Vietnamese claimed 'a very glorious victory' and said 62,500 Chinese had been killed or wounded and 280 tanks destroyed. General Wu Xiuquan, the Chinese Deputy Chief of Staff, said on 2 May that 20,000 Chinese and 50,000 Vietnamese had been killed or wounded. The latter figures are likely to be the more accurate. During the brief invasion the Chinese virtually razed to the ground the four provincial capitals of Cao Bang, Lang Son, Lao Kay and Cam Duong.

Cambodia/Kampuchea

Cambodia became a French protectorate in 1863 and achieved independence by gradual stages between 1953 and 1955. For the next 15 years the political life of the country was dominated by the pro-communist Prince Norodom Sihanouk, first as King, then as Head of Government after he had abdicated in favour of his father and, finally, following his father's death in 1960, as Head of State. In March, 1970, while he was on holiday in France, he was deposed in a military coup, headed by General Lon Nol, and went into exile in Peking. The new government was anxious to preserve Cambodia's neutrality during the Vietnam War but, faced with the loss of bases and supply lines essential to operations in S. Vietnam, the N. Vietnamese began to take over the sparsely populated north and north-east provinces and to foment disaffection in the rest of the country. They supported Sihanouk's government-in-exile and the extreme left Khmer Rouge movement, which Sihanouk himself had tried to suppress while in power.

1971

21–22 January: Vietnamese suicide squads raid Phnom Penh airport and reduce the miniscule Cambodian air force to rubble.

April: Lon Nol resigns after suffering a stroke but is persuaded to resume office later in the year.

1973

By now most of the area east of the Mekong River was under North Vietnamese control, as well as some territory along the southern frontier. The Government retained control of about a quarter of the rural areas, most of the major towns and three-fifths of the population.

1975

The end of the stalemate was hastened by an increase of supplies to the Khmer Rouge by the North Vietnamese at the same time as the US virtually halved the sums allocated for aid to Cambodia. Sharp inflation, government inefficiency and corruption further reduced supplies reaching the fighting units. In early February the Mekong River supply route was cut and Phnom Penh fell on 17 April. Having taken the capital, the Khmer Rouge drove the entire population of over 2 million people out into the countryside, regardless of age or infirmity. This new régime, head by Pol Pot, is generally regarded as the cruellest of modern times. The number of those who died between April, 1975, and January, 1979, will never be known, but has been estimated at between 2 and 3 million people, between a third and a half of the population.

1978

On 25 December the Vietnamese invaded the country and the lightly armed Khmer Rouge forces were quickly swept aside.

1979

Phnom Penh fell on 7 January and a puppet régime was installed under Heng Samrin. The country was renamed the People's Republic of Kampuchea. The country found itself in the throes of a new civil war as Pol Pot's Khmer Rouge, once more the guerillas, fought the Vietnamese occupation forces, of which, by December, there were estimated to be 200,000 in the country.

1983

April: Thai planes attack Vietnamese troops dug in on Thai territory in pursuit of Khmer Rouge guerillas.

No end to the confrontation is in sight.

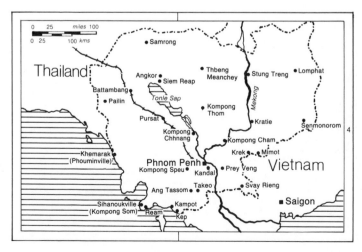

The Hukbalahap Revolt in the Philippines 1945–54

The Philippine Islands were discovered by Ferdinand Magellan in 1521 and conquered by the Spaniards in 1565. The Islands were ceded to the USA on 10 December, 1898, after the Spanish–American War. During the Second World War they were occupied by the Japanese and the Republic of the Philippines was proclaimed on 4 July, 1946. The Hukbalahap Movement, usually abbreviated to 'Huk', (the word means 'People's Anti-Japanese Army' in Tagalog) was a revolutionary guerrilla force originally recruited and trained by the Philippine Communist Party (PKP) to fight the Japanese. After the war the Huks continued the fight, under the leadership of Luis Taruc, a dedicated Communist, against the new 'neo-colonialist' régime. The suggestion that they operated under direct orders from Russia is now discredited, but some of their leaders had certainly been trained in Moscow. At one time Taruc claimed that he had 30,000 men under arms and a further million peasant supporters. This may have been an exaggeration but certainly at one time five provinces were partly under his control and a large area north of Manila was sarcastically known as 'Huklandia'. However, the increasing demands and reprisals the Huks imposed on the peasants, the threat to American bases in the Philippines during the Korean War and the appointment, in 1950, of Ramon Magsaysay as Secretary of National Defence acted together to crush the rebellion. In 1951 resistance spread to a number of regions beyond central Luzon and included Leyte, Mindanao, Mindoro, Negros and Panay, but it gradually petered out as a result of Magsaysay's tactics. By the end of the year the backbone of the revolt had been broken and the Huks retired to the mountains. Sporadic fighting continued until Taruc surrendered in 1954.

PART VIII

Central and South America

Civil Wars and Guerrilla Movements in South America

COLOMBIA

The independence of Colombia was proclaimed by Simón Bolivar on 17 December, 1819, but the Republic did not assume its present boundaries until 1903. In 1948 civil war broke out between the Conservatives and the Liberals and authoritative sources estimate that some 200,000 people lost their lives in the *violencia*, as it was known, between then and 1958. General Rojas Pinilla, who was President from 1953 to 1957, put an end to the worst of the *violencia* but some of the troublemakers turned guerrilla and, styling themselves the Revolutionary Armed Forces (FARC), are still in the field. An urban guerrilla movement emerged in the mid-70s called the April 19 movement, familiarly known as M19. It announced its arrival by stealing Bolivar's sword from a museum outside Bogotá. It would now like to become a legal political party.

VENEZUELA

Venezuela formed part of the Spanish colony of New Granada until 1821 when it became part of the Federal Republic of Colombia, the present independent state being formed on 1830. In October, 1945, a revolt broke out against the revolutionary government of General Medina and the leader of the revolt, Rómulo Betancourt, assumed the Presidency after a 3-day struggle. In 1952 Perez Jimenez became President but was overthrown in 1958 after a brief uprising in which at least 600 people died in Caracas; Betancourt returned to office. Between 1961 and 1964 the Communist-inspired National Liberation Armed Forces (FALN) waged full-scale urban guerrilla warfare against the government, but the overwhelming support given to Betancourt in December, 1963, showed that the mass of the people were sick of violence and thereafter what support FALN had was mostly from Cuba. Its *raison d'être* was largely removed in 1969 by the legalization of the Communist Party. The country remained relatively free from guerrilla activity until 1982 when there were several shoot-outs between police patrols and bands of armed left-wing terrorists.

BRAZIL

Brazil belonged to Portugal from 1500 until 1822 when it became an independent empire under Dom Pedro I, son of the refugee King Joao IV of Portugal. On 15 November 1889 Dom Pedro II was dethroned and a republic proclaimed. The main post-war guerrilla movement in Brazil since 1945 was called 'MR-8', led by Carlos Marighela, an ex-federal deputy. Between 13 and 16 July, 1969, MR-8 blew up all the television stations in São Paolo and on 4 September kidnapped the American Ambassador, Charles Burke Elbrick, exchanging him 2 days later for 15 political prisoners. Marighela died in that year but, as the author of a booklet called *A Handbook of Urban Guerrilla Warfare*, his influence remained great. In 1970 and 1971 kidnappings became commonplace but organized guerrilla protest was prevented by the dreaded 'Death Squad' whose bloody actions so appalled the nation that it was disbanded in 1971.

BOLIVIA

Bolivia, named after Simón Bolivar, the 'Liberator', became independent in 1825 but lost her strip of the Pacific coast to Chile in 1884. On 20 July, 1946, after an armed attempt had been made to overthrow his government, President Villarroel formed a military government whereupon fighting broke out between his supporters and opponents. Armed students stormed the palace and Villarroel was lynched in the main square of La Paz. Nearly 1000 people died in fierce fighting throughout the capital. In 1952 the Movimiento Nacionalista Revolucionario (MNR), in revenge for its defeat after Villarroel's death, staged a revolution in which another 1000 people were killed and Victor Paz Estenssoro became President. In 1967 a poorly-organized anti-government campaign, led by the Argentinian-born revolutionary Ernesto(Che) Guevara, was destroyed, largely because it failed to mobilize the peasants. Presidents of Bolivia have come and gone with bewildering rapidity of recent years but each military coup has stopped just this side of bloodshed.

PERU

Peru remained under Spanish rule until 1821. Its early post-war history was comparatively uneventful though there was large-scale Indian unrest throughout the 1960s. In 1965 a group calling itself the Movement of the Revolutionary Left (MIR) was put down by the Army. In the late 1970s emerged a Maoist guerrilla group called Sendero Luminoso (the Shining Path) which has since presented a dangerous armed challenge to the government. It appeals to the most impoverished among the Indians and draws its inspiration from the writings of José Carlos Mariátegui, whose 'Shining Path' its adherents profess to follow. In March 1982 150 Sendero guerrillas attacked a prison in Ayacucho and let out 250 prisoners.

URUGUAY

Uruguay was under Portuguese rule in the 17th century, then under Spanish rule for 100 years before gaining independence in 1828. The Tupamaros, a pro-Chinese communist group, began in 1963 as a protest movement among the sugar-cane workers in N. Uruguay. By 1969, during which year they stole $¼m from banks and casinos, they enjoyed wide popular support among the people, who looked on them as Robin Hoods. In 1970 the Army captured their leader, Raul Séndic. In January, 1971 the Tupamaros kidnapped the British Ambassador, Mr Geoffrey Jackson, and held him for 8 months, while in September in a mass breakout from Punta Carretas prison Séndic and 106 other guerrillas escaped. But in 1972 President Bordaberry launched an all-out drive against the Tupamaros, Sénic was recaptured and 2000 other guerrillas taken. Within a year the Tupamaros were broken. Since 1973 Uruguay has been governed by presidential rule with military support.

The map shows South America with grid references A, B, C, D across the top and 1, 2, 3 down the side. Labeled features include:

VENEZUELA — Caracas
Orinoco
GUYANA
SURINAM
FRENCH-GUIANA
COLOMBIA — Bogota
ECUADOR — Quito
Amazon
PERU — Lima
BRAZIL — Brasília
BOLIVIA — La Paz
PARAGUAY
Rio de Janeiro
Paraná
CHILE — Santiago
URUGUAY
Buenos Aires — Montevideo
ARGENTINA

CHILE

Chile was under Spanish rule until 1810 when a revolutionary war which ended with the Battle of the Maipo River (5 April 1818) achieved the independence of the nation. As a result of the 1970 elections Dr Salvador Allende became the first ever democratically elected Marxist head of state, but his régime led to increasing social and economic chaos and on 11 September, 1973, Chile experienced its first coup in 49 years when army and airforce units attacked the palace. Allende, it was said, committed suicide; Augusto Pinochet became President and Chile was turned overnight from a turbulent leftist democracy to a rightist authoritarian state. Though Pinochet's repressive régime has done much to restore the health of the country's economy, Chile's traditional democratic freedoms remain in abeyance.

ARGENTINA

Argentina's independence from Spain was proclaimed in 1816. In February, 1946, Juan Perón was elected President, his success then and later depending largely on the popularity of his wife Evita. She died in 1952 and in 1956 Perón was overthrown. In June, 1956, a revolt by Peronista army officers against the ruling military junta was easily crushed and the leaders and others shot. Throughout the 1970s guerrilla activity mounted steadily, the main groups being the Ejército Revolucionario del Pueblo (ERP) or People's Revolutionary Army and the Peronist Montoneros. In 1973 Perón returned from exile and was again elected President but he died after only 9 months in office and his place was taken by his second wife, Isabel. Thereafter, terrorist activity and political violence increased to such an extent that in November, 1974, the Chief of Police declared a state of siege. Matters deteriorated further in 1975 with Montoneros mounting open attacks on Army barracks and a leftist guerrilla attack on an arsenal near Buenos Aires in which 100 people were killed. In the 12 months to May 1975 the fascist 'death squad' Alianza Anticomunista Argentina executed over 1000 leftists. Isabel Perón was deposed in March 1976 and the country was ruled for 7 years by a series of military juntas who were very far from scrupulous about the methods used to deal with terrorists. In 1979 Amnesty International put the number of people who have 'disappeared' at 15–20,000 and the fate of the *desaparecidos* remains a highly sensitive issue. On 2 April, 1982, Argentine troops invaded the Falkland Islands.

In October, 1983, Raul Alfonsin was elected President and immediately after his inauguration in December instituted a rigorous examination of the past. Most of the Falkland Islands War commanders are now facing trial and the fate of the *desaparecidos* is under close scrutiny.

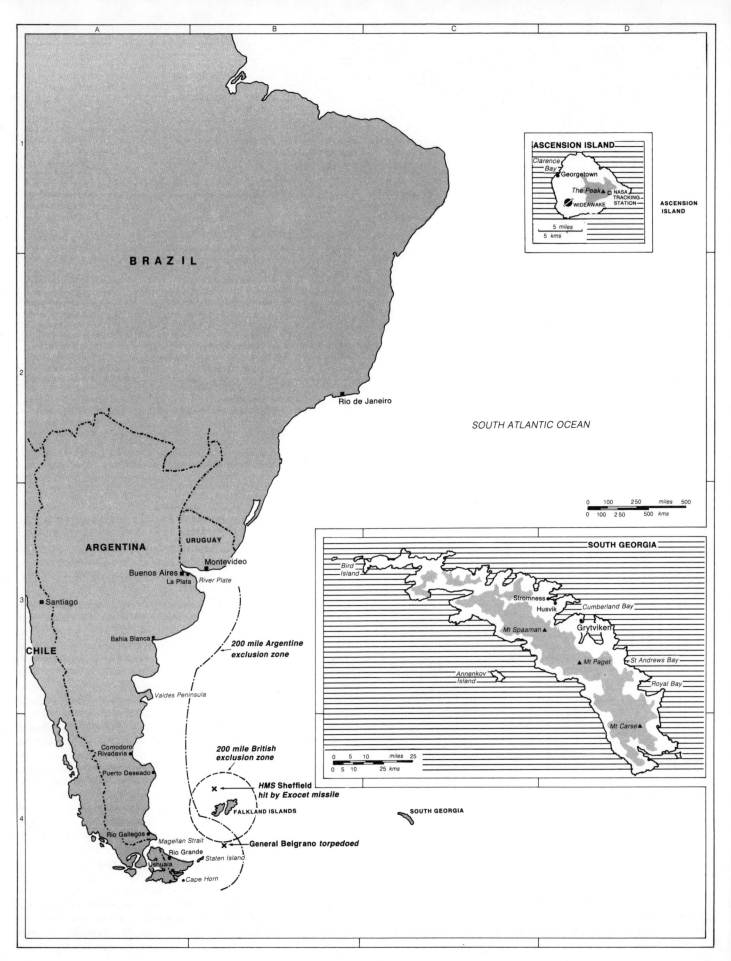

ASCENSION ISLAND

Clarence Bay ☐
● Georgetown
The Peak ▲ ☐ NASA TRACKING STATION
⊗ WIDEAWAKE

5 miles
5 kms

ASCENSION ISLAND

BRAZIL

■ Rio de Janeiro

SOUTH ATLANTIC OCEAN

0 100 250 *miles* 500
0 100 2 50 *500 kms*

ARGENTINA

URUGUAY

Buenos Aires ■■ ● Montevideo
La Plata ● *River Plate*

● Santiago

CHILE

Bahia Blanca ●

Valdes Peninsula

Comodoro Rivadavia ●
Puerto Deseado ●

200 mile Argentine exclusion zone

200 mile British exclusion zone

✕ ← **HMS** Sheffield *hit by Exocet missile*

Rio Gallegos ●
Magellan Strait
Rio Grande ●
Ushuaia ● *Staten Island*
● *Cape Horn*

FALKLAND ISLANDS

✕ **General Belgrano** *torpedoed*

SOUTH GEORGIA

SOUTH GEORGIA

Bird Island

Stromness ●
Husvik ● *Cumberland Bay*
Mt Spaaman ▲ **Grytviken** ●

Mt Paget ▲ *St Andrews Bay*

Annenkov Island

Royal Bay

Mt Carse ▲

0 5 10 *miles* 25
0 5 10 *25 kms*

86

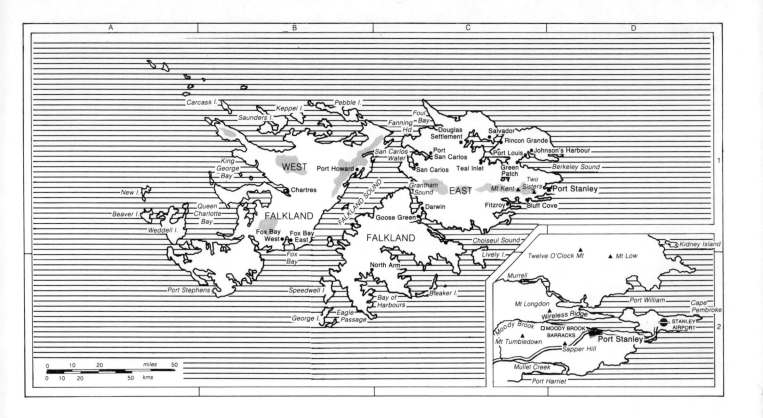

The Recapture of the Falkland Islands, 1982

The Falkland Islands were discovered in 1592 by the English explorer John Davis and named by one Captain Strong in 1690 in memory of Lucius Cary, 2nd Viscount Falkland, an unenthusiastic royalist who was nevertheless called 'the example of the ideal cavalier' and was killed at the Battle of Newbury in 1643. The first settlement was established by the French in 1764, but was sold to Spain in 1767. The islands were without permanent inhabitants until 1820 when possession was taken by the Republic of Buenos Aires. In 1833 Great Britain occupied the islands and expelled the Argentine soldiers and colonists, thereby sowing the seeds of a grievance which smouldered for the next 149 years and finally burst into flames in April, 1982.

The main events of the Battle for the Falkland Islands were as follows:

2 April	500 Argentine troops invade the Falkland Islands. The garrison of 81 Royal Marines at Port Stanley surrenders.
4 April	Argentine forces seize the island of South Georgia after strong resistance by 22 Royal Marines who shot down a helicopter, holed a warship and killed 3 of the invaders before being overwhelmed.
5 April	Lord Carrington resigns as Foreign Secretary and is replaced by Mr Francis Pym. First Task Force ships sail from Portsmouth.
7 April	Britain declares a 200-mile war zone round the Falklands.
25 April	Royal Marines, landing from helicopters, recapture S. Georgia. After attacks by Naval helicopters, the Argentine submarine Santa Fe is run aground and her crew surrender.
1 May	RAF Harriers and Vulcans attack Port Stanley airfield. 3 Argentine aircraft shot down.
2 May	Argentine cruiser General Belgrano sunk by Tigerfish torpedoes 36 miles outside the exclusion zone, with loss of 368 lives.
4 May	HMS Sheffield hit by Exocet missile; 20 men killed.
15 May	Royal Marines land on Pebble Island, destroy 11 Argentine aircraft and withdraw.
21 May	British troops establish bridgehead at San Carlos. HMS Ardent sunk by air attack; 24 killed. 20 Argentine aircraft shot down.
23 May	HMS Antelope sunk; 2 killed. 9 Argentine aircraft shot down.
24 May	7 Argentine aircraft shot down.
25 May	HMS Coventry sunk by bombs; 19 killed. Container ship Atlantic Conveyor abandoned after being hit by an Exocet missile; 12 killed.
28 May	2nd Bn. Parachute Regiment take Darwin and Goose Green. British casualties 17 killed, including Lt-Col. H. Jones; 31 wounded.
30 May	Royal Marines advancing on northern pincer route from San Carlos take Douglas Settlement and Teal Inlet.
2 June	British troops take Mount Kent.
8 June	Landing ships Sir Tristram and Sir Galahad sunk by air attack during landing at Bluff Cove; 56 killed. HMS Plymouth badly damaged by bombs. British troops build up bridgehead S. of Port Stanley.
8–9 June	11 more Argentinian aircraft shot down.
11 June	HMS Glamorgan hit by an Exocet missile. 9 killed
13 June	British forces take Mount Tumbledown.
14 June	Argentinian forces under General Menendez surrender to Major-General Jeremy Moore in Port Stanley.

In all 255 members of the Task Force were killed and 777 were wounded. There were no authoritative figures for Argentine casualties.

Central America

The independent states of Central America include Guatemala, Honduras, Nicaragua, Costa Rica, El Salvador, Panama and Belize. For about 300 years most of the region was governed by Spain, after which followed a brief period of federation between 1821 and 1838, when the states became independent republics. Belize, which had never been under Spanish rule, was recognized as a British colony in 1862 and called British Honduras. In 1973 it was renamed Belize and was granted independence on 21 September, 1981.

GUATEMALA

Invasion of Guatemala 18 June 1954

On 18 June, 1954, exiled Guatemalans, led by Colonel Carlos Castillo Armas, invaded Guatemala from Honduras and ousted the pro-communist President Arbenz, after a campaign lasting 10 days, throughout which the U.S. Ambassador, John Puerifoy, was actively contriving that the Arbenz régime should be replaced by an anti-communist administration. Indeed, it is generally accepted that the invasion only succeeded thanks to aerial bombardments made by CIA aircraft flown by North Americans and Nationalist Chinese. Castillo Armas became and remained President until he was assassinated in July, 1957.

HONDURAS

The Honduras/Nicaragua Border Dispute, 1957

On 18 April, 1957, Nicaraguan troops crossed the Coco River and occupied the small Honduran town of Morocon. An area of 4,500,000 acres north of the Coco River had been in dispute between the two countries since King Alfonso XIII of Spain had awarded it to Honduras in 1906. The issue was revived when Honduras created a new political department, Gracias à Dios, in the disputed area on 21 February, 1957. This was strongly resented in Nicaragua and led to the occupation of Morocon. On 1 May the town was recaptured by a Honduran battalion with air support; 35 Nicaraguan soldiers were killed. A 5-nation peace commission appointed by the O.A.S. obtained a ceasefire on 6 May and the matter was referred to the UN. Gracias à Dios remains part of Honduras.

The Football War, July 1969

In July, 1969, hostilities broke out between Honduras and El Salvador. The war lasted from 14 to 30 July and was known as the Football (or Soccer) War because it was triggered off by El Salvador's defeat of Honduras in the qualifying round of a World Cup football match. The deeper cause lay in the presence of 300,000 semi-skilled Salvadorean workers living in Honduras where they had obtained jobs at the expense of less skilled Hondurans. The football match was followed by riots which led to the death of two Salvadoreans and the expulsion of 11,000 others. On 14 July Salvadorean troops crossed the frontier and advanced in a two-pronged attack on Tegucigalpa. On 30 July the O.A.S. persuaded the Salvadorean Government to withdraw its forces. Some 4000 Hondurans were killed during the invasion, the majority being civilians killed during 'mopping up' operations. The most serious consequence for El Salvador was the loss of Honduras as a convenient sponge to absorb her surplus workforce.

EL SALVADOR 1980

In October, 1979, a popular coup in El Salvador resulted in the replacement of a military dictatorship by a military-civilian junta. Civil War between Government forces and 5,000 to 6,000 Marxist-led guerrillas, styling themselves the Faraibundo Marti National Liberation Front (FMLN), started in 1980 and has so far claimed some 35,000 lives, the vast majority of them civilians killed by security forces and right-wing death squads. The US supports the Govern-

THE FOOTBALL WAR, July 1969

🌿 Towns bombed by Salvadorean airforce

Nacaome Towns taken by Salvadorean troops

Oil refinery destroyed by Honduran airforce

Border crossing by Salvadorean armoured column

ment but has agreed to a limit of 55 military advisers, another example of the West tying one hand behind its back while fully aware that it can expect no such courtesy in return. In spite of one of the US adviser's statement that 'By our standards the Salvadorean Army is just plain bad,' the U.S.-directed Operation Goodwill, based on the 'hearts and minds' principle and launched in June, 1983, appears to be succeeding. Says its commander, Colonel Reinaldo Golcher, 'This has changed the direction of the entire war.' But even assuming the success of Operation Goodwill, there is no quick end to the fighting in sight.

NICARAGUA

Severe unrest began in January, 1978, with the murder of Pedro Joaquin Chamorro Cardenal, the editor of the influential paper *La Prensa*, leader of the Democratic Liberation Union (UDEL) and the most serious opponent of President Anastasio Somoza, whose family had ruled Nicaragua, with the ungentle aid of the National Guard, since 1933. By September, 1978, the unrest had turned into open civil war. The FSLN (Frente Sandinista de Liberación Nacional), the guerrilla movement opposing Somoza, was named after Augusto César Sandino who led a resistance force against Americans occupying Nicaragua in 1927–33. He was shot in 1934, probably on the orders of Somoza's father, who was himself killed by a Sandinist in 1954. The FSLN gained worldwide notoriety in December, 1974, with the seizure of a large number of important hostages at a party in Managua. Thereafter the main events leading up to and during the Civil War were as follows:

1977
October — FSLN attack National Guard posts at San Carlos, Esquipulas, Masaya and Managua.

1978
26 Feb–1 March — Fighting in Masaya and León.
19 July — FSLN guerrillas launch rockets from the roof of the Intercontinental Hotel in Managua on to the nearby National Guard training school.

7 April	FSLN take Esteli; fighting at Condega and El Sauce.
14 April	National Guard retake Esteli; 1000 people killed.
28–9 May	FSLN launch double offensive – 1) around Rivas and Peña Blanca 2) around Puerto Cabezas.
5 June	FSLN take León and Matagalpa.
12 June	FSLN entrenched in the slum quarters of Managua.
23 June	Government forces begin intensive bombardment of Managua, causing estimated 10–12,000 civilian casualties. FSLN now holding León, Diriamba, Chichigalpa, Masaya, Somotillo, Ocotal, Esteli and Matagalpa.
27–8 June	FSLN withdraw from Managua to prevent further civilian casualties.
6 July	FSLN take Jinotepe and San Marcos.
17 July	Somoza resigns and flees to Miami.
18 July	5-Man FSLN provisional junta assumes power.

The expulsion of Somoza and the National Guard did not, however, bring peace to Nicaragua. Many of the National Guardsmen took refuge in Honduras and from there, with US support, began to plot the overthrow of the Sandinista régime. Border raids started in 1981 and by March, 1983, were thought to have cost about 400 lives on each side, by which time the rebels had established a permanent presence inside Nicaragua. These rebels, 5000 strong and known officially as the Nicaraguan Democratic Front (FDN), are usually referred to as the *contras*. The FDN enjoys little popular support in Nicaragua because many of its members formerly belonged to Somoza's hated National Guard. The FDN are not the only group opposing the Sandinistas. From across the Costa Rican border to the south raids are mounted by 1500 rebels under command of Edén Pastora, a dissident Sandinist who, styling himself Commander Zero, was the military architect of the Sandinista victory in 1979. They call themselves the Democratic Revolutionary Front (ARDE). A third guerrilla faction, a 3000-strong band of disaffected Miskito, Sumo and Rama Indians, operate in the border area on the east coast. There is, however, no cooperation between the three groups. The Sandinistas, in the summer of 1983, had 25,000 regular troops, 25,000 in the reserves, 80,000 in the militia and 8000 in paramilitary forces – a total of 138,000 men. There are also thought to be some 2000 Cuban military advisers in Nicaragua. Despite the military ineptitude of the Sandinists and the acknowledged US support of the FDN, under the transparent excuse of preventing arms being sent from Nicaragua through Honduras to the Salvadorean guerrillas, the balance of power nevertheless seemed too uneven to give the rebels much chance of success.

Recently, however, they changed their tactics from conventional attacks on towns and villages to attacks on the economic arteries of the country. On 11 October 1983 they blew up five large storage tanks at Corinto, which contained a large portion of Nicaragua's fuel reserves. On 14 October they blew up the pipeline from Puerto Sandino to Managua.

COSTA RICA

Civil War March–April 1948

Civil war broke out in Costa Rica early in March, 1948, following the annulment by President Picado of the recent presidential elections which had resulted in a majority for Señor Otilio Ulate over the Government-sponsored candidate, Dr Rafael Calderon Guardia. By 30 March the Army of National Liberation, led by Colonel José Figueras, was in control of the town of San Isidro. During the following month the rebels had gained control of all the southern part of the country, including the port of Limón. On 20 April they took Cartago and entered San José on the 24th. President Picado resigned and a revolutionary junta was set up in which Figueras

22 August	FSLN guerrillas, led by a girl of 22, occupy the National Palace in Managua and take 1000 hostages, all but 70 of whom later escaped or were set free. Somoza was forced to meet the demands of the guerrillas who were then flown to Panama.
25 August	500 teenagers take over town of Matagalpa after severe fighting with the National Guard.
9 September	Heavy fighting in Masaya, León, Esteli, Chinandega and Diriamba.
25 September	Somoza agrees to O.A.S.-sponsored mediation; negotiations last until January, 1979, when talks break down and fighting recommences.

became Foreign Minister and Minister of Justice & Public Security.

Invasion of Costa Rica 10 December 1948
On 10 December, 1948, Costa Rica was invaded from across the Nicaraguan border by a force of 1000 supporters of ex-President Calderon Guardia. The town of La Cruz was taken by the rebels and Costa Rica accused Nicaragua of supporting the rebels, a charge which Nicaragua vehemently denied. By 17 December the invaders had been driven back over the border. An OAS Commission absolved Nicaragua of any participation in the invasion but blamed her for taking no steps to prevent it.

Invasion of Costa Rica 11 January 1955
On 11 January, 1955, Costa Rica was invaded by a rebel force of Costa Rican exiles who crossed the border from Nicaragua, with the backing of the Nicaraguan President, Anastasio Somoza, and the apparent intention of overthrowing the Costa Rican President, Dr Figueras. After an 11-day campaign and the intervention of the OAS, the insurgent force was driven back across the Nicaraguan border. 'Pausing only to take undisputed possession of [Villa Quesada's] beer supply [the rebels] betook themselves hastily off in the direction of the Nicaraguan frontier' (*The Times* 14.1.55).

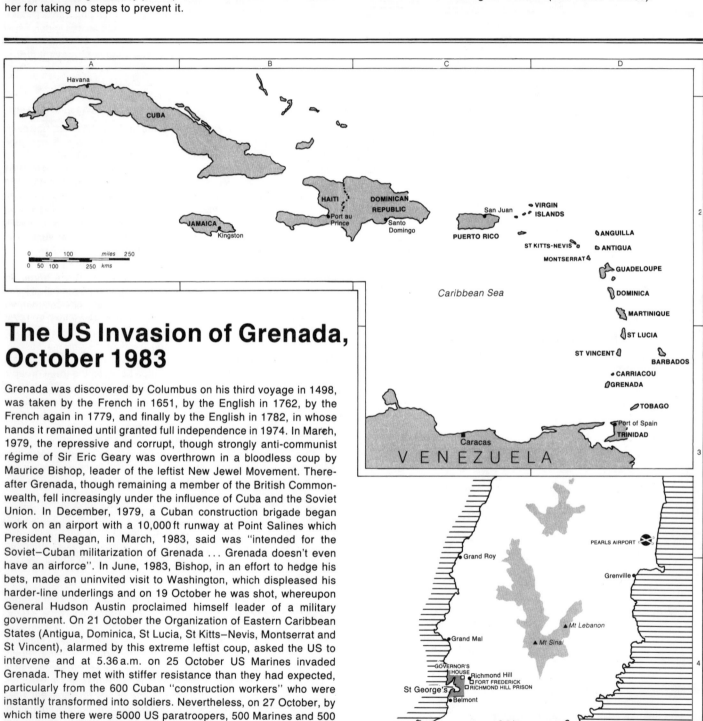

The US Invasion of Grenada, October 1983

Grenada was discovered by Columbus on his third voyage in 1498, was taken by the French in 1651, by the English in 1762, by the French again in 1779, and finally by the English in 1782, in whose hands it remained until granted full independence in 1974. In March, 1979, the repressive and corrupt, though strongly anti-communist, régime of Sir Eric Geary was overthrown in a bloodless coup by Maurice Bishop, leader of the leftist New Jewel Movement. Thereafter Grenada, though remaining a member of the British Commonwealth, fell increasingly under the influence of Cuba and the Soviet Union. In December, 1979, a Cuban construction brigade began work on an airport with a 10,000 ft runway at Point Salines which President Reagan, in March, 1983, said was "intended for the Soviet–Cuban militarization of Grenada ... Grenada doesn't even have an airforce". In June, 1983, Bishop, in an effort to hedge his bets, made an uninvited visit to Washington, which displeased his harder-line underlings and on 19 October he was shot, whereupon General Hudson Austin proclaimed himself leader of a military government. On 21 October the Organization of Eastern Caribbean States (Antigua, Dominica, St Lucia, St Kitts–Nevis, Montserrat and St Vincent), alarmed by this extreme leftist coup, asked the US to intervene and at 5.36 a.m. on 25 October US Marines invaded Grenada. They met with stiffer resistance than they had expected, particularly from the 600 Cuban "construction workers" who were instantly transformed into soldiers. Nevertheless, on 27 October, by which time there were 5000 US paratroopers, 500 Marines and 500 Rangers on the island, Admiral Wesley McDonald reported that all "major military objectives were secured", but later admitted that "scattered pockets of resistance remained". 11 US servicemen were reported killed and 67 wounded. Details of Cuban and Grenadian casualties were not released.

90

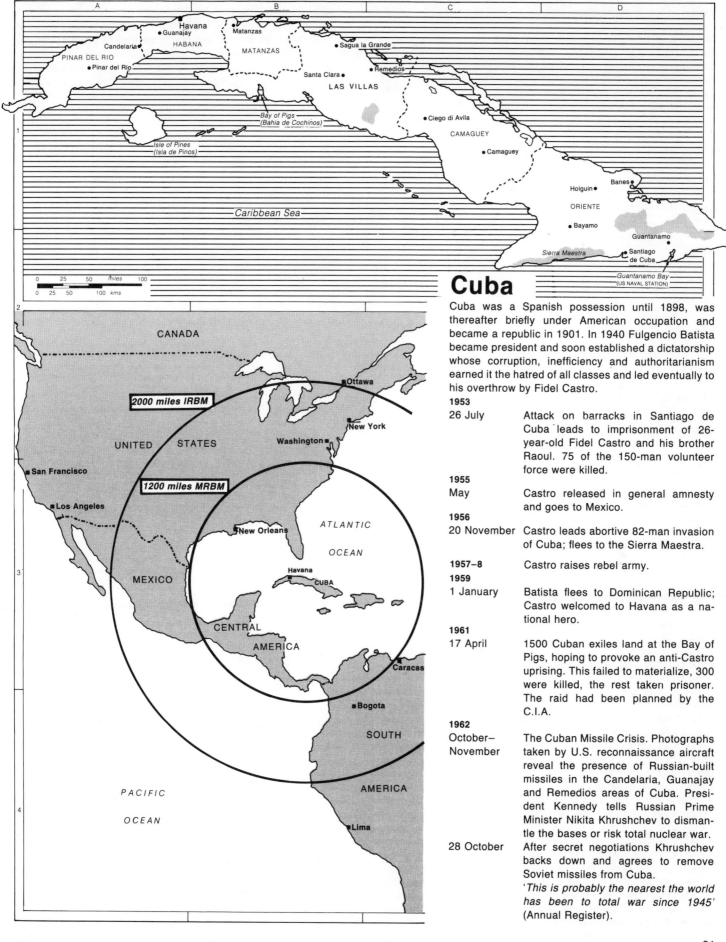

Cuba

Cuba was a Spanish possession until 1898, was thereafter briefly under American occupation and became a republic in 1901. In 1940 Fulgencio Batista became president and soon established a dictatorship whose corruption, inefficiency and authoritarianism earned it the hatred of all classes and led eventually to his overthrow by Fidel Castro.

1953

26 July	Attack on barracks in Santiago de Cuba leads to imprisonment of 26-year-old Fidel Castro and his brother Raoul. 75 of the 150-man volunteer force were killed.

1955

May	Castro released in general amnesty and goes to Mexico.

1956

20 November	Castro leads abortive 82-man invasion of Cuba; flees to the Sierra Maestra.

1957–8 Castro raises rebel army.

1959

1 January	Batista flees to Dominican Republic; Castro welcomed to Havana as a national hero.

1961

17 April	1500 Cuban exiles land at the Bay of Pigs, hoping to provoke an anti-Castro uprising. This failed to materialize, 300 were killed, the rest taken prisoner. The raid had been planned by the C.I.A.

1962

October– November	The Cuban Missile Crisis. Photographs taken by U.S. reconnaissance aircraft reveal the presence of Russian-built missiles in the Candelaria, Guanajay and Remedios areas of Cuba. President Kennedy tells Russian Prime Minister Nikita Khrushchev to dismantle the bases or risk total nuclear war.
28 October	After secret negotiations Khrushchev backs down and agrees to remove Soviet missiles from Cuba.

'This is probably the nearest the world has been to total war since 1945' (Annual Register).

TEXT INDEX

GAZETTEER

Atta, Nigeria   37 C4
Attopeu, Laos   79 A3
Auchi, Nigeria   37 C1
Aurès Mts, Algeria   33 B1
Awabi, Oman   23 C3
Awali, R, Lebanon   17 B3
Awash, Ethiopia   45 B2
Ayios Dhometios, Cyprus   6 C1
Ayios Theodoros, Cyprus   6 C2
Aziziyat, Syria   13 D1
Azumini, Nigeria   37 D4

Baa, Indonesia   75 C4
Baabda, Lebanon   20 A1
Baadarane, Lebanon   17 B3
Baalbek, Lebanon   16 B1, 17 C2
Bab el Mandeb, Aden   24 C2
Bac Kan, Vietnam   77 C1
Bac Ninh, Vietnam   77 C2
Bacolod, Philippines   82 B1
Bac Quang, Vietnam   77 B1
Badakhshan, Region, Afghanistan   59 C1
Badawi, Lebanon   17 B1
Badgam, Kashmir   54 B3
Badulla, Ceylon   60 B2
Bafatá, Guinea-Bissau   41 C2
Baghdad, Iraq   25 D1, 27 A2, 27 C1
Bagram, Afghanistan   59 C2
Bahawalpur, Pakistan   56 A2
Bahawalpur, Prov, Pakistan   52 B1
Bahia Blanca, Argentina   86 A3
Bahla, Oman   23 C4
Bahmanshir, R, Iran   26 D4
Bahrain, I, Arabian Gulf   27 D2, 28 B2
Bahr el Ghazal, Prov, Sudan   44 D2
Bahr el Ghazal, R, Sudan   44 D2
Baikal, L, USSR   67 C1
Bakelalan, Brunei   75 C2
Bakenu, Sarawak   75 A2
Bakhti, USSR   67 B1
Bakri Ridge, Aden   22 C4
Baku, USSR   25 D1
Balai Ringin, Sarawak   74 B4
Balaton, L, Hungary   4 B2
Balat Sait, Oman   23 C4
Bali, I, Indonesia   73 B2
Balikpapan, Indonesia   73 B1
Balipara, India   66 B4
Ballycastle, N Ireland   7 D1
Ballymena, N Ireland   7 D1
Baluchistan, Prov, Pakistan   52 A1
Baluza, Sinai   14 C1
Bananera, Guatemala   88 D1
Bandar Abbas, Iran   27 D2, 28 D2
Bandar Khomeini, Iran   27 C3
Bandjermasin, Indonesia   73 B1
Bandung, Indonesia   73 C2
Banes, Cuba   91 D1
Bangalore, India   53 B3
Bangar, Brunei   75 B1
Bangka I, Indonesia   73 A1
Bangkok, Thailand   76 A1
Bangui, Central African Rep   39 A1
Banihal Pass, Kashmir   54 B4
Baniyas, Syria   13 D1
Ban Me Thuot, Vietnam   79 B3
Bann, R, N Ireland   7 C1
Bao Loc, Vietnam   80 D1
Baram R, Malaysia   75 A2
Bardai, Chad   35 A1
Bardera, Somalia   45 C3
Barentu, Ethiopia   46 A2
Bario, Sarawak   75 C2
Barisal, Bangladesh   57 D2
Baramula, Kashmir   54 A3
Barmer, India   56 A2
Barro, Guinea-Bissau   41 C2
Bartolomeu Dias, Mozambique   42 B3
Barzan, Iraq   25 D1, 27 A1
Baskinta, Lebanon   17 B2
Basra, Iraq   26 C3, 27 C1, 27 C3
Bassein, Burma   58 A3
Batavia, Indonesia   73 B1
Bathurst, Gambia   41 C2
Batinah Coast, Oman   23 D1
Batna, Algeria   33 B1
Batong Duri, Brunei   75 B1
Batroun, Lebanon   17 B2

Battambang, Cambodia   81 C4
Batu Pahat, Malaya   72 B4
Bau, Sarawak   74 B4
Baucau, Indonesia   75 D4
Bayamo, Cuba   91 D1
Bayn al Gidr, Aden   22 D4
Bchamoun, Lebanon   20 A1
Beaufort Castle, Lebanon   17 B4
Beaver I, Falkland Is   87 A1
Becheré, Lebanon   17 C2
Beersheba, Israel   10 A2, 10 B2, 15 D3
Behbehan, Iran   27 D3
Beidha, Yemen   23 A1, 23 B3
Beihan, Yemen   23 B1, 23 B3, 24 D1
Beiltung I, Indonesia   73 B1
Beilul, Ethiopia   46 D3
Beira, Mozambique   42 B2, 45 D2
Beirut, Lebanon   12 D1, 16 A1, 17 B3, 18 A1, 19 D1, 20 A1
Beitbridge, Zimbabwe   49 C4
Beit-ed-Din, Lebanon   17 B3
Beit Hanina, Israel   13 A3
Beit Iksa, Israel   13 A3
Beiting, China   63 B2
Beit Kika, Israel   13 A3
Beit Meri, Lebanon   20 B1
Beit Safafa, Israel   13 A4
Beit Samuel, Israel   13 A3
Bekaa Valley, Lebanon   17 B3, 20 C1
Bekasi, Indonesia   73 C2
Békéscsaba, Hungary   4 C2
Belet Uen, Somalia   45 C2
Belfast, N Ireland   7 D2, 8 A1, 8 C4
Belfast L, N Ireland   7 D1
Belmont, Grenada   90 C4
Belmopan, Belize   88 D1
Ben Cat, Vietnam   79 A4
Bende, Nigeria   37 B4, 37 D4
Bengal, India   52 D2
Benguela, Angola   40 A3, 41 A3
Benguela, District, Angola   40 A3
Benguela Railway, Angola   41 A3
Beni-Abbès, Algeria   34 B1
Benin, Bight of, Nigeria   36 A3
Benin City, Nigeria   36 B3, 37 C1
Benin R, Nigeria   37 C2
Beni Ounif, Algeria   34 C1
Beni Sueif, Egypt   12 B2
Beni Yakov Bridge, Israel   14 C4
Bent Jbail, Lebanon   17 B4
Bentong, Malaya   72 B3
Benue R, Nigeria   36 C2
Benue Plateau, Prov, Nigeria   36 C2
Bepe Hills, Zimbabwe   48 C3
Berbera, Somalia   45 C1
Berkeley Sound, Falkland Is   87 C1
Berlin, Germany   2 B2
Bergen, Norway   8 D4
Betano, Indonesia   75 D4
Bethlehem, Israel   10 A1, 13 A4, 13 C4
Betong, Malaya   72 A2
Bhamdoun, Lebanon   20 B1
Bhairab Bazar, Bangladesh   57 D1
Bhairawa, India   55 A3
Bhimbar, Kashmir   54 A4
Bhojpur, Nepal   55 A3
Bhuj, India   56 A3
Biafra, Prov, Nigeria   36 B3
Biar Bet, India   56 A2
Biawak, Malaysia   74 D4
Bibilieu, Indonesia   75 D4
Biddu, Israel   13 A3
Bie, District, Angola   40 B3
Bien Hoa, Vietnam   79 A4, 80 B3
Bigair, Wadi, Aden   22 C4
Bihar, State, India   52 C2, 53 C2
Bijagos I, Guinea-Bissau   41 C2
Billiton I, Indonesia   73 B1
Biltine, Chad   35 B3
Binh Dinh, Vietnam   79 B3
Binh Son, Vietnam   79 B2
Biratnagar, Nepal   55 A3
Birchenough Bridge, Zimbabwe   48 D4, 49 D3
Bird I, South Georgia   86 B3
Birganj, Nepal   55 A3
Bir Gifgafa, Sinai   11 C1, 12 C2, 13 A2, 14 C1
Bir Hasana, Sinai   11 D1, 12 A2, 13 A2
Birket-al-Moza, Oman   23 D4

Bir Lahfan, Sinai   13 A2
Bir Lahlou, Spanish Sahara   34 B2
Bir Moghrein, Mauritania   34 A2, 34 B2
Bir Thamada, Sinai   12 C2, 13 A2
Biskra, Algeria   33 B2
Bismuna, Nicaragua   89 B1
Bissau, Guinea-Bissau   41 C2
Bizerta, Tunisia   33 D1, 33 D2
Bizerta, Lake, Tunisia   33 D3
Black R, Vietnam   77 B2
Blanco, C, Spanish Sahara   34 A2
Bleaker I, Falkland Is   87 C2
Blida, Algeria   33 A1
Bloody Ridge, Korea   69 B4
Bluefields, Nicaragua   89 B3
Blue Nile R, Sudan   45 A1
Bluff Cove, Falkland Is   87 C1
Bmariam   20 B1
Boa, Yemen   24 D1
Boaco, Nicaragua   89 A2
Bobonaro, Indonesia   75 D4
Bodele Depression, Chad   35 A2
Bodø, Norway   8 D3
Boende, Zaire   39 A2
Bogota, Colombia   85 B1, 91 B4
Bogra, Bangladesh   57 C1
Bojador, C, Spanish Sahara   34 A2
Boké, Guinea-Bissau   41 C2
Bokoro, Chad   35 A3
Bol, Chad   35 A3
Bolamo, Guinea-Bissau   41 C2
Bolovens Plateau, Laos   79 A3
Boma, Zaire   38 C3
Bombay, India   52 B2
Bomdila, India   55 C3, 66 B4
Bondo, Zaire   39 B1
Bône, Algeria   33 C1
Bongor, Chad   35 A3
Bonny, Nigeria   37 A4
Bor, Sudan   45 A2
Boran, Wadi, Aden   22 C3
Bori, Nigeria   37 A4
Borneo, Indonesia   73 B1
Bosaso, Somalia   45 D1
Bostan, Iran   27 C3
Bou Izakaren, Morocco   34 B2
Bou Saada, Algeria   33 A1
Bourj-al-Brajneh (Beirut), Lebanon   18 B2
Brahmanbaria, Bangladesh   57 D1
Brahmaputra R, India   55 B3, 55 C2, 57 D1, 66 B2, 66 B3, 66 B4
Bramiye, Lebanon   17 A3
Brasilia, Brazil   85 C2
Bratislava, Czechoslovakia   4 B1, 5 B2
Breslau, Poland   5 B1
Brno, Czechoslovakia   5 B2
Brunei Town   75 B1
Brunei Bay   75 C1
Buba, Guinea-Bissau   41 C2
Bubaque, Guinea-Bissau   41 C2
Bu Craa, Spanish Sahara   34 B2
Budapest, Hungary   4 C2, 5 C2
Buenos Aires, Argentina   85 B3, 86 A3
Bukavu, Zaire   39 C2
Bukhara, USSR   59 B1
Bukit Knuckle, Sarawak   74 A4
Bukittingi, Indonesia   73 A1
Bulawayo, Zimbabwe   49 B3, 49 D1
Bulbar, Wadi, Aden   22 C4
Bumba, Zaire   39 A1
Bunia, Zaire   39 C1
Buraimi, Oman   23 D1
Burao, Somalia   45 C2
Burdinie, Somalia   45 D2
Buru I, Indonesia   73 C1
Bushehr, Iran   28 B1
Busira R, Zaire   39 A2
Buta, Zaire   39 B1
Butmiye, Syria   13 D1
Butuan, Philippines   82 B2
Butwal, Nepal   55 A3

Cabinda, Angola   40 A2, 41 A3
Cabora-Bassa Dam, Mozambique   42 B2
Cacine, Guinea-Bissau   41 C2
Cagayan de Ora, Philippines   82 B2
Cahama, Angola   40 B4
Cairo, Egypt   11 D3, 12 B2, 19 B1

Caiundo, Angola 40 B4
Calabar, Nigeria 36 C3, 37 B4, 37 D4
Calai, Angola 40 C4
Calapan, Philippines 82 A1
Calcutta, India 52 D2, 53 D2, 57 C2
Calivigny, Grenada 90 C4
Calliste, Grenada 90 C4
Calulo, Angola 40 B3
Calunda, Angola 40 D3
Camabatela, Angola 40 B2
Camaguey, Cuba 91 C1
Camaguey, Prov, Cuba 91 C1
Cam Duong, Vietnam 77 B1
Cameron Highlands, Malaya 72 B3
Cam Ranh Bay, Vietnam 79 A4, 79 B4
Camu Peninsula, Vietnam 79 A4
Candelaria, Cuba 91 A1
Candia, Crete 3 B3
Canea, Crete 3 B3
Cangamba, Angola 40 C3
Can Tho, Vietnam 79 A4, 80 A4
Canton, China 64 B4
Cao Bang, Vietnam 77 C1, 81 D1
Capitol Hill, Korea 69 B4
Capodistria, Yugoslavia 2 C4
Capo Gracios a Dios, Nicaragua 89 B1
Caprivi Strip, Namibia 40 C4
Caracas, Venezuela 85 B1, 90 C2, 91 C3
Carcass I, Falkland Is 87 B1
Carlsbad, Czechoslovakia 5 A1
Carmona, Angola 40 B2, 41 A3
Carnotan, Guatemala 88 D1
Carse, Mt, South Georgia 86 D4
Cartago, Costa Rica 89 B3
Casablanca, Morocco 34 B1
Cashel, Zimbabwe 48 D3, 49 D3
Cassai R, Zaire 40 C2
Cassinga, Angola 40 B4
Catete, Angola 40 A3
Catió, Guinea-Bissau 41 C2
Caxito, Angola 41 A3
Cazombo, Angola 40 D3
Cebu, Philippines 82 B1
Cela, Angola 40 B3
Celebes, Indonesia 73 C1
Cero de Hule, Honduras 88 D2
Ceské Budĕjovice, Czechoslovakia 5 A2
Ceuta, Morocco 34 B1
Chad, L, Chad 35 A3, 36 D1
Chaghara R, India 54 D3
Chainpur, Nepal 55 A3
Chaku, India 55 C3
Chalatenango, El Salvador 88 D2
Chalna, Bangladesh 57 C2
Chamdo, Tibet 66 C2
Champerico, Guatemala 88 C2
Chandernagore, India 52 D2
Chandigarh, India 54 C2
Chandpur, Bangladesh 57 D2
Changane R, Mozambique 42 B3
Changchun, China 63 D1
Changjin Reservoir, Korea 69 B1
Changkiakow, China 63 A2
Changsha, China 64 B3
Changtu, China 63 C2
Changwu, China 62 D3, 63 C2
Chan Muang, Vietnam 77 B1
Chao Phu, Vietnam 79 A4
Chardzou, USSR 59 B1
Chari R, Chad 35 A3
Chartres, Falkland Is 87 B1
Chatilla (Beirut), Lebanon 18 A2
Chauk, Burma 58 A2
Cheba, Lebanon 17 B4
Chechon, Korea 69 D1
Chefod, China 63 C3
Chekiang, Prov, China 63 C4, 64 D3
Chemba, Mozambique 42 B2
Chemlan, Lebanon 20 A1
Chenab R, Pakistan 54 A4, 54 B2, 56 B1,
  57 A1, 59 D3
Chengchow, China 63 A3
Chengte, China 63 B2
Chengting, China 63 A3
Chengtu, China 66 D2
Chengtzukai, China 63 D1
Chengwu, China 63 B3
Chen Pao I, USSR 67 D1

Chentai Rly, China 63 A3
Che Pass, Tibet 66 A3
Cherchell, Algeria 32 D1
Cherchen, China 66 A1
Cheribon, Indonesia 73 C2
Chhamb, Kashmir 56 B1, 57 B1
Chiaohsien, China 63 C2
Chibemba, Angola 40 B4
Chibuto, Mozambique 42 A3
Chicapa R, Angola 40 C2
Chicha Well, Chad 35 B2
Chichigalpa, Nicaragua 89 A2
Chihli Gulf, China 63 B3
Chilfa, Lebanon 17 C2
Chimaniman Mts, Mozambique 48 D4
Chinaja, Guatemala 88 C1
Chinandega, Nicaragua 89 A2
Chinchow, China 63 C2
Chinde, Mozambique 42 C2
Chindwin R, Burma 55 D3, 58 A1
Chinhovi, Zimbabwe 49 C2
Chiniot, Pakistan 56 B1
Chinju, Korea 68 B4
Chinkiang, China 63 B4
Chin-Men I, Taiwan 64 D4
Chinwangtao, China 63 B2
Chios I, Greece 3 C2
Chip Chap R, Kashmir 54 C1
Chipinga, Zimbabwe 48 D4, 49 D3
Chipyong, Korea 68 B3, 69 B4
Chiquimula, Guatemala 88 D2
Chiredzi, Zimbabwe 49 C4
Chirundi, Zambia 49 B1
Chita, USSR 67 D1
Chitequeta, Angola 40 B4
Chitral, Pakistan 56 B1
Chittagong, Bangladesh 57 D2
Chiumbe R, Angola 40 C2
Choiseul Sound, Falkland Is 87 C1
Chokochoko, Nigeria 37 C4
Choluteca, Honduras 88 D2
Chonan, Korea 68 B3
Chongchon, R, Korea 69 B1
Chongjin, Korea 69 B1, 69 C1
Chongju, Korea 68 B4, 69 A1
Chonju, Korea 68 B4, 69 A2
Chon Thanh, Vietnam 80 B3
Chor, Pakistan 57 A2
Chorwon, Korea 68 B3, 69 A4, 69 C1, 69 C2
Chosan, Korea 69 A1
Chouafat (Beirut), Lebanon 18 B3
Chouf Hills Lebanon 17 B3, 20 B1
Chtaura, Lebanon 17 B3, 20 C1
Chuchow, China 64 B3
Chuhsien, China 63 A3
Chumdo, China 55 D2
Chunchon, Korea 68 B3, 69 B4, 69 C1
Chungju, Korea 69 A2
Chungking, China 62 D4, 64 A3
Chusul, Kashmir 54 C1
Chwarta, Iraq 27 B1
Ciego di Avila, Cuba 91 C1
Clarence Bay, Ascension I 86 D1
Clear R, Vietnam 77 B1
Coban, Guatemala 88 C1
Cochinos, Bahia de, Cuba 91 B1
Coco R, Nicaragua 89 B1
Coleraine, N Ireland 7 C1
Colomb-Béchar, Algeria 34 B1
Colombo, Sri Lanka 52 B3, 53 C3, 60 A2
Comayagua, Honduras 88 D2
Comodoro Rivadavia, Argentina 86 A4
Comilla, Bangladesh 57 D1
Conakry, Guinea-Bissau 41 D2
Condega, Nicaragua 89 A1
Congo, R, Zaire 38 D2, 39 A1
Congo Brazzaville, Zaire 38 D3
Coquilhatville, Zaire 39 A2
Corinth, Greece 3 B2
Corinto, Nicaragua 88 D2
Cox's Bazar, Bangladesh 57 D2
Crater, Aden 22 B3
Cres I, Yugoslavia 2 D4
Crete 3 B3, 15 B4
Cross R, Nigeria 37 B3, 37 D4
Crossmaglen, N Ireland 7 C2
Cuando R, Angola 40 C4

Cuando Cubango, Angola 40 C4
Cuangar, Angola 40 C4
Cuango, Angola 40 B2
Cuango R, Angola 38 D3, 40 B2
Cuanza R, Angola 40 B3
Cuanza-Norte, District Angola 40 A3
Cuanza-Sul, District Angola 40 A3
Cubango, Angola 40 C4
Cuchi, Angola 40 B4
Cuilo R, Angola 40 C3
Cuito, Angola 40 B3
Cuito Cuanavale, Angola 40 C4
Cuito R, Angola 40 C4
Cumberland Bay, South Georgia 86 D3
Cunene R, Angola 40 B4
Cuvelai, Angola 40 B4
Cuvo R, Angola 40 B3
Cuxhaven, West Germany 8 D4
Cyclades Is, Greece 3 B2

Dabat, Ethiopia 46 A3
Dacca, Bangladesh 57 D1
Dahab, Sinai 11 D2
Dahr-el-Baidar Pass, Lebanon 20 C1
Dailekh, Nepal 54 D3
Dairen, China 63 C2
Dakhla, Spanish Sahara 34 A2
Da Lat, Vietnam 79 B4
Dalhousie, India 54 C2
Daman, India 52 B2
Damansky I, USSR 67 D1
Damara Land, Namibia 43 B2
Damascus, Syria 12 D1, 14 D3, 16 B2,
  17 C3, 19 D1
Damba, Angola 40 B2
Damiya Bridge, Jordan 13 D3
Damour, Lebanon 17 B3, 20 A1
Damour R, Lebanon 17 B3
Dan, Israel 13 D1
Danaba, Aden 22 C3
Da Nang, Vietnam 76 B1, 77 D4, 79 B2
Dange R, Angola 40 B2
Danube R, Hungary 2 A2, 4 B2
Daoud, Algeria 33 B1
Darbat, Wadi, Oman 24 C4
Darjeeling, India 55 B3
Dar Lac Plateau, Vietnam 79 B3
Darma Pass, Kashmir 54 D2
Darra Ridge, Oman 24 A4
Dar Sa'ad, Aden 22 B2
Darsana, Bangladesh 57 C1
Darwin, Falkland Is 87 C1
Darwin, Mt, Zimbabwe 49 C2
Das I, Arabian Gulf 28 B2
Daudkandi, Bangladesh 57 D1
Daulat Beg Oldi, Kashmir 54 C1
Daurakpa, Tibet 66 A2
Davao, Philippines 82 B2
David, Panama 89 B4
Debrecen, Hungary 4 D2
Defa, Oman 24 A4
Dehra Dun, India 54 C2
Deir el Quamar, Lebanon 17 B3
Delhi, India 52 B1, 53 B1, 54 C3, 56 B2
Dellys, Algeria 33 A1
Demba, Zaire 39 A3
Demchok, India 54 D2
Deniyaya, Ceylon 60 A2
Deraa, Syria 14 D4
Dera Ismail Khan, Pakistan 56 A1
Deversoir, Egypt 12 C2
Dezful, Iran 27 C3
Dezh Shahpur, Iran 27 B1
Dhala, Yemen 23 A1, 23 A3
Dhalbir, Wadi, Aden 22 C4
Dhali, Cyprus 6 C1
Dhankuta, Nepal 55 A3
Dhekelia, Cyprus 6 D1
Dhernia, Cyprus 6 D1
Dhofar, Prov., Oman 23 C2, 24 A4
Dhola, China 55 C3
Dhubsan, Wadi, Aden 22 D4
Dhura'a, Wadi, Aden 22 D4
Dibrugarh, India 55 D3
Diego Suarez, Madagascar 50 D1
Dien Bien Phu, Vietnam 77 A2, 77 A3, 78 D1
Digboi, India 55 D3
Dihok, Iraq 27 A1

Dili, Indonesia   75 D4
Dilolo, Zaire   39 A4
Dinajpur, Bangladesh   57 C1
Dipolog, Philippines   82 B2
Diredawa, Ethiopia   45 C2
Diriamba, Nicaragua   89 A2
Dirico, Angola   40 C4
Diu, India   52 B2
Diyala, R, Iraq   27 B2
Djkarta, Indonesia   73 B1, 73 C2
Djibouti, Somalia   45 C1
Djidjelli, Algeria   33 B1
Doba, Chad   35 A3
Doha, Arabian Gulf   27 D2, 28 B2
Dombodema, Zimbabwe   49 A4
Domo, Ethiopia   45 D2
Dong Dang, Vietnam   77 C1, 81 D1
Dong Ha, Vietnam   79 A2
Dong Hoi, Vietnam   79 A2
Dong Khe, Vietnam   77 C1
Donguena, Angola   40 B4
Dong Xoai, Vietnam   79 B4
Dorog, Hungary   4 B2
Doshi, Afghanistan   59 C2
Douglas Settlement, Falkland Is   87 C1
Down, Co, N Ireland   7 D2
Downpatrick, N Ireland   7 D2
Do Xa, Vietnam   79 B3
Drama, Greece   3 B1
Draya, Tibet   66 C2
Dresden, East Germany   5 A1
Dubai, Arabian Gulf   23 D1, 28 C2
Duino, Yugoslavia   2 C3
Dukan, Iraq   27 B1
Dundalk, Eire   7 C2
Dungannon, N Ireland   7 C2
Dungiven, N Ireland   7 C1
Dusa Mareb, Somalia   45 C2
Dwarka, India   56 A3

Eagle Passage, Falkland Is   87 B2
Eastern States, India   52 C2
Ebocha, Nigeria   37 A4, 37 C4
Edd, Ethiopia   46 D3
Edinburgh, Scotland   8 D4
Edward L, Zaire   39 C2
Eger, Hungary   4 C1
Eha-Amufu, Nigeria   37 B3
Ehor, Nigeria   37 C1
Eil, Somalia   45 D2
Eilat, Israel   10 C2, 11 D1, 12 D2, 13 B2, 15 D3
Ein Gev, Israel   13 D2
Eizariya, Israel   13 B4
Eket, Nigeria   37 B4
Ekpoma, Nigeria   37 C1
El Aïoun, Spanish Sahara   34 A2, 34 B2
El Al, Israel   14 C4
El Arish, Sinai   10 A2, 11 D1, 12 A2, 12 C2, 13 A2, 15 D3
El Auja, Israel   10 A2
Elbe R, West Germany   2 A1
El Bur, Somalia   45 D2
El Burg, Yemen   24 C1
El Cap, Egypt   14 C1
Elele, Nigeria   37 C4
Elisabethville, Zaire   39 C4
El Jicard, Guatemala   88 D1
El Kuntilla, Sinai   12 B2
El Manzala L, Egypt   11 A4
El Mansura, Egypt   12 B2
El Mersa, Morocco   32 B4
El Minya, Egypt   12 B3
El Naamé, Lebanon   20 A1
Elpitiya, Ceylon   60 A2
El Prado, Guatemala   88 C1
El Sauce, Nicaragua   89 A2
El Tasa, Sinai   14 C1
El Thamad, Sinai   11 D1, 13 A2, 15 D3
El Tina, Egypt   14 C1
El Tur, Sinai   11 D2, 13 A3, 15 D4
Embu, Kenya   47 B2
Enniskillen, N Ireland   7 B2
Enugu, Nigeria   37 A3
Episkopi, Cyprus   6 C2
Equatoria, Prov, Sudan   45 A2
Erigavo, Somalia   45 D1
Ergig R, Chad   35 A3

Eritrea, Prov, Ethiopia   45 B1
Erne, L, N Ireland   7 B2
Er Rumman, Jordan   15 D2
Erzurum, Turkey   25 C1
Esbjerg, Denmark   8 D4
Escondido R, Nicaragua   89 B3
Esquipulas, Nicaragua   89 A2
Esteli, Nicaragua   89 A2
Euphrates R, Iraq   25 C1, 27 B3, 27 C1
Everest, Mt, Nepal   55 A3

Fada, Chad   35 B2
Fahud, Oman   23 D1
Fair I, Scotland   8 D4
Faizabad, Afghanistan   59 C1
Fakeh, Iran   27 C3
Fakfak, New Guinea   73 D1
Faku, China   63 C2
Falkland Is,   86 B4
Falkland Sound, Falkland Is   87 B1
Faluja, Israel   10 D1
Famagusta, Cyprus   6 D1, 19 D1
Fanning Head, Falkland Is   87 C1
Faradje, Zaire   39 C1, 44 D3
Farafangana, Madagascar   50 D2
Farah, Afghanistan   59 A2
Farasan Is, Red Sea   23 A2
Faraya, Lebanon   17 B2
Faridkot, India   57 B1
Faridpur, Bangladesh   57 D1
Farim, Guinea-Bissau   41 C2
Faroes Is, Atlantic Ocean   8 C4
Farsia, Spanish Sahara   34 B2
Faya-Largeau, Chad   35 B2
Fayid, Egypt   12 C2, 14 D2
Fazilka, India   57 B1
Fengsiang, China   62 D3, 63 B4
Fen Ho R, China   63 A3
Feni, Bangladesh   57 D2
Ferfer, Somalia   45 C2
Fermanagh, Co, N Ireland   7 B2
Ferryville, Tunisia   33 C3
Ferozepore, India   57 B1
Fianarantsoa, Madagascar   50 C2
Fida, Yemen   24 C1
Figuig, Morocco   32 C3, 34 C1
Fiq, Syria   13 D2
Firq, Oman   23 C4
Fitri, L, Chad   35 A3
Fitzroy, Falkland Is   87 C1
Fiume, Yugoslavia   2 D4
Flores I, Indonesia   73 C2
Florina, Greece   3 A1
Foochow, China   64 D3, 65 D3
Fort Archambault, Chad   35 B3
Fort-Dauphin, Madagascar   50 C3
Fort Hall, Kenya   47 B2
Fort Lamy, Chad   35 A3
Fort Victoria, Zimbabwe   49 C3, 49 D1
Forur I, Arabian Gulf   28 C2
Fouhsin, China   63 C2
Foul Bay, Falkland Is   87 C2
Fowning, China   63 B4
Fox Bay, Falkland Is   87 B1
Foyle, L, N Ireland   7 C1
Foyle, R, N Ireland   7 C1
Fuhsien, China   62 D3
Fujaireh   28 D2
Fuka, Iraq   27 C3
Fukien, Prov., China   64 C3
Fulacunda, Guinea-Bissau   41 C2
Fushih, China   62 D3
Fuyu, China   63 C1

Gabela, Angola   40 B3
Gabes, Tunisia   33 D2
Gabredare, Ethiopia   45 C2
Gadot, Israel   13 D1
Gadra, Pakistan   56 A2, 57 A2
Gafsa, Tunisia   33 C2
Gago Coutinho, Angola   40 C4
Gakem, Nigeria   36 C3
Galilee, Sea of, Israel   13 D2, 14 C4
Galkayo, Somalia   45 D2
Galle, Ceylon   60 A2
Galwan R, Kashmir   54 C1
Gandak R, India   55 A3
Ganges, R, India   54 C3, 56 B2, 57 C1

Gangtok, Sikkim   55 B3, 66 B2
Gardez, Afghanistan   59 C2
Garissa, Kenya   47 D2
Garmdasht, Iran   26 D3
Gartok, China   54 D2
Gatooma, Zimbabwe   49 B2
Gatow, West Germany   2 A1
Gawara, Iraq   27 B1
Gaza, Sinai, 10 A1, 10 B1, 10 D1, 11 D1, 12 B2, 12 D2, 13 B2, 14 A1
Gaza Strip, Sinai   11 D1
General Machado, Angola   40 B3
George I, Falkland Is   86 B2
Georgetown, Ascension I   86 D1
Gerlogubi, Ethiopia   45 C2
Geunyeli, Cyprus   6 C1
Gezenti, Chad   35 B1
Ghardaia, Algeria   33 A3
Ghazir, Wadi, Oman   24 C4
Ghazni, Afghanistan   59 C2
Ghazze, Lebanon   17 B3
Gidi Pass, Sinai   14 C2
Gilgil, Kenya   47 B2
Gilgit, Kashmir   54 B1, 56 B1
Giradeh, Sinai   13 A2
Githunguri, Kenya   47 B2
Goa, India   52 B3
Goascoran, Honduras   88 D2
Gobabis, Namibia   43 C2
Go Cong, Vietnam   79 A4
God Dere, Ethiopia   45 C2
Golaghat, India   55 C3
Golan Heights, Israel   13 D1, 14 B1, 17 B4
Goldogob, Ethiopia   45 D2
Gondar, Ethiopia   46 A3
Gonen, Israel   13 D1
Goose Green, Falkland Is   87 C1
Gorizia, Italy   2 C3
Gotiwaldov, Czechoslovakia   5 B2
Goulimine, Morocco   32 A4, 34 B1, 34 B2
Gouro, Chad   35 B2
Gracias, Honduras   88 D2
Gracias a Dios, Prov, Nicaragua   89 A1
Grammos, Mt, Greece   3 A1
Granada, Nicaragua   89 A2
Grande de Matagalpe R., Nicaragua   89 A2
Grand Mal, Grenada   90 C4
Grand Reef, Zimbabwe   48 D3
Grand Roy, Grenada   90 C4
Grantham Sound, Falkland Is   87 C1
Great Bitter L, Egypt   14 C2
Great Kabylia Mts, Algeria   33 A1
Great Nama Land, Namibia   43 B2
Great Zab R, Iraq   25 A4, 27 A1
Greco, C, Cyprus   6 D1
Green Patch, Falkland Is   87 C1
Grenville, Grenada   90 D4
Grimsby, England   8 D4
Grootfontein, Namibia   43 B1
Grytviken, South Georgia   86 D3
Gualan, Guatemala   88 D1
Guanajay, Cuba   91 A1
Guantanamo, Cuba   91 D2
Guatemala City, Guatemala   88 C2
Guelma, Algeria   33 B1
Guelta Zemmour, Mauritania   34 B2
Gujarat, State, India   52 B2, 53 B2
Gujrat, Pakistan   54 A4
Gulmarg, Kashmir   54 A3
Gumbang, Indonesia   74 A4
Gurais, Kashmir   54 B2
Gurkha, Nepal   55 A3
Gurreh, Iran   27 D4
Gwanda, Zimbabwe   49 B4
Gwelo, Zimbabwe   49 B3, 49 D1
Gweru, Zimbabwe   49 B3
Gyamda Dzong, Tibet   66 A3
Gyangtse, Tibet   66 B2
Gyöngyös, Hungary   4 C1
Győr, Hungary   4 B2

Habana, Prov, Cuba   91 A1
Habarane, Ceylon   60 A2
Habarut, Oman   23 C2
Habban, Yemen   23 B1, 23 B3
Habib, Oman   23 C4
Habil Sabaha, Aden   22 C3
Hajib, Aden   22 C4

Hadeth, Lebanon   18 B2
Hadong, Korea   68 B4
Hagaif, Oman   24 B4
Ha Giang, Vietnam   77 B1, 81 C1
Hagunia, Spanish Sahara   34 B2
Hai Duong, Vietnam   77 C2
Haifa, Israel   10 A1, 10 C1, 10 D1, 13 B2
Haiphong, Vietnam   77 C2, 79 A1, 81 D1
Hairatan, Afghanistan   59 B1
Haitan Tao I, China   65 D3
Hajjah, Yemen   24 C1
Haj Omran, Iraq   25 D1, 27 B1
Halabja, Iraq   27 B1
Halmahera, I, Indonesia   73 C1
Halul I, Arabian Gulf   28 B2
Halwara, India   56 B1
Hamadan, Iran   25 D1, 27 D1
Hambantota, Ceylon   60 B2
Hamburg, West Germany   8 D4
Hamdan, Prov, Yemen   24 C1
Hamra, Oman   23 C4
Ham Tan, Vietnam   79 A4
Han R, Korea   68 B3, 69 A1, 69 A4, 69 B2
Hangchow, China   63 C4, 64 D3
Hangye, Korea   69 B4, 69 D2
Hankow, China   63 A4, 64 C3
Hanoi, Vietnam   76 B1, 77 C2, 79 A1, 81 D1
Hantan, China   63 A3
Hanyang, China   63 A4
Haon, Israel   13 D2
Haouza, Mauritania   34 B2
Haradh, Yemen   24 C1
Haraincha, Nepal   55 B3
Harar, Ethiopia   45 C2
Harare, Zimbabwe   49 C2, 49 D1
Harbin, China   63 D1
Harbours, Bay of, Falkland Is   87 C2
Hardinge Bridge, Bangladesh   57 C1
Hargeisa, Somalia   45 C2
Harib, Yemen   23 A1, 23 B3, 24 D1
Haris, Lebanon   17 A4
Hartley, Zimbabwe   49 C2
Hasbaya, Lebanon   17 B3
Hauf, Yemen   23 C2, 24 A4
Havana, Cuba   90 A1, 91 A1, 91 B3
Havel R, West Germany   2 A1
Hawfi, Aden   22 D4
Hawr-al-Hammar, Iraq   27 C3
Hawr-al-Hawizah, Iraq   27 C3
Hazm, Yemen   24 D1
Hazmiyé, Lebanon   18 B2
Hebron, Israel   10 A1, 10 D1, 13 C4
Hegyeshalom, Hungary   4 B1
Heimatain, Prov, Yemen   24 C1
Helmand R, Afghanistan   59 B3
Helwan, Egypt   12 B2
Hengyang, China   64 B3
Henrique de Carvalho, Angola   40 C3, 41 B3
Herat, Afghanistan   59 A2
Hermon, Mt, Lebanon   13 D1, 14 C3, 17 B3
Hijar, Oman   23 C4
Hili, Bangladesh   57 C1
Hill 1179, Korea   69 B4
Himachal Pradesh, State, India   53 B1
Himalaya Mts, Nepal   54 D2
Hindu Kush, Afghanistan   59 C2
Hingurakgoda, Ceylon   60 B2
Hirran, Wadi, Yemen   24 C1
Hitaura, Nepal   55 A3
Ho Chi Minh City, Vietnam   80 B3
Hodeidah, Yemen   23 A3, 24 C2
Hodna Mts, Algeria   33 B1
Hoengsong, Korea   69 B4
Hofei, China   63 B4
Hoi An, Vietnam   79 B2
Hoi Xuan, Vietnam   77 B2
Holguin, Cuba   91 D1
Homs, Syria   17 D1
Honan, Prov, China   63 A4
Honduras, Gulf of,   88 D1
Hon Gay, Vietnam   79 A1
Hongchon, Korea   69 B4
Hong Kong   64 C4
Hopeh, Prov, China   63 A2
Hormuz I, Arabian Gulf   28 D2
Hormuz, Strait of, Arabian Gulf   23 D1, 28 D2

Horn, C, Chile   86 A4
Hotse, China   63 A3
Hoveyzeh, Iran   27 C3
Hsia-Men, China   64 D4
Hsiangyuan, China   63 A3
Hsiliao Ho, R, China   63 C1
Hsilanmulun Ho, R, China   63 B1
Hsinanchen, China   63 B3
Hsingning, China   64 C4
Hsinhailing, China   63 B3
Hsuchang, China   63 A3
Huaian, China   63 B4
Huai Ho R, China   63 B4
Huaiyin, China   63 B4
Hualien, Taiwan   65 D4
Huambo, Angola   40 B3, 41 A3
Huambo, District, Angola   40 B3
Hué, Vietnam   77 D4, 79 B2
Hufuf, Saudi Arabia   28 A2
Huila, District, Angola   40 B4
Hula, L, Israel   10 B1
Hull, England   8 D4
Hulutao, China   63 C2
Humbe, Angola   40 B4
Humeidat, Yemen   24 C1
Hunan, Prov, China   62 D4, 64 B3
Hungtze, L, China   63 B4
Hung Yen, Vietnam   77 C2
Hupeh, Prov, China   63 A4, 64 B3
Hurghada, Egypt   12 C3
Husvik, South Georgia   86 D3
Hwaiju, China   63 B2
Hwaiyuan, China   63 B4
Hwange, Zimbabwe   49 A3
Hwang Ho R, China   63 B3
Hyderabad, India   53 B2
Hyderabad, State, India   52 B2
Hyderabad, Pakistan   56 A2, 57 A2
Hyesanjin, Korea   69 A1, 69 B1

Ibadan, Nigeria   36 A3, 37 B1
Ibo, Mozambique   42 C1
Ibri, Oman   23 D1
Ichuan, China   62 D3
Idah, Nigeria   37 A3, 37 D1
Ifni, Morocco   34 B1, 34 B2
Ifon, Nigeria   37 C1
Igarra, Nigeria   37 C1
Ihsien, China   63 C2
Ijebu Ode, Nigeria   37 B1
Ikolo, Nigeria   37 A3
Ikom, Nigeria   37 B3
Ikot Ekpene, Nigeria   37 B4, 37 D4
Ilam, Iran   27 B2
Ilam, Nepal   55 B3
Iloilo, Philippines   82 B1
Ilorin, Nigeria   36 A2
Imjin R, Korea   68 B3, 69 A4, 69 B1
Imo R, Nigeria   37 A4, 37 C4
Inchas, Egypt   12 B2
Inchon, Korea   68 A3, 68 C3, 69 A4
Indus R, Pakistan   54 A2, 54 C1, 56 A1, 57 A1, 57 A2, 59 D2
Inhambane, Mozambique   42 B3
Inje, Korea   69 B4, 69 D2
Insein, Burma   58 B3
Inverness, Scotland   8 C4
Inyazura, Zimbabwe   48 C3
Ipoh, Malaya   72 A2
Iraklion, Crete   3 B3
Irbid, Jordan   15 D1
Irkutsk, USSR   67 C1
Irrawaddy R, Burma   55 D3, 58 A2
Isbouia, Morocco   32 A4
Isele-Uku, Nigeria   37 D1
Isha Baidoa, Somalia   45 C3
Ishkashim, Afghanistan   59 D1
Ishui, China   63 B3
Isiolo, Kenya   47 C2
Islamabad, Kashmir   54 B3, 59 D2
Ismailia, Egypt   11 C1, 12 C2, 13 A2, 14 C1, 14 D1
Isawiya, Israel   13 B3
Itu, Nigeria   37 D4
Iwo, Nigeria   36 A3
Iwon, Korea   69 C1
Izabal, Guatemala   88 D1
Izabal, L, Guatemala   88 D1

Izki, Oman   23 D4

Jadong R, Korea   68 A3
Jadotville, Zaire   39 C4
Jaffa, Israel   10 A1, 10 B1
Jaffna, Ceylon   60 A1
Jaipur Hat, Bangladesh   57 C1
Jaisalmer, India   57 A2
Jalalabad, Afghanistan   59 C2
Jalapa, Guatemala   88 C2
Jamalpur, Bangladesh   57 D1
Jambu, Sarawak   74 D4
Jambur, Iraq   27 B1
Jamestown, Nigeria   37 B4
Jammu, Kashmir   54 B4, 57 B1
Jammu and Kashmir State, India   53 B1
Jamnagar, India   56 A3
Jamuna R, Bangladesh   57 D1
Janakpur, Nepal   55 A3
Jan Mayen I, Arctic Ocean   8 C3
Jannina, Greece   3 A1
Jars, Plain of, Laos   77 A2, 78 D1
Jauf, Prov, Yemen   24 D1
Java, Indonesia   73 B2
Jaydebpur, Bangladesh   57 D1
Jbail, Lebanon   17 B2
Jdaidé, Lebanon   20 B1
Jdira, Mauritania   34 B2
Jdita, Lebanon   20 C1
Jebel Akhdar, Oman   23 D1
Jebel Barouk, Lebanon   20 C1
Jebel Haqla, Aden   22 D4
Jebel Huriyah, Aden   22 D4
Jebel Knisse, Lebanon   20 C1
Jebel Libni, Sinai   12 A2, 12 C2, 13 A2
Jebel Ouarksis, Morocco   34 B2
Jebel Widina, Aden   22 D4
Jehol, China   63 B2
Jenin, Israel   13 C2
Jerash, Jordan   15 D2
Jerusalem, Israel   10 A1, 10 C1, 10 D1, 12 D1, 13 A4, 13 C4, 14 B1, 19 D1
Jesselton, Malaysia   73 B1
Jessore, Bangladesh   57 C2
Jezzine, Lebanon   16 A2, 17 B3
Jhangar, Kashmir   54 A4
Jhapa, Nepal   55 B3
Jhelum, Pakistan   54 B2
Jhelum R, Pakistan   54 B2, 56 B1, 57 A1
Jibjat, Oman   24 C3
Jigjiga, Ethiopia   45 C2
Jihana, Yemen   24 D1
Jihlava, Czechoslovakia   5 B2
Jinotega, Nicaragua   89 A2
Jinotepe, Nicaragua   89 A2
Jiquilisco, El Salvador   88 D2
Jiye, Lebanon   17 B3
Jizan, Saudi Arabia   24 C1
João Belo, Mozambique   42 A4
Jodhpur, India   56 B2, 57 B2
Jogjakarta, Indonesia   73 D2
Johnson's Harbour, Falkland Is   87 C1
Johore Bahru, Malaya   72 B4
Johore, State, Malaya   72 B3
Jordan, R, Jordan   10 B1, 13 D3, 15 D2
Jorhat, India   55 C3
Jounie, Lebanon   17 B2
Juba, Sudan   45 A2
Juba R, Somalia   45 C3
Juffa, Oman   24 D4
Jukao, China   63 C4
Jullundur, India   54 C2
Jumla, Nepal   54 D2
Jumna R, India   54 C3
Junagadh, India   56 A3
Junagadh, State, India   52 A2
Junction Gate, Zimbabwe   48 D4
Jutiápa, Guatemala   88 C2
Jyekundo, China   66 C1

Kabrit, Egypt   12 C2
Kabul, Afghanistan   59 C2
Kadisha, Lebanon   17 C2
Kaesong, Korea   68 A3, 69 A1, 69 A4, 69 D4
Kafr el Mar, Syria   13 D2
Kafr Naffakh, Syria   13 D1
Kafr Shams, Syria   14 D3
Kahuta, Pakistan   57 B1

Kaifeng, China   63 A3
Kailali, Nepal   54 D3
Kairouan, Tunisia   33 D1
Kaiyuan, China   63 C2
Kajokaji, Sudan   45 A2
Kakopetria, Cyprus   6 C1
Kalabakan, Malaysia   75 D1
Kalait, Chad   35 B2
Kalat, Pakistan   56 A2
Kalamai, Greece   3 A2
Kalémié, Zaire   39 C3
Kalgan, China   63 A2
Kaliakar, Bangladesh   57 D1
Kalimantan, Indonesia   75 D2
Kalimantan Prov, Indonesia   73 B1, 74 C4
Kalimpong, India   66 B2
Kalkilya, Israel   13 B3
Kallafo, Ethiopia   45 C2
Kalwapur, Nepal   54 D3
Kamah, Oman   23 C4
Kamaran I, Red Sea   23 A3
Kambing I, Indonesia   75 C4
Kambos, Cyprus   6 C1
Kamina, Zaire   39 B3
Kampong Cham, Cambodia   79 A4
Kampot, Cambodia   81 C4
Kanchow, China   64 C3
Kanchuan, China   62 D3
Kandahar, Afghanistan   59 B3
Kandal, Cambodia   81 D4
Kandy, Ceylon   52 C3, 60 A2
Kangnung, Korea   68 B3, 69 C4
Kangping, China   63 C2
Kanjarkot, India   56 A2
Kano, Nigeria   36 C1
Kanowit, Sarawak   74 D3
Kansong, Korea   69 B4, 69 D1, 69 D2
Kantara, Sinai   11 C1, 12 C2, 13 A2, 14 C1, 15 C3
Kaocheng, China   63 A3
Kaohsiung, Taiwan   65 D4
Kaomi, China   63 B3
Kaotsi Rly, China   63 B3
Kapoeta, Sudan   45 A2
Kaposvár, Hungary   4 B2
Kapyong, Korea   69 B4
Karachi, Pakistan   52 A2, 56 A2
Karakal, India   52 B3
Karakoram Mts, Kashmir   54 C1
Karakoram Pass, Kashmir   54 C1
Karameh, Jordan   13 D3
Karasburg, Namibia   43 C3
Karavas, Cyprus   6 C1
Kardhitsa, Greece   3 A1
Kargil, Kashmir   54 C1, 56 B1, 57 B1
Kariba, Zimbabwe   49 B2
Kariba L, Zambia   49 A2
Karkheh R, Iran   27 C2
Karlovy Vary, Czechoslovakia   5 A1
Karora, Ethiopia   46 B1
Karouba, Tunisia   33 C3
Karun R, Iran   26 D3, 27 C3
Kasai R, Zaire   39 A3
Kashmir,   *see* Jammu and Kashmir
Kasserine, Tunisia   33 C1
Kasur, Pakistan   56 B1
Kataragama, Ceylon   60 B2
Kathiawar, State, India   52 A2
Kathua, India   54 C2
Katire, Sudan   45 A2
Katmandu, Nepal   55 A3, 66 A2
Katowice, Poland   5 C1
Kayfoun, Lebanon   17 B3
Kazakhstan SSR, USSR   67 B1
Kecskemét, Hungary   4 C2
Kedah, State, Malaya   72 A2
Keelung, Taiwan   65 D3
Keetmanshoop, Namibia   43 B2
Kegalia, Ceylon   60 A2
Kekirawa, Ceylon   60 A2
Kelantan, State, Malaya   72 B2
Kelantan R, Malaya   72 B2
Kent, Mt, Falkland Is   87 C1
Kenya, Mt, Kenya   47 B2
Kep, Cambodia   81 C4
Keppel I, Falkland Is   87 B1
Kepulauan Is, Indonesia   75 C4
Kerala, State, India   53 B3

Keran, Kashmir   54 A2
Keren, Ethiopia   46 B2
Kermanshah, Iran   25 D1, 27 C2
Keyfoun, Lebanon   20 B1
Kfar Falous, Lebanon   17 B3
Kfar Matta, Lebanon   20 A1
Kfar, Melhkl, Lebanon   17 B3
Kfar Szold, Israel   13 D1
Khabarovsk, USSR   67 D1
Khadr, Israel   13 A4
Khaimah, Arabian Gulf   28 C2
Khaldé, Lebanon   17 B3, 20 A1
Khalkis, Greece   3 B2
Khanaquin, Iraq   25 D1, 27 B2
Khanja, Yemen   24 D1
Khan Yunis, Sinai   10 A1, 12 A2, 13 A2
Kharg I, Persian Gulf   27 D4, 28 A1
Khasab   28 D2
Khartoum, Sudan   45 A1
Khatima Pass, Sinai   14 C1
Khemarak, Cambodia   81 C4
Khem Karan, India   56 B1, 57 B1
Khenchela, Algeria   33 B1
Khe Sanh, Vietnam   79 A2
Khetal, Bangladesh   57 C1
Khinzemane, India   55 C3
Khirbet Rouha, Lebanon   17 B3
Khisfin, Syria   13 D2
Khojak Pass, Afghanistan   59 B3
Khokhropar, Pakistan   56 A2
Khong, Laos   79 A3
Khong Sedone, Laos   79 A2
Khormaksar, Aden   22 B2
Khorramabad, Iran   27 C2
Khorramshahr, Iran   26 D3, 27 C3
Khosrowabad, Iran   26 D4
Khost, Afghanistan   59 C2
Khotang, Nepal   55 A3
Khowlan, Prov, Yemen   24 C1
Khulna, Bangladesh   57 C2
Khuzestan, Prov, Iran   27 C3
Khyber Pass, Afghanistan   59 D2
Kiambu, Kenya   47 B2
Kiangsi, Prov, China   63 A4, 64 C3
Kiangsu, Prov, China   63 B4
Kidney I, Falkland Is   87 D1
Kienhsien, China   62 D3
Kienyang, China   62 D3
Kifri, Iraq   27 B2
Kikwit, Zaire   39 A3
Kimpo, Korea   68 D3, 69 C2, 69 A4
Kindu, Zaire   39 B2
Kingchwan, China   62 D3
King George Bay, Falkland Is   87 B1
Kingston, Jamaica   90 B2
King Ho R, China   62 D3
Kinshasa, Zaire   38 D3, 40 B2, 41 A3
Kingsiang, China   63 B3
Kintai, China   63 D1
Kipushi, Zaire   39 C4
Kirin, China   63 D1
Kirkuk, Iraq   25 B4, 25 D1, 27 A1
Kisangani, Zaire   39 B2
Kishenganga R, Kashmir   54 A2
Kishtwar, Kashmir   54 C1
Kiukiang, China   63 B4, 64 C3
Kivu, L, Zaire   39 C2
Kling Kang Mts, Indonesia   74 C4
Kluan, Sarawak   74 B4
Kluang, Malaya   72 B4
Kodok, Sudan   45 A2
Kohima, India   55 C3
Koi Sanjaq, Iraq   25 B4
Kokkina, Cyprus   6 B1
Kolwezi, Zaire   39 B4
Komati Poort, South Africa   42 A4
Komotini, Greece   3 B1
Kompong Cham, Cambodia   81 D4
Kompong Chhnang, Cambodia   81 C4
Kompong Som, Cambodia   81 C4
Kompong Speu, Cambodia   81 D4
Kompong Thom, Cambodia   81 D4
Kongka la Pass, Kashmir   54 C1
Kongolo, Zaire   39 C3
Konitsa, Greece   3 A1
Konji, Korea   68 B4
Kontum, Vietnam   79 B3
Koper, Yugoslavia   2 C4

Kophinou, Cyprus   6 C1
Korat, Thailand   78 D3
Kordestan, Prov, Iran   27 B1
Kormakiti, Cape, Cyprus   6 C1
Körös R, Hungary   4 C2
Koro Toro, Chad   35 B2
Košice, Czechoslovakia   5 D2
Kota Bharu, Malaya   72 B2
Kota Kinabulu, Sabah   73 B1
Kotchandpur, Bangladesh   57 C1
Kotli, Kashmir   54 A4
Koukaba, Lebanon   17 B3
Kowpangtse, China   63 C2
Krakow, Poland   5 C1
Kratie, Cambodia   79 A3, 81 D4
Krek, Cambodia   81 D4
Krk I, Yugoslavia   2 D4
Ktima, Cyprus   6 B2
Kuala Belait, Brunei   75 A1
Kuala Lumpur, Malaya   72 B3
Kuang-Chou, China   64 B4
Kuantan, Malaya   72 B3
Kuchar, Yemen   24 C1
Kuching, Sarawak   73 B1, 74 B4
Kufow, China   63 B3
Kum R, Korea   68 B4
Kumbum, China   66 D1
Kumchong, Korea   68 B4
Kumhwa, Korea   69 A4, 69 D1, 69 D2
Kumira, Bangladesh   57 D2
Kumsong, Korea   69 B4
Kunar R, Afghanistan   59 D2
Kunduz, Afghanistan   59 C1
Kuneitra, Syria   13 D1, 14 C3, 17 B4
Kungchuling, China   63 C1
Kunsan, Korea   68 A4
Kuntilla, Sinai   11 D1, 13 B2, 15 D3
Kunuri, Korea   69 B1
Kupang, Indonesia   75 C4
Kupeikou, China   63 B2
Kurunegala, Ceylon   60 A2
Kushka, USSR   59 A2
Kushtia, Bangladesh   57 C1
Kutch, State, India   52 A2
Kuwait   27 C4, 28 A1
Kwale, Nigeria   37 D2
Kwangju, Korea   68 B4
Kwangsi, Prov, China   64 A4
Kwangtung, Prov, China   64 B4
Kwara, Prov, Nigeria   36 A2
Kweilin, China   64 B4
Kwekwe, Zimbabwe   49 B3
Kwilu R, Zaire   39 A3
Kykko Monastery, Cyprus   6 C1
Kyrenia, Cyprus   6 C1
Kyrenia Mts, Cyprus   6 C1

Labe, Guinea-Bissau   41 D2
Labuan I, Sabah   75 B1
La Cruz, Costa Rica   89 A3
Ladakh Mts, Kashmir   54 C1
La Drang R, Vietnam   79 B3
Laghouat, Algeria   33 A2
Lagos, Nigeria   36 A3, 37 A1
La Güera, Spanish Sahara   34 A2
Lahej, Yemen   23 A2
Lahore, Pakistan   52 B1, 54 B2, 56 B1, 57 B1, 59 D3
Lai, Chad   35 A3
Laibach, Yugoslavia   2 D3
Lai Chau, Vietnam   77 A1, 81 C1
Lai Khe, Vietnam   80 B3
Laiochung, China   63 C2
Laiwu, China   63 B3
Laiyang, China   63 C3
Laksham, Bangladesh   57 D2
Lalamusa, Pakistan   54 A4
Lalmanirhat, Bangladesh   57 C1
Lamia, Greece   3 A2
Lanak Pass, Kashmir   54 D1
Lanchow, China   66 D1
Lanfeng, China   63 A3
Lang Son, Vietnam   77 C1, 81 D1
Lang Vei, Laos   79 A2
Lao Kai, Vietnam   77 B1, 81 C1
La Paz, Bolivia   85 B2
Lapithos, Cyprus   6 C1
La Plata, Argentina   86 A3

Larak I, Arabian Gulf   28 D2
Lari, Kenya   47 B2
Larissa, Greece   3 A1
Larnaca, Cyprus   6 D1
Larne, N Ireland   7 D1
Las Anod, Somalia   45 D2
Las Villas, Prov, Cuba   91 B1
Latrun, Israel   13 B4
La Union, El Salvador   88 D2
Lautem, Indonesia   75 D4
Lawas, Brunei   75 C1
Lebanon, Mt, Grenada   90 D4
Lebanon, Mts of, Lebanon   17 B3
Lebouriate, Morocco   34 B2
Leça, Indonesia   75 D4
Lefka, Cyprus   6 C1
Lefkoniko, Cyprus   6 D1
Leh, Kashmir   54 C1, 56 B1
Leipzig, E Germany   5 A1
Lekef, Tunisia   33 C1
Lempa R, El Salvador   88 D2
León, Nicaragua   89 A2
Léopoldville, Zaire   38 D3
Lesbos, I, Greece   3 C1
Lesser Zab R, Iraq   25 A4, 27 A1
Lethoom, Aden   22 D4
Leyte I, Philippines   82 B1
Lharigao, Tibet   66 C2
Lhasa, Tibet   66 A3, 66 B2
Lho Dzong, Tibet   66 C2
Liao Ho, R, China   63 C2
Liaotung, Gulf of, China   63 C2
Liaotung Pen, China   63 C2
Liaoyang, China   63 C2
Liberia, Costa Rica   89 A3
Lien R, China   63 B3
Lienshui, China   63 B4
Lima, Peru   85 A2, 91 B4
Limassol, Cyprus   6 C2, 11 D3
Limbang, Sarawak   75 B1
Limón, Costa Rica   89 B3
Limpopo R, South Africa   42 A3
Linfen, China   63 A3
Linggadjati, Indonesia   73 C2
Lingling, China   64 B3
Lingpi, China   63 B4
Linyi, China   63 B3
Linyu, China   62 D3
Linz, Austria   5 A2
Lisburn, N Ireland   7 D2
Litani R, Lebanon   17 B3, 19 C1
Little Kabylia Mts, Algeria   33 B1
Little Aden, Aden   22 A3
Little Quemoy I, China   65 C4
Liuan, China   63 B4
Liuchow, China   64 A4
Lively I, Falkland Is   87 C1
Liverpool, England   8 D4
Livingstone, Zimbabwe   48 D2
Ljubljana, Yugoslavia   2 D3
Lobit, Angola   40 A3
Loc Chao, Vietnam   79 A1
Lochwan, China   62 D3
Loemba, L, Zaire   39 B3
Lohit R, India   55 D3
Loka, Sudan   45 A2
Lomani R, Zaire   39 B2
Lombok I, Indonesia   73 B2
Lomphat, Cambodia   81 D4
London, England   8 D4
Londonderry, N Ireland   7 A1, 7 C1
Londonderry Co, N Ireland   7 C1
Longdon, Mt, Falkland Is   87 D2
Longju, India   55 C3
Long Seridan, Sarawak   75 B2
Long Thien, Laos   78 D2
Loronyo, Sudan   45 A2
Los Angeles, USA   91 A3
Los Chiles, Costa Rica   89 A3
Los Palos, Indonesia   75 D4
Lourenço Marques, Mozambique   42 A4
Low, Mt, Falkland Is   87 D2
Lowestoft, England   8 D4
Loyang, China   63 A3
Lualaba R, Zaire   39 B3
Luanda, Angola   40 A2, 41 A3
Luanda, District, Angola   40 A3, 40 C3
Luang Prabang, Laos   76 A1, 77 A2, 78 D1

Luangue R, Angola   40 C2
Luau, Angola   40 B3
Lubango, Angola   40 A4
Lublin, Poland   5 D1
Lubong Tanah, Malaysia   74 D4
Lucknow, India   54 D3
Lüderitz, Namibia   43 B2
Ludhiana, India   54 C2
Luena, Angola   40 C3
Luena R, Angola   40 C3
Lugenda R, Tanzania   42 B1
Luke the Gook's Castle, Korea   69 B3
Luluabourg, Zaire   39 A3
Lumumbashi, Zaire   39 C4
Lundu, Sarawak   74 A4
Lunghai Rly, China   63 A3
Lungué-Bungo R, Angola   40 C3
Lurgan, N Ireland   7 D2
Luristan, Prov, Iran   27 B2
Lusaka, Zambia   49 A1
Lusambo, Zaire   39 B3
Lushun, China   63 C2
Luso, Angola   40 C3, 41 B3
Lutong, Sarawak   75 A1
Luxor, Egypt   12 C4
Luzon I, Philippines   82 A1
Lvov, USSR   5 D1
Lysi, Cyprus   6 D1

Ma'alla, Aden   22 B3
Maaten es Sarra, Libya   35 B1
Mabda, Yemen   24 C1
Mabhès, Mauritania   34 B2
Macedonia, Prov, Yugoslavia   3 A1
Madaba, Jordan   15 D2
Madai, Chad   35 B2
Madhya Pradesh, State, India   53 B2
Madina do Boé, Guinea-Bissau   41 C2
Madium, Indonesia   73 D2
Madras, India   52 C3, 53 C3
Madras, State, India   53 B3
Madura I, Indonesia   73 B2
Mafraq, Jordan   12 D1, 15 D2
Magelang, Indonesia   73 D2
Magellan Strait, Chile   86 A4
Magura, Bangladesh   57 C1
Magwe, Burma   58 B2
Magwe, Sudan   45 A2
Mahabad, Iran   27 B1
Mahagi, Zaire   39 D1
Maharastra, State, India   53 B2
Mahé, India   52 B3
Mahfid, Yemen   23 B1
Mahnaqa, Lebanon   17 B2
Maho, Ceylon   60 A2
Maidi, Yemen   24 C1
Maiduguri, Nigeria   36 D1
Majnoon, I, Iraq   26 C3
Majunga, Madagascar   50 C1
Makale, Ethiopia   46 B3
Makassar, Indonesia   73 C1
Makurdi, Nigeria   36 C2, 37 B2
Malacca, Malaya   72 B3
Malahah, Aden   22 C3
Malakal, Sudan   45 A2
Malanje, Angola   40 B3
Malanje, District, Angola   40 B3
Malatya, Turkey   25 C1
Maliana, Indonesia   75 D4
Malvernia, Mozambique   42 A3, 49 D4
Mamurah, Oman   24 C4
Manado, Indonesia   73 C1
Managua, Nicaragua   89 A2
Managua, L, Nicaragua   89 A2
Manamah, Bahrein   28 B2
Manatuto, Indonesia   75 D4
Manawar, Kashmir   54 A4
Manchuria, Prov, China   63 C1
Mandalay, Burma   58 B2
Mandali, Iraq   27 B2
Manila, Philippines   82 A1
Manipur, State, India   52 D2, 53 D2
Manokwari, New Guinea   73 D1
Manono, Zaire   39 C3
Mansoura, Cyprus   6 B1
Manston, Oman   24 A4
Mao, Chad   35 A3
Mao Khe, Vietnam   77 C2

Mapande Mts, Zimbabwe   48 D4
Mapien, Yemen   24 C1
Mapu, Sarawak   74 B4
Maputo, Mozambique   42 A4
Maquela do Zombo, Angola   40 B2
Marabada Hills, Zimbabwe   48 C4
Maragheh, Iran   25 D1
Mar Elias, Israel   13 A4
Mari, Cyprus   6 C2
Marib, Yemen   23 B3, 24 D1
Maridi, Sudan   44 D2
Mariental, Namibia   43 B2
Marjayoun, Lebanon   17 B4
Marol, Kashmir   54 C1
Marrakech, Morocco   34 B1
Marromeu, Mozambique   42 B2
Marsabit, Kenya   47 C1
Marudi, Malaysia   75 A2
Masada, Syria   13 D1
Masan, Korea   68 B4, 69 A2
Masaya, Nicaragua   89 A2
Mascara, Algeria   32 C1
Mas Hagar, Aden   22 C4
Masshad, Iran   59 A1
Massaguet, Chad   35 A3
Massakory, Chad   35 A3
Massawa, Ethiopia   45 B1, 46 B2
Matadi, Zaire   38 D3, 40 A2
Matagalpa, Nicaragua   89 A2
Matala, Angola   40 B4
Matanzas, Cuba   91 B1
Matanzas, Prov, Cuba   91 B1
Matara, Ceylon   60 A2
Matara, Yemen   24 C1
Matil Fawq, Aden   22 C4
Matsu, China   64 D3, 65 D3
Maubara, Indonesia   75 D4
Maur, Wadi, Yemen   24 C1
Mavangwe Hills, Zimbabwe   48 C3
Mavinga, Angola   40 C4
Maymyo, Burma   58 B2
Mazar-i-Sharif, Afghanistan   59 B1
Mazraa (Beirut), Lebanon   18 A1
Mazrat Beit Jan, Israel   14 C3
Mbandaka, Zaire   39 A2
Mdeirej, Lebanon   20 B1
Mecheria, Algeria   32 C2
Medan, Indonesia   73 A1
Medenine, Tunisia   33 D2
Medinat al Haq, Oman   24 C4
Meerut, India   54 C2
Mehran, Iran   27 B2
Mehsàna, India   56 A3
Meihokow, China   63 D2
Meihsien, China   64 C4
Meiktila, Burma   58 A2
Mejdel Anjar, Lebanon   17 C3
Mekong Delta, Vietnam   79 A4, 80 B4
Mekong R.,   66 D2, 77 B3, 78 C1, 79 A2, 81 D4
Melilla, Morocco   34 B1
Melousha, Cyprus   6 C1
Melsetter, Zimbabwe   48 D4, 49 D3
Mengyin, China   63 B3
Menongue, Angola   40 B4
Mentekab, Malaya   72 B3
Menzel-abd-er-Rahmane, Tunisia   33 D3
Menzel-Bourgiba, Tunisia   33 C3
Menzel-Djemil, Tunisia   33 D3
Merauke, Indonesia   73 D2
Mers el Kébir, Algeria   32 C1
Mersing, Malaya   72 B3
Meru, Kenya   47 C2
Metsavo, Greece   3 A1
Meyrouba, Lebanon   17 B2
Mezer, Israel   13 C2
M'Gasen, Mauritania   34 B2
Mhaldee, Lebanon   17 B3
Michih, China   62 D3
Mid-Western Prov, Nigeria   36 B3
Migyitun, China   55 C2
Mimot, Cambodia   81 D4
Mindanao I, Philippines   82 B2
Mindolling, Tibet   66 A3
Mindoro I, Philippines   82 A1
Mingaladon, Burma   58 B3
Mirbat, Oman   23 D2, 24 D4
Miri, Malaysia   75 A1
Mirpur, Kashmir   54 B1

Mirzapur, Bangladesh   57 D1
Miskolc, Hungary   4 C1
Misrah, Wadi, Aden   22 C4
Mitla Pass, Sinai   14 C2
Miyun, China   63 B2
Moatize, Mozambique   42 B2
Moçambique, Mozambique   42 C2
Moçâmedes, Angola   40 A4, 41 A3
Moçâmedes, District, Angola   40 A4
Mocha, Yemen   23 A3, 24 C2
Moc Hoa, Vietnam   80 A3
Mocimboa da Praia, Mozambique   42 C1
Mocuba, Mozambique   42 B2
Mogadishu, Somalia   45 C3
Mogga, Aden   22 C4
Mokpo, Korea   68 A4, 69 A2
Mombasa, Kenya   47 D4
Monaragala, Ceylon   60 B2
Mon Cay, China   64 A4, 77 D1, 81 D1
Monfalcone, Italy   2 C3
Mongalla, Sudan   45 A2
Mongkus, Sarawak   74 B4
Mongo, Chad   35 B3
Mongua, Angola   40 B4
Monou, Chad   35 B2
Montevideo, Uruguay   85 C3, 86 B3
Monywa, Burma   58 A2
Moody Brook R, Falkland Is   87 C2
Mora, Cyprus   6 C1
Morales, Guatemala   88 D1
Moramanga, Madagascar   50 D2
Morocon, Honduras   89 A1
Morondava, Madagascar   50 C2
Morotai I, Indonesia   73 C1
Morphou, Cyprus   6 C1
Mosonmagyaróvár, Hungary   4 B1
Mosquito Coast, Nicaragua   89 B1
Mosul, Iraq   25 A4, 25 D1, 27 A1, 27 C1
Moukhtara, Lebanon   17 B3
Moulmein, Burma   58 B3
Moundou, Chad   35 A3
Moung Khoua, Laos   77 A2
Mount Zion, Israel   13 A4
Moussoro, Chad   35 A3
Moxico, Angola   40 C3
Moyale, Kenya   45 B3
Moyo, Uganda   45 A3
Mtanda Range, Zimbabwe   48 C3
Muar, Malaya   72 B4
Mudia, Yemen   23 B1
Mudugh, Reg, Somali Rep   45 D2
Mugasyl, Oman   24 B4
Mukalla, Yemen   23 B3
Mukden, China   63 C2
Mukur, Afghanistan   59 C2
Mullaghmore, Eire   7 B2
Mullet Creek R, Falkland Is.   87 C2
Multan, Pakistan   56 A1, 57 A1
Mungla, Bangladesh   57 C2
Mungyong, Korea   68 B4
Munsan, Korea   69 A4, 69 C1, 69 C2, 69 D4
Muong Sing, Laos   78 C1
Muong Suoi, Laos   78 D1
Murree, Pakistan   54 B1
Murrel R, Falkland Is   87 C1
Musandam Pen, Oman   23 D1, 28 D2
Muscat, Oman   23 D1
Musi, Sarawak   74 B4
Musian, Iran   27 C3
Musjed Soleyman, Iran   27 C3
Mussende, Angola   40 B3
Mutarara, Mozambique   42 B2
Mutare, Zimbabwe   49 D3
Muti, Oman   23 D4
Mutumbara, Zimbabwe   48 D3
Muzaffarabad, Kashmir   54 B1
Mweiga, Kenya   47 B2
Mweru, L, Zaire   39 C4
Myera, Mali   42 B1
Myitkyina, Burma   58 B1
My Lai, Vietnam   79 B3
Mymensingh, Bangladesh   57 D1
Mysore, State, India   52 B3, 53 B3
My Tho, Vietnam   79 A4, 80 B4
Mzick, Mauritania   34 B2

Nabatiyeh, Lebanon   17 B4
Nabi Chit, Lebanon   20 D1

Nabiyu I, Arabian Gulf   28 C2
Nablus, Israel   10 A1, 10 C1, 13 C3
Nabq, Sinai   11 D2
Nacala, Mozambique   42 C1
Nacaome, Honduras   88 D2
Nachingwea, Tanzania   42 C1
Naepyong, Korea   69 B4, 69 D2
Nagaland, India   53 D2
Nagar Parkar, Pakistan   57 A2
Nagchuka, Tibet   66 B2
Nagykanizsa, Hungary   4 B2
Nahariya, Israel   10 A1
Naheez, Wadi, Oman   24 C4
Nairobi, Kenya   47 B3
Naivasha, Kenya   47 B3
Najran, Saudi Arabia   23 A2, 24 C1
Nafka, Ethiopia   46 B1
Na Khang, Laos   78 D1
Nakhl, Sinai   11 D1, 12 A2, 13 A2, 15 D3
Nakhon Phanom, Thailand   78 D2
Nakuru, Kenya   47 B2
Nam Bac, Laos   78 D1
Nam Dinh, Vietnam   77 C2
Namibe, Angola   40 A4, 41 A3
Nam Oum, R, Vietnam   77 A4
Nampula, Mozambique   42 C2
Nam Tha, Laos   78 D1
Namwon, Korea   69 A2
Nanchang, China   64 C3
Nanchi I, China   64 D3
Nanhsiung, China   64 C4
Nanking, China   63 B4
Nankow, China   63 B2
Nanning, China   64 A4
Nantung, China   63 C4
Nanukan I, Indonesia   75 D1
Nanyang, L, China   63 B3
Nanyuki, Kenya   47 B2
Naqqura, Israel   16 A2, 17 A4
Narayanganj, Bangladesh   57 D1
Naro Moru, Kenya   47 B2
Narsingdi, Bangladesh   57 D1
Narvik, Norway   8 D3
Na Sam, Vietnam   77 B2
Nasir, Sudan   45 A2
Nasirabad, Bangladesh   57 D1
Natanya, Israel   10 A1, 10 D1
Natkong R, Korea   68 B4
Naushera, Kashmir   54 A4
Nautanwa, India   55 A3
Nazareth, Israel   10 A1, 10 C1, 13 C2
Nazwa, Oman   23 C4, 23 D1
N'Djamena, Chad   35 A3
Ndola, Zambia   39 C4
Neac Luong, Vietnam   80 A3
Neagh, L, N Ireland   7 C2
Nedong, Tibet   66 A3, 66 B2
Negev, Reg, Israel   10 D2
Négrine, Algeria   33 C2
Negri Sembilan, State, Malaya   72 B3
Negros I, Philippines   82 B1
Neisse R, Poland   2 B2
Nembrala, Indonesia   75 C4
New I, Falkland Is   87 A1
New Orleans, USA   91 B3
Newry, N Ireland   7 D2
New York, USA   91 B2
Ngangala, Sudan   45 A2
N'Giva, Angola   40 B4
Nglia Lo, Vietnam   77 B1
Ngunza, Angola   40 A3
Nha Trang, Vietnam   79 B3
Niah, Sarawak   75 A2
Nicaragua, L, Nicaragua   89 A3
Nicosia, Cyprus   6 C1, 11 D3
Nienchuangchi, China   63 B3
Niger R, Nigeria   36 B2, 37 A3, 37 C4, 37 D1
Nilang, India   54 D2
Nimule, Sudan   45 A3
Ningpo, China   63 C4, 64 D3
Ninh Binh, Vietnam   77 C2
Nisab, Yemen   23 B1
Nitsana, Israel   15 D3
Nkalagu, Nigeria   37 B3
Nnewi, Nigeria   37 C4
No, L, Sudan   44 D2
Noakhali, Bangladesh   57 D2
Nonsan, Korea   68 B4

North Arm, Falkland Is   87 B2
North Central Prov, Nigeria   36 B2
North Eastern Prov, Nigeria   36 D1
North Lakhimpur, India   55 C3
North West Frontier Prov, Pakistan   52 B1
North Western Prov, Nigeria   36 A1
Nova Chaves, Angola   40 C3
Nova Freixo, Mozambique   42 B1
Nouakchott, Mauritania   34 A2
Nova Lisboa, Angola   40 B3, 41 A3
Novo Redondo, Angola   40 A3, 41 A3
Nsukka, Nigeria   36 B3, 37 A3
Nuanetsi R, Zimbabwe   42 A3
Nueiba, Sinai   15 D4
Nueva Segovia, Prov, Nicaragua   89 A2
Nugal, Region, Somalia   45 D2
Nungan, China   63 D1
Nuqayr, Aden   22 C4
Nuwara Eliya, Ceylon   60 A2
Nyàmandhlovu, Zimbabwe   49 A3
Nyanda, Zimbabwe   49 C3
Nyanyadzi, Zimbabwe   48 D4
Nyasa, L, Zambia   39 D4, 42 B1
Nyeri, Kenya   47 B2
Nyerol, Sudan   45 A2
Nzara, Sudan   44 D2

Oban, Nigeria   37 B4
Obbia, Somalia   45 D2
Obilagu, Nigeria   37 A4
Obubra, Nigeria   37 B3
Ocotal, Nicaragua   89 A2
Octepeque, Honduras   88 D2
Ocussi Ambeno, Indonesia   75 C4
Oder R, Poland   2 B2
Ofusu, Nigeria   37 C1
Ogaden, Reg, Ethiopia   45 C2
Ogoja, Nigeria   37 B3
Ogugu, Nigeria   37 A3
Oguta, Nigeria   37 C4
Ogwashi Uku, Nigeria   37 D1
Ohaba, Nigeria   37 C4
Ohafia, Nigeria   37 B4, 37 D4
Ohopoho, Namibia   40 B4
Ojhakati, Namibia   40 B4
Okahandja, Namibia   43 B2
Okene, Nigeria   37 C1
Okigwe, Nigeria   37 A4
Okitpupa, Nigeria   37 B1
Olakwo, Nigeria   37 C4
Old Baldy, Mt, Korea   69 A4
Olives, Mount of, Israel   13 B4
Olomuc, Czechoslovakia   5 B2
Omagh, N Ireland   7 C2
Oman, Gulf of,   28 D2
Omararu, Mozambique   43 B1
Ondangua, Namibia   40 B4, 43 B1
Ondo, Nigeria   37 B1
Ongjin, Korea   68 A3
Onitsha, Nigeria   36 B3, 37 A3, 37 D1
Opari, Sudan   45 A2
Opobo, Nigeria   37 A4
Oradea, Romania   4 D2
Oran, Algeria   32 C1, 34 C1
Orashi R, Nigeria   37 A4
Ore, Nigeria   36 A3, 37 B1
Oriente, Prov, Cuba   91 D1
Orinoco R, Venezuela   85 B1
Orissa, State India   52 C2, 53 C2
Orkney Is, Scotland   8 D4
Orleansville, Algeria   32 D1
Orlu, Nigeria   37 A4, 37 C4
Oron, Nigeria   37 B4
Osan, Korea   68 B3
Oshogbo, Nigeria   36 A3
Oslo, Norway   8 D4
Ostrava, Czechoslovakia   5 C1
Otjiwarongo, Namibia   43 B1
Ottawa, Canada   91 B2
Ouarsenis Mts, Algeria   32 D1
Oubangui, R, Central African Rep.   39 A1
Oudh, State, India   52 B1
Oujda, Morocco   32 C2
Oum Chalouba, Chad   35 B2
Oum Hadjer, Chad   35 B3
Ounianga Kébir, Chad   35 B2
Ouri, Chad   35 B1
Ovamboland, Region, Namibia   40 B4, 43 B1

Romani, Sinai　11 C1, 13 A2, 14 C1, 15 C3
Rosh Pinna, Israel　13 D1
Roti I, Indonesia　75 C4
Rovigno, Yugoslavia　2 C4
Rovuma, R, Tanzania　42 C1
Royal Bay, South Georgia　86 D3
Rudolph, L, Kenya　45 A3, 47 B1
Ruines, Morocco　32 A4
Rukumkot, Nepal　54 D3
Rumah Pasang, Malaysia　75 A2
Rumaila, Iraq　27 C3
Rumbek, Sudan　44 D2
Rupa, India　55 C3
Rusape, Zimbabwe　49 D3
Rustaq, Oman　23 D1

Sabah　73 B1, 75 D2, 82 A2
Sabangu, Korea　69 B4
Sabanguo, Korea　69 D2
Sabatik I, Indonesia　75 D1
Sabi R, Zimbabwe　42 A3
Sableh, Iran　27 C3
Sabrah (Beirut), Lebanon　18 A2
Sada, Yemen　24 C1
Sá da Bandeira, Angola　40 A4, 41 A3
Sadiya, India　55 D3
Safad, Israel　10 A1
Saglia la Grande, Cuba　91 B1
Saharan Atlas Mts, Algeria　32 C2
Saharanpur, India　54 C2
Saïda, Algeria　32 C2
Saigon, Vietnam　76 B2, 79 A4, 80 B3, 81 D4
St Andreas, C, Cyprus　6 D1
St Andrews Bay, South Georgia　86 D3
St Antonio de Zaire, Angola　40 A2, 41 A3
St Catherine's Monastery, Sinai　15 D4
St Georges, Grenada　90 C4
Saiq, Oman　23 D4
Sakiet, Tunisia　33 C1
Salal, Chad　35 A2
Salalah, Oman　24 C4
Salang Iunnel, Afghanistan　59 C2
Salazar, Angola　41 A3
Salif, Yemen　23 A3
Salima, Lebanon　20 B1
Salines Pt, Grenada　90 C4
Salisbury, Zimbabwe　49 C2, 49 D1
Salonika, Greece　3 B1
Salt, Jordan　10 B1, 15 D2
Salvador, Falkland Is　86 C1
Salween R, Burma/Tibet　58 B2, 66 C2
Samar I, Philippines　82 B1
Samarkand, USSR　59 B1
Samba, Pakistan　54 B4
Samchok, Korea　68 B3, 69 A1, 69 C2, 69 C4
Same, Indonesia　75 D4
Sam Neua, Laos　77 B2, 78 D1
Samrong, Cambodia　81 C4
Samtrong, Laos　78 D1
Sana, Yemen　23 A3, 24 C1
San Carlos, Falkland Is　87 C1
San Carlos, Nicaragua　89 A3
San Carlos Water, Falkland Is　87 C1
Sandala, Israel　13 C2
San Fernando, Nicaragua　89 A2
San Francisco, USA　91 A3
San Francisco Gotera, El Salvador　88 D2
San Isidro, Costa Rica　89 B3
San José, Costa Rica　89 B3
Sanju, Korea　68 B4
San Juan, Puerto Rico　90 C2
San Juan R, Nicaragua　89 B3
San Juan del Norte, Nicaragua　89 B3
San Juan del Sud, Nicaragua　89 A3
San Luis, Guatemala　88 D1
San Marcos, Nicaragua　89 A2
San Miguel, El Salvador　88 D2
San Pedro de Copan, Honduras　88 D2
San Pedro Sula, Honduras　88 D1
San Salvador, El Salvador　88 D2
Santa Ana, El Salvador　88 D2
Santa Clara, Cuba　91 B1
Santa Clara, Nicaragua　89 A2
Santa Comba, Angola　41 A3
Santa Rosa, Costa Rica　89 A3
Santa Rosa de Copan, Honduras　88 D2
Santiago, Chile　85 B3, 86 A3
Santiago de Cuba, Cuba　91 D2

Santo Domingo, Dominican Rep.　90 C2
Santo Tomas, Guatemala　88 D1
San Vicente, El Salvador　88 D2
Sao Dominigos, Guinea-Bissau　41 C2
Sao Salvador, Angola　41 A3
Sapele, Nigeria　37 C2
Sapper Hill, Falkland Is　87 D2
Saqqez, Iran　27 B1
Sarafand, Lebanon　17 A3
Saravane, Laos　79 A2
Sarawak　73 B1, 74 B4, 75 D2
Sardar, India　56 A2
Sarfait, Oman　24 A4
Sargodha, Pakistan　56 B1
Sarh, Chad　35 B3
Sariwon, Korea　69 A1
Sassa, Syria　14 D3
Sassabaneh, Ethiopia　45 C2
Saunders I, Falkland Is　87 B1
Saurimo, Angola　40 C3
Savannakhet, Laos　79 A2
Save R, Mozambique　42 A3
Scopus, Mt, Israel　13 B3
Sebaco, Nicaragua　89 B2
Sebal, Guatemala　88 C1
Selangor, State, Malaya　72 B3
Se la Pass, India　55 C3
Semara, Spanish Sahara　34 A2, 34 B2
Semarang, Indonesia　73 D2
Semengo, Sarawak　74 B4
Semipalatinsk, U.S.S.R.　67 B1
Senmonorom, Cambodia　81 D4
Seoul, Korea　68 B3, 68 D3, 69 A1, 69 A4,
　69 B2, 69 C1, 69 C2, 69 D4
Sepone, Laos　79 A2
Seram I, Indonesia　73 C1
Serdang, Brunei　75 B1
Serdeh Band, Afghanistan　59 C2
Seremban, Malaysia　72 B3
Seria, Brunei　75 A1
Serian, Sarawak　74 B4
Serpa Pinto, Angola　40 B4, 41 A3
Serudong, Sabah　75 D1
Sétif, Algeria　33 B1
Sewa, Mozambique　42 B2
Sezana, Yugoslavia　2 D3
Sfax, Tunisia　33 D2
Shaab Sharah, Aden　22 C4
Shabani, Zimbabwe　49 C3
Shab Tem, Aden　22 C3
Shacheng, China　63 B2
Shafat, Israel　13 A3
Shanghai, China　63 C4
Shanghaikwan, China　63 B2
Shambe, Sudan　44 D2
Shansi, Prov, China　63 A3
Shantung, Prov, China　63 B3
Shaohing, China　63 C4
Shao-Hsing, China　64 D3
Sharaijah, Oman　23 D4
Shargung la Pass, Tibet　66 C2
Sharhani, Iraq　27 C3
Sharjah, Oman　23 D1
Sharm el Sheikh, Sinai　11 D2, 12 A3, 13 A3,
　15 D4
Shatt-al-Arab, Iraq　26 D4, 27 C3
Shawa Hills, Zimbabwe　48 C3
Shear, Israel　13 D1
Shebelle, R, Somalia　45 C3
Shedda, Yemen　24 C1
Sheikh Abdul Aziz, Israel　13 A3
Sheikh Othman, Aden　22 B2
Sheikh Sho'eyb I, Arabian Gulf　28 C2
Shensi, Prov, China　62 D3
Shentsa, Tibet　66 B2
Shenyang, China　63 C2
Sher Khan, Afghanistan　59 C1
Shetland Is, Scotland　8 D4
Shigatse, Tibet　66 B2
Shihchiachuang, China　63 A3
Shihchiuso, China　63 B3
Shillong, India　55 C3
Shindand, Afghanistan　59 A2
Shipki Pass, Kashmir　54 C2
Shiraz, Iran　27 D2, 28 B1
Shisr, Oman　23 C2
Shopando, Tibet　66 C2
Shuangcheng, China　63 D1

Shuang-Feng, China　64 B3
Shuangliao, China　63 C1
Shugden, Tibet　66 C2
Shupiyan, Kashmir　54 B3
Shuqra, Yemen　23 B2, 23 B3
Shyok, Kashmir　54 C1
Shyok R, Kashmir　54 C1
Sialkot, Pakistan　54 A4, 56 B1, 57 B1
Siam, Gulf of, Thailand　76 A2
Sian, China　62 D3
Siangtan, China　64 B3
Sib, Oman　23 D1
Sibu, Sarawak　74 D3
Sidi-Abdallah, Tunisia　33 C3
Sidi Ahmed, Tunisia　33 C3
Sidi bel Abbès, Algeria　32 C1
Sidi Ifni, Morocco　32 A4
Sidon, Lebanon　16 A2, 17 A3
Siem Reap, Cambodia　81 C4
Sierra Maestra, Cuba　91 D2
Sihanoukville, Cambodia　78 D4, 81 C4
Sikang, Prov, China　66 D2
Silgarhi, Nepal　54 D2
Silimpopon, Sabah　75 D1
Silva Porto, Angola　40 B3, 41 A3
Silvicola, Indonesia　75 D4
Simla, India　52 B1, 54 C2
Simmanggang, Sarawak　74 C4
Sinai, Mt, Grenada　90 C4
Sind, Prov, Pakistan　52 A2, 57 A2
Singapore, Malaysia　72 B4, 73 A1
Sining, China　66 D1
Sinkiang, Prov, China　54 C1, 66 A1
Sinoia, Zimbabwe　49 C2
Sinuiju, Korea　69 A1
Siptang, Sabah　75 C1
Sirri I, Arabian Gulf　28 C2
Sirwah, Yemen　24 D1
Sittang, R, Burma　58 B2
Skardu, Kashmir　56 B1
Skarinou, Cyprus　6 C1
Skikda, Algeria　33 B1
Slave I, Aden　22 B2
Sligo, Eire　7 B2
Sligo Bay, Eire　7 B2
Sobat R, Sudan　45 A2
Sofar, Lebanon　20 B1
Sohar, Oman　23 D1
Sohmor, Lebanon　17 B3
Sokota, Ethiopia　46 B3
Sokoto, Nigeria　36 A1
Somotillo, Nicaragua　89 A2
Somoto, Nicaragua　89 A2
Sonamarg, Kashmir　54 B3
Songsin, Korea　69 A1, 69 C1
Son La, Vietnam　77 B2, 81 C1
Son Tay, Vietnam　77 C2
Soochow, China　63 C4
Sopron, Hungary　4 A2
Sopur, Kashmir　54 A3
Souk Ahras, Algeria　33 C1
Souk el Gharb, Lebanon　20 B1
Soummam R, Algeria　33 A1
Sousse, Tunisia　33 D1
Southern Kurdistan, Region, Iraq　25 B4,
　27 B1
South Georgia, I, Atlantic Ocean　86 C4
Souvannakhili, Laos　79 A2
Spaaman, Mt., South Georgia　86 D3
Spanggur, Kashmir　54 C1
Speedwell I, Falkland Is　87 B2
Spilia, Cyprus　6 C1
Spree R, East Germany　2 A1
Springbok, South Africa　43 B3
Srinagar, Kashmir　54 B1, 54 B3, 56 B1,
　57 B1
Ssuping, China　63 C1
Stanleyville, Zaire　39 B2
Stapleford, Zimbabwe　48 D3
Stass, Sarawak　74 A4
Staten I, Argentina　86 B4
Stefanie, L, Ethiopia　45 B2
Strabane, N Ireland　7 C1
Strangford, L, N Ireland　7 D2
Stromness, South Georgia　86 D3
Stung Treng, Cambodia　79 A3, 81 D4
Sturma R, Bulgaria　3 B1
Suchon, Korea　68 B4

Suchow, China   63 B3
Sudh, Oman   24 D4
Sudong, Korea   69 A1
Sudr, Sinai   11 C1, 13 A2, 15 C3
Suez, Egypt   11 C1, 11 D3, 12 C2, 13 A2,
  14 A1, 14 C2, 14 D2, 15 C3
Suez Canal, Egypt   11 B4, 11 C1, 12 C2,
  14 D1
Suez, Gulf of, Egypt   11 C2, 12 C2, 14 C2
Suhsien, China   63 B4
Sui, Pakistan   56 A2
Suihsien, China   63 A3
Suining, China   63 B4
Suiteh, China   62 D3
Sukabumi, Indonesia   73 C2
Sukarnapura, New Guinea   73 D1
Sukchon, Korea   69 A1
Sukkur, Pakistan   56 A2
Sulawesi I, Indonesia   73 C1
Sulaymaniyah, Iraq   25 B4, 25 D1, 27 B1
Suleimanki, Pakistan   57 B1
Sumail, Oman   23 D3
Sumatra, Indonesia   73 A1
Sumba I, Indonesia   73 C2
Sumbawa I, Indonesia   73 B2
Sumhuran, Oman   24 C4
Sunchon, Korea   69 A1, 69 A2
Sungari R, China   63 C1
Sungari Reservoir, China   63 D1
Sungei Patani, Malaya   72 A2
Sungei Siput, Malaya   72 A2
Sur, Oman   23 D1
Surabaya, Indonesia   73 B2, 73 C2
Surakarta, Indonesia   73 D2
Susangerd, Iran   27 C3
Sutlej R, Pakistan   54 B2, 56 B1, 57 A1
Suwaiq, Oman   23 D1
Suweilih, Jordan   15 D2
Suwon, Korea   69 C1
Svay Rieng, Cambodia   81 D4
Swakopmund, Namibia   43 B2
Swatow, China   64 C4
Sylhet, Bangladesh   57 D1
Szechwan, Prov, China   62 D4, 64 A3
Szeged, Hungary   4 C2
Székesfehérvár, Hungary   4 B2
Szepingkai, China   63 C1
Szolnok, Hungary   4 C2
Szombathely, Hungary   4 A2

Tabelbala, Algeria   34 B1
Tabriz, Iran   25 D1
Tachen Is, China   65 D3
Tacloban, Philippines   82 B1
Tadajirht, Morocco   34 B2
Tandozinze, Cabinda   40 A2
Taedong R, Korea   69 B1
Taegu, Korea   68 B4, 69 C2
Taejon, Korea   68 B4, 69 A2, 69 B2
Taepori, Korea   69 C4, 69 D1, 69 D2
Taepyong, Korea   68 B4
Tafudaret, Spanish Sahara   34 B2
Tahushan, China   63 C2
Taian, China   63 B3
Taichung, Taiwan   65 D4
Taierchwang, China   63 B3
Tailai, China   63 C1
Tainan, Taiwan   65 D4
Taipei, Taiwan   64 D4, 65 D4
Taiping, Malaya   72 A2
Taiyuan, China   63 A3
Taiz, Yemen   23 A2, 23 A3, 24 C2
Takeo, Cambodia   81 D4
Taksang, India   55 C3
Tali, Sudan   44 D2
Tamatave, Madagascar   50 D2
Tambura, Sudan   44 D2
Taming, China   63 A3
Tam Ky, Vietnam   79 B2
Tana, L, Ethiopia   45 B1
Tanahmerah, New Guinea   73 D1
Tan An, Vietnam   80 B4
Tananarive, Madagascar   50 D2
Tangail, Bangladesh   57 D1
Tanganyika, L, Zaire   39 C3
Tangku, China   63 B2
Tangshan, China   63 B2, 63 B3
Tanimbar I, Indonesia   73 D2

Tankse, Kashmir   54 C1
Tan-Tan, Morocco   34 B2
Tanuf, Oman   23 C4
Tanyang, Korea   68 B3
Taobat, Kashmir   54 A2
Taolaichao, China   63 D1
Taonan, China   63 C1
Taoyuan, China   64 B3
Taqa, Oman   24 C4
Tarfaya, Spanish Sahara   34 A1, 34 B2
Tarim, Yemen   23 B2
Tasek Bera, Swamp, Malaya   72 B3
Tashihkao, China   63 C2
Tata, Hungary   4 B2
Tata, Morocco   34 B1
Tatabánya, Hungary   4 B2
Tatung, China   63 A2, 65 D4
Tawahi, Aden   22 A3
Tawang, India   55 C3, 66 A4
Tawau, Malaysia   75 D1
Tawenkow, China   63 B3
Tawi Atair, Oman   24 C4
Taym Basin, Aden   22 D3
Taym, Wadi, Aden   22 D3
Tay Ninh, Vietnam   79 A4, 80 A3
Teal Inlet, Falkland Is   87 C1
Tebedu, Sarawak   74 B4
Tebessa, Algeria   33 C1
Tegel Airport, West Germany   2 A1
Tegucigalpa, Honduras   88 D2
Tehchow, China   63 B3
Teheran, Iran   27 D1
Teixeira da Silva, Angola   40 B3
Teixeira de Sousa, Angola   40 D3
Teixeira Pinto, Guinea-Bissau   41 C2
Tejutla, El Salvador   88 D2
Tel Aviv, Israel   10 A1, 10 B1, 10 D1, 12 D1,
  13 B3, 14 A1
Tel el Ful, Israel   13 A3
Tel Kazir, Israel   13 D2
Telok Anson, Malaysia   72 A3
Tempelhof Airport, West Germany   2 A1
Tenancingo, El Salvador   88 D2
Ténès, Algeria   32 D1
Tenghsien, China   63 B3
Tepoi, Sarawak   74 B4
Terhathum, Nepal   55 B3
Termez, USSR   59 C1
Tesseni, Ethiopia   46 A2
Tete, Mozambique   42 B2
Tezpur, India   55 C3, 66 B2, 66 B4
Thai Binh, Vietnam   77 C2
Thai Nguyen, Vietnam   77 C1
Thakhek, Laos   79 A2
Thakurgaon, Bangladesh   57 C1
Thanh Hoa, Vietnam   77 C2
Thateng, Laos   79 A2
That Khe, Vietnam   77 C1
Thaton, Burma   58 B3
Thayetmyo, Burma   58 A2
Thbengmeanchey, Cambodia   81 D4
The Hook, Mt, Korea   69 A4
Thika, Kenya   47 B2
Thio, Ethiopia   46 C2
Thomson's Falls, Kenya   47 B2
Thumier, Aden   22 C4
Thumrait, Oman   23 C2
Thysville, Zaire   38 D3
Tiberias, Israel   13 D2, 15 C1
Tiberias, L, Israel   10 B1, 13 D2, 14 C4, 15 D1
Tibesti Mts, Chad   35 B2
Tibiyat, Lebanon   20 B1
Tiemcen, Algeria   32 C2
Tientsin, China   63 B2
Tifariti, Mauritania   34 B2
Tiginert, Morocco   32 A4
Tigre, Region, Ethiopia   45 B1
Tigris R, Iraq   25 A4, 25 D1, 27 B2, 27 C1
Tilomar, Indonesia   75 D4
Tilouine, Morocco   32 A4
Timisoara, Romania   4 C2
Timor I, Indonesia   73 C2
Tindja, Tunisia   33 C3
Tindouf, Algeria   34 B1, 34 C2
Tingtao, China   63 B3
Tinjar R, Sarawak   75 A2
Tiran, Strait of, Sinai   11 D2, 12 D3
Tirat Zvei, Israel   13 D2

Tiszar R, Hungary   4 C2
Tithwal, Kashmir   54 A3, 56 B1
Titule, Zaire   39 B1
Tizi Ouzou, Algeria   33 A1
Tiznit, Morocco   32 B4, 34 B1
Tjibadak, Indonesia   73 C2
Tjolotjo, Zimbabwe   49 A3
Tokchon, Korea   69 B1
Tonle Sap, L, Cambodia   79 A3, 81 C4
Tonj, Sudan   44 D2
Tonking, Gulf of, Vietnam   77 D3, 79 B4
Torgchon, Korea   68 B3
Torit, Sudan   45 A2
Tou Morong, Vietnam   79 B3
Toungoo, Burma   58 B2
Tozeur, Tunisia   33 C2
Trakhonas, Cyprus   6 C1
Tramare, Wadi, Aden   22 C4
Travancore, State, India   52 B3
Trengganu, State, Malaya   72 B2
Triangle Hill, Korea   69 B4
Trieste, Yugoslavia   2 C3
Trigu, L, Tibet   66 A3
Trikkala, Greece   3 A1
Trikomo, Cyprus   6 D1
Trincomalee, Sri Lanka   60 B1
Tringgus, Sarawak   74 B4
Tripoli, Lebanon   16 A1, 17 B1
Tripoli, Libya   19 A1
Tripolis, Greece   3 A2
Tripura, State, India   52 D2, 57 D1
Tro la Pass, Tibet   66 C2
Trondheim, Norway   8 D3
Troodos, Cyprus   6 C1
Trujillo, Honduras   89 A1
Trung Ha, Vietnam   77 C2
Tsangchan, China   63 B3
Tsangpo R, China   55 C2
Tsetang, Tibet   66 A3
Tsinan, China   63 B3
Tsinghai, Prov, China   66 C1
Tsingkiang, China   63 B4
Tsingtao, China   63 C3
Tsingyuan, China   63 B2, 63 D2
Tsining, China   63 B3
Tsinpu Railway, China   63 B3
Tsitsihar, China   63 C1
Tsona Dzong, Tibet   66 A4
Tsowhsien, China   63 B3
Tsumeb, Namibia   43 B1
Tuan Giao, Vietnam   77 A1
Tubas, Israel   13 C3
Tuléar, Madagascar   50 C2
Tulkarm, Israel   10 A1, 10 D1, 13 C3
Tumbledown, Mt, Falkland Is   87 C2
Tunb I, Arabian Gulf   28 C2
Tungchow, China   63 B2
Tunghai, China   63 B3
Tunghua, China   63 D2
Tungi, Bangladesh   57 D1
Tungkwan, China   62 D3
Tungliao, China   63 C1
Tungliao Ho R, China   63 C1
Tungting, L, China   64 B3
Tunis, Tunisia   19 A1, 33 D1
Tunliu, China   63 A3
Tur, Israel   13 B4
Tutong, Brunei   75 B1
Tuyen Quang, Vietnam   77 B1
Tuy Hoa, Vietnam   79 B3
Tuz Khurmatu, Iraq   27 B2
Twelve o'Clock Mt, Falkland Is   87 D1
Two Sisters, Mt, Falkland Is   87 C1
Tyre, Lebanon   10 A1, 16 A2, 17 A4
Tyrone Co, N Ireland   7 C2
Tzeyang, China   63 B3

Ubiaja, Nigeria   37 D1
Ubon, Thailand   79 A3
Udaipur, India   56 B2
Udhampur, Kashmir   54 B4
Udine, Italy   2 C3
Udon, Thailand   78 D2
Uele R, Zaire   39 B1
Uga, Nigeria   37 A3
Ugep, Nigeria   37 B4
Ughelli, Nigeria   37 C2
Uige, Angola   40 B2